THE ART OF SYLVIA PLATH

Photograph by Rollie McKenna

The art of
SYLVIA PLATH

A Symposium

Edited by Charles Newman

*Selected criticism, with a complete
bibliography, checklist of criticism,
and an appendix of uncollected
and unpublished work.*

Indiana University Press
Bloomington & London

FIRST MIDLAND BOOK EDITION 1971

PUBLISHED IN CANADA BY FITZHENRY & WHITESIDE LIMITED,
DON MILLS, ONTARIO
LIBRARY OF CONGRESS CATALOG CARD NUMBER: 75-85096
ISBN: 0-253-20148-9
MANUFACTURED IN THE UNITED STATES OF AMERICA

This book is for those who will
return to the poetry without it.

PUBLISHER'S NOTE

Charles Newman graduated from Yale in 1960, did graduate work at Balliol College, Oxford, and is currently Associate Professor of English at Northwestern University, Evanston, Illinois, and editor of the *TriQuarterly* review, an international review of arts, letters, and opinion. A first novel, *New Axis*, was published by Calder and Boyars in 1968.

CONTENTS

9

ACKNOWLEDGEMENTS

Needless to say, I am alone responsible for the selection of this material as well as my own commentary. I am particularly grateful to Professors Richard Ellmann and Moody Prior who, simply through their generosity of spirit, encouraged me to complete this project. I am also indebted to the Northwestern University Research Committee, whose grant made it possible for me to do initial research on this book, and to Ted and Olwyn Hughes who read the manuscript and offered helpful suggestions.

'Sylvia Plath' by A. Alvarez, by permission of the author; 'On Sylvia Plath' by A. E. Dyson, reprinted with emendations from *TriQuarterly* 7 by permission of the editor and author; 'Notes on the Chronological Order of Sylvia Plath's Poems' by Ted Hughes, by permission of the author; 'The Barfly Ought to Sing' by Anne Sexton, reprinted entire from *TriQuarterly* 7 by permission of the editor and author; 'Candor is the Only Wile' reprinted with emendations from *TriQuarterly* 7 by permission of the editor and author; 'Notes Towards a Biography' by Lois Ames, reprinted with emendations from *TriQuarterly* 7 by permission of the editor and author; 'Sylvia Plath and confessional poetry' by M. L. Rosenthal, reprinted with emendations from *The New Poets*. Oxford University Press, 1967, by permission of the author and publishers; 'Dying is an Art' by George Steiner, reprinted from *Language and Silence*, Faber and Faber Ltd., and Atheneum, 1967, by permission of the author and publishers; 'Warnings from the Grave' by Stephen Spender, reprinted entire

INTRODUCTION

I was aware of Sylvia Plath's poetry in literary magazines as early I think as 1960, and marvelled like everyone at the poems published posthumously in 1963. But the circumstances surrounding that publication created the illusion that the 'last poems' had been produced, somehow, *in vacuo*. Actually, they struck me then as a culmination of prior themes and techniques rather than a new departure, and my personal reaction, insufficient perhaps, was that a poet had perfected her art, not that a brilliant young woman had died.

These two facts have nevertheless become inseparable, and it was my concern from the first that poetry of this order should not be obscured by the myths of its origin. I wanted only, as another writer of her generation, as an appreciative reader, to place her work in a serviceable perspective, indicate something of the real measure of her achievement. For if criticism cannot illuminate writing as contemporary and overwhelming as Sylvia Plath's, then as far as I am concerned, it is of practically no use at all. Here then, is criticism which accepts the risk of not being definitive.

Some of these essays—now two years later emendated as you might expect—were first collected in a literary review I edit. Since then, I have tried to account for most obvious gaps with commissioned commentary from people I felt most qualified to fill them. Accessory contributions are reprints of material written for other more particularized occasions. As such, this collection provides no particular overview, and, in fact, I have resisted editing what may strike the casual reader as repetitious, or to strategically oppose what seem to be contradictions in judgment, so that these patterns themselves might be preserved for evaluation.

Such wide variety of methodologies, however, tell us something that no synthesis could. It is interesting that no one here begins from the same critical presuppositions; few quote the same poetry in support of their points; all seem driven to amplify her effort by allusions to other literature. That she should strike such a variety of responses in such a wide spectrum of commentators, is itself the best testimony to the richness of her work.

This volume's purpose is not commemorative. It is simply to begin a discussion of her work, her life, and the cultural history from which they sprang and now serve, one step at a time. It is a sorting-out process that the reader himself will have to continue, if this book is to serve its modest if persistent purpose.

Any attempt to evaluate her importance must ultimately confront two criticisms. The first treats her work as a handful of shocking, autobiographical poems, blown out of proportion by commentary of which this book, say, is only the first. But this is a poet who published over 170 poems, a novel, a verse play, six stories and a respectable amount of expository prose in something less than a decade, and the greater part of it is worthy of attention even when it must compete with the best of the 'last' poems. In this regard, I have tried to indicate through the selection of materials and in my own writing, how organic her development was, and why the uniqueness of the last poems should not over-shadow the admirable apprenticeship which made them possible.

The second charge is that her work—again haunted by the last poems—is merely fashionable; that is, a drowning cry which is authentic simply because it is a drowning cry, in the current mode of existential *angst*. Again, I have tried to establish that she speaks from a definite poetic tradition, and that she speaks to our present condition in a manner which in no way depends upon the platitudinous despair and derivative techniques which have characterized so much American poetry of the last decade.

She now belongs to that large and excellent company of American poets who, because of their relatively small body of work, and the singularity of their themes, must be termed *kleine-meisters*. For my own part, I believe her work as fully important to our generation as that of, say, Hart Crane or John Crowe Ransom were to theirs.

Finally, one should note how frequently the contributors, ultimately imply the question: Given the premises of *her* poetry, what *good* is art? That question cannot be answered in criticism, but it might be worth pointing out that like much of contemporary art, the real terror of her poetry derives from the fact that it actually bypasses life to question the function and value of art itself. For those who find this impulse anti-humanistic, or indicative of mental illness, I can only recall Jung's distinction between James Joyce's fantasies and those of his patients:

'They are falling . . . he is diving.'

Charles Newman
Evanston, Illinois
1968

PART I

CANDOR IS THE ONLY WILE
The Art of Sylvia Plath
CHARLES NEWMAN

Is God Love's adversary?

THE AWFUL BIRTHDAY OF OTHERNESS

'When I was learning to creep,' she tells us, 'my mother set me down on the beach to see what I thought of it. I crawled straight for the coming wave and was just through the wall of green when she caught my heels.'[1]

The courting of experience that kills is characteristic of major poets, and even if we discount the artist's hindsight, Sylvia Plath seems to have been so preoccupied from the beginning.

Breath, that is the first thing. Something is breathing. My own breath? The breath of my mother? No, something else, something larger, farther, more serious, more weary . . .

That breath, discounting our own hindsight now, is both the echo of her future voice, as well as her first sense of 'Otherness', with whom, in a variety of guises, she will argue the possibility of existence throughout her life.

It is her mother, who inadvertently, gives first shape to that breath, even if it is only through reading Matthew Arnold aloud—

> Where the sea snakes coil and twine
> Dry their mail and bask in the brine

and, by suggesting that the sea can be captured through language, provides her daughter with a 'new way of being happy'. The child responds by coding the sea for herself—not with basking snakes albeit—but her grandmother's phone number, OCEAN

N.B. The title and all italicized lead quotations are Emily Dickinson's. The section titles in roman are Sylvia Plath's.

[1] Narrative quotations in this section from 'Context', *London Magazine*, February, 1962. (See Appendix for complete text.) All citations to poetry refer to first publication, unless otherwise indicated.

1212-W.[2] And with the typical good sense of the modern poet, she reverses Arnold's poetics and endows the sea with the characteristics of her own mind.

> I think the sea swallowed dozens of tea sets—tossed in abandon off liners, or consigned to the tides by jilted brides. I collected a shiver of china bits, with borders of larkspur and birds or braids of daisies. No two patterns ever matched.

It is not surprising then, to find in the last poems, that Nature herself is equated with, even regulated by, the mind.

> In a pit of rock
> The sea sucks obsessively,
> One hollow the whole sea's pivot.
>
> > 'Contusion'[3]

On the occasion of the birth of her brother, her first rival, her second sense of 'Otherness', the sea provides a sign—an antidote to the loss of her specialness.

> I flung the starfish against the stone. Let it perish. It had no wit . . . but a piece of the sea . . . might any minute pitch at my feet a sign . . . out of the pulp of kelp, still shining with a wet, fresh smell, reached a small brown hand . . . what it was was a monkey. Not a real monkey; but a monkey of wood. Heavy with the water that it swallowed, and scarred with tar, it crouched on its pedestal, remote and holy, long muzzled and oddly foreign. I brushed it and admired its delicately carved hair. It looked like no monkey I had ever seen eating peanuts and moony-foolish. It had the noble pose of a simian Thinker. I realize now that the totem I so lovingly undid from its caul of kelp . . . was a sacred baboon.
> So the sea perceiving my need, conferred a blessing. My baby brother took his place in the house that day, but so did my marvelous and (who knew?) even priceless baboon . . .[4]

The confrontation of 'Otherness' requires that imagination become equal to experience. She appropriates the sea by collecting

---

[2] 'Ocean 1212-W', *The Listener*, August 29, 1963. (See pp. 266–72 for complete text.)
[3] *The Observer*, February 17, 1963.
[4] 'Ocean 1212-W'.

from it a banquet set of seachina; she accepts her brother by resurrecting her own totem of him. All babies come from the same place. There is no division between the world and her wilful representation of it. 'The state of being in love threatens to obliterate the boundaries between ego and object . . .',[5] Freud warns us.

Her mind and the world, her sea and the real sea do not divide until she is nine. Then:

My father died, we moved inland.

> *I rose because he sank*
> *I thought it would be opposite.*

ELECTRA ON THE AZALEA PATH

My mother said: you died like any man.
How shall I age into that state of mind?
I am the ghost of an infamous suicide,
My own blue razor rusting in my throat.
Oh pardon the one who knocks for pardon at
Your gate, father—your hound-bitch, daughter, friend.
It was my love that did us both to death.
                    'Electra on the Azalea Path'[6]

Clearly, the loss of the father, the ambiguous hand of the mother will remain her central preoccupations. And she can accept them only by universalizing their memory.

From the mercury-backed glass
Mother, grandmother, greatgrandmother
Reach hag hands to haul me in,
And an image looms under the fishpond surface
Where the daft father went down
With orange duck-feet winnowing his hair
                    'All the Dead Dears'[7]

[5] Freud, *Civilization and its Discontents.*
[6] *Hudson Review,* Fall, 1960.
[7] *The Grecourt Review,* November, 1957.

23

These formative years, the dialectic they propose, conforms to critical preoccupations all too nicely. Freudian analysis is perhaps inescapable—sibling rivalry simultaneous with guilt at the father's death, the vengeful urge to get back to the father through the mother, the lovingly expressed Death-wish.

I AM VERTICAL
But I would rather be horizontal[8]

one poem begins, and the critic beginning here may hang the rest of her work on the thought-rack of Eros and Thanatos. Yet the situation, as Freud himself would recognize, is that love and death instincts are in fact indivisible here; 'Originally the ego includes everything . . . the notion of limitless extension and oneness with the universe . . . the feeling . . . described as . . . "oceanic" . . .'[9]

> What I want back is what I was
> Before the bed, before the knife,
> Before the brooch-pin and the salve
> Fixed me in this parenthesis;[10]
>   'The Eye-mote'

It is fairer both to Freud and the poetry, if we approach this art in terms of rhetorical rather than psychological analysis. This is not because we should avoid treating art as substitute gratification, but because it commits us to a misleading dialectical framework, between X an unfulfilled wish, and Y its unsublimated expression. For present purposes, it doesn't really matter whether we interpret the wish as sexual or aesthetic, or whether it is dictated by personality or culture. What is important is that we recognize that the expression (and by implication the nature of the wish) changes as the artist develops. It is the form of the expression, and not the neurosis from which it may or may not issue, which concerns us, and which we can evaluate, celebrate. For Sylvia Plath, that sense of 'Otherness'—the larger, weary breath which accompanied her from the very first—takes varying form and voice as

---

[8] 'I am Vertical', *Critical Quarterly*, Summer, 1961.
[9] S. Freud, *op. cit.*
[10] *Chelsea Review*, May, 1960.

she matures. Her entire body of work can be seen as dialogue with an 'Other', but it is not a dialectic in any academic sense, for her voice and her interlocutor metamorphize as the context of her private quarrel is enlarged.[11]

In avoiding irresponsible gossip about that *Other*, we should recall that generation of critics which obscured Emily Dickinson's poetry either to identify or protect 'real people'—the ostensible correlatives of her work. Not only did this excite the very excesses it meant to control, but reduced the finest love lyrics by an American of her century to a sensationalistic confessional.

The cult which obscured Emily Dickinson's poetry in its posthumous appearance has much in common with that which now attends Sylvia Plath's work. Similar legends surround their respective objects of affection. It was suggested that Emily held her father in something more than esteem, that her nephew bore the wish-fulfilling burden of her childlessness. Potential suitors appeared as eligible young house-guests only to be banished by a tyrannical father and subsequently die of a broken heart, or as a married man of the cloth, whose sinful proposals Emily herself dismissed. The most recent scholarship suggests that she experienced her 'love' vicariously through her sister's affair,[12] while others have stressed the mystical, fleshless nature of her 'perfect lover'.[13]

The point is that although each 'character' in fact existed, and may indeed be traced through specific poems, this love poetry is

[11] Ludwig Wittgenstein's choppy logic is equal to Freudian imagination here . . . 'Freud considers the majority of dreams to be *camouflaged* with fulfilments; and in this case they simply don't fulfil the wish. Ex hypothesi the wish is not allowed to be fulfilled, and something else is hallucinated instead. If the wish is cheated in this way, then the dream can hardly be called a fulfilment of it. Also, it becomes impossible to say whether it is the wish or the censor that is cheated. Apparently both are, and the result is that neither is satisfied. So that, the dream is not an hallucinated satisfaction of anything." [*sic*] from 'Conversations on Freud' *Lectures & Conversations*, compiled from Notes taken by Rush Rhees and others, University of California Press, Los Angeles, 1966.

To translate this into the literary critic's vocabulary, if the dream can stand for the poem, then that 'something else [which is] hallucinated' is what is important about the poem, whether it bears any relation to the 'wish' or not. We are used to calling that 'something else', the *persona*.

[12] See Richard B. Seawall, 'The Lyman Letters; New Light on Emily Dickinson', *The Massachusetts Review*, Autumn, 1965.

[13] The least pretentious argument for this point of view is Olive H. Rabe's 'Emily Dickinson as Mystic', *The Colorado Quarterly*, Winter, 1966.

best understood as the reverberations of sensibility against actuality—a poet's unity of fancy more than a woman's case-history. For both poets, the brother/father, husband/lover relationships are finally significant as they effect the poet's chosen *personae*—just as it is the poet's imitative sea and not the real sea which attracted Sylvia from the first. Such a distinction has nothing to do with protecting 'real people', but only to distinguish poetry as craft from autobiography. This is not unimportant, for the irony and grief of Sylvia Plath's poetry issues from the tension between her imagination and experience, the urge to make them one again.

When Emily says,

> *The sweeping up the heart*
> *And putting love away*
> *We shall not use again*
> *Until eternity*

and Sylvia says,

> And round her house she set
> Such a barricade of barb and check
> Against mutinous weather
> As no mere insurgent man could hope to break
> With curse, fist, threat
> Or love, either.
>
> 'Spinster'[14]

they bespeak the artist's isolation, not the spinster's loneliness. Further, we can best understand Sylvia's obsession with death, not in terms of a Freudian post-mortem, but rather from within a poetic tradition that extends back through Emily to Anne Bradstreet and Edward Taylor, a tradition in which the imaginative realization of dying is the determining, climactic experience of living. 'Life is death we're lengthy at,' Emily writes in 1863, 'death the hinge to life.' Or, to hear her put it in what we call a more 'positive' way: 'my business is circumference.'

No American poet of her era treated the theme of love with more candour than Emily Dickinson, and Sylvia Plath carries the

---

[14] *London Magazine*, June, 1958.

tradition to equal heights at mid-century. What lifts their work above the commonplace is the totality of their affections and the fastidiousness with which they express them. Both cut through popular sociology by acknowledging the terrifying ambiguity of the female role, and then by universalizing their very feminism. That is to say, by rejecting the traditional pose of the 'heroine', they give us the woman as 'hero'—a protagonist who not only undergoes the central action of a work, but a character whom men as well as women may view as an actor in a destiny possible for them.[15]

The essential difference between their approaches binds them all the closer. For while Emily was obsessed with the paradox of *giving* love in a Christian context, Sylvia Plath, in her day of abstract philanthropy and evanescent relationships, dramatizes the difficulty of knowing or *accepting* love. Emily speaks for both when she says,

> *We learn by contrast to admire*
> *the beauty that enchains us*
> *And know the object of desire*
> *by that which pains us.*

> *They thought it queer I didn't rise*
> *I thought a lie would be queerer.*

ON THE DIFFICULTY OF CONJURING UP A DRYAD

'She has no objection to becoming a Christian', a report card of Emily's tells us, but it is clear that she will settle for no institutionalized sensibility. She did not set out to question the reality of religious myth, it was simply that its forms were not capacious enough for her poetic energies. And as we might expect, Sylvia subjects secular classical models to the same firm scrutiny as Emily did the biblical. Both took seriously Whitman's dictum to

[15] For an impressive elaboration of 'The Woman as Hero', see Carolyn Heilbrun's essay by that title in *The Texas Quarterly*, Winter, 1965.

find an aesthetic which would 'meet modern discoveries face to face'.

'*The Bible is an antique volume / Written by faded men*', Emily tells us playfully, and Sylvia echoes her in 'On the Decline of Oracles',

> Worthless such vision to eyes gone dull
> That once descried Troy's towers fall,
> Saw evil break out of the north.[16]

Or more specifically,

> This is not death, it is something safer.
> The wingy myths won't tug at us any more:
> > 'Flute notes from a Reedy Pond'[17]

She then goes on to systematically undermine Gothic imagery as well.

> They are the last romantics, these candles;
> Upside down hearts of light tipping wax fingers,
> And the fingers, taken in by their own haloes,
> Crown milky, almost clear, like the bodies of saints.
> It is touching, the way they'll ignore
>
> A whole family of prominent objects
> Simply to plumb the deeps of an eye.
> . . .
>
> In its hollow of shadows, its fringe of reeds,
> And the owner past thirty, no beauty at all
> Daylight would be more judicious,
> Giving everybody a fair hearing.

> > > > 'Candles'[18]

Like Emily, she sensed that the Gothic[19] was simply an importunate regurgitation of the classical mode, and a nostalgia particu-

---

[16] *Poetry*, September, 1959.
[17] *Texas Quarterly*, Winter, 1960.
[18] *The Listener*, November 17, 1960.
[19] Several critics have pointed out the Gothic influence in Sylvia's early work, but they have neglected to note how often she uses it ironically.

larly crippling to a female narrator. Within the gothic or classical traditions, one could be merely a 'heroine'. A poem might possibly be both oracular and feminist, but it was a personal medium or nothing.

In fact, Emily is in many ways the beginning, and Sylvia the culmination of the movement whereby the imagination, sated with the abstraction of myth, is driven back to the concrete. Emily astounds us because she presages the Imagist manifesto, and Sylvia does because she demonstrates how flexible that tradition is when metrical lyricism and narrative momentum are restored to it.

There is, of course, a price the modern poet must pay, in terms of perception, if not vision. When adopting the *persona* of Electra, for instance, she admits ruefully that in order to give magnitude to her father's memory, she must 'borrow the stilts of an old tragedy'. But while she goes through the motions of self-mockery, and while she is at first simply turning a cliché upon itself, she is gradually asserting her own strict vision. The tone of the following is apologiac, for example, but its intention is just the opposite:

> But no hocus-pocus of green angels
> Damasks with dazzle the threadbare eye;
> 'My trouble, doctor is: I see a tree,
> And that damn scrupulous tree won't practice wiles
> > To beguile sight:
> > E.g., by cant of light
> > Concoct a Daphne:
> > My tree stays tree.
> > 'On the Difficulty of Conjuring up a Dryad'[20]

Trusting that affirmation of rigorous optics, we know where we are.

> > Now, in valleys narrow
> > And black as purses, the house lights
> > Gleam like small change.
> > > 'Wuthering Heights'[21]

[20] *Poetry*, July, 1957.
[21] *The New Statesman*, March 16, 1962.

Capacity to terminate
Is a Specific Grace.

I AM SILVER AND EXACT

Abstraction and archaic usage are not limited to classical models or gothic sentiment. Indeed, for the contemporary poet, the debt to an immediate past may be more burdensome. Sylvia Plath's work is most remarkable in its struggle with modern influences.

Her first published work was thoroughly researched, initially employing that most complicated of French forms, the Villanelle. Her final work is spontaneous, achieving her own definition of greatness, 'born all of a piece . . . poems possessed . . . as by the rhythms of their own breathing . . .'[22]

The development between these two periods is astounding, in that her ability to deal with larger themes and her technical virtuosity keep precise pace with one another. She experiments with an extremely wide variety of forms and modes.[23]

Yet, as with Emily, the despair at not being equal to her craft remains a constant theme.

> Seek no stony camera-eye to fix
> The passing dazzle of each face
> In black and white, or put on ice
> Mouth's instant flare for future looks;
> Stars shoot their petals, and suns run to seed,
> However you may sweat to hold such darling wrecks
> Hived in honey in your head.
>
> 'Epitaph for Fire and Flower'[24]

---

[22] 'Context', *op. cit.*

[23] The only form she tried which fails as a whole, it seems to me, are the dramatic monologues in her radio play, 'Three Women'. Here, the many fine lines—lines which frequently turn up slightly altered in the *Ariel* poems—seem to dissipate their effect within this narative structure. Further, the strength of many of her poems lies in the fact that the 'self' is capable of mastering several voices to correspond to the divisions of the self, whereas in the play, the three distinct speaking agencies sound too much like a single self. This objection might of course be overridden by the inflexion of the actors and astute directing. In any case, it seems clear that the play is a bridge between *The Colossus* and *Ariel*.

[24] *Poetry*, January, 1957. (See pp. 244-5 for complete text.)

It is when such self-preoccupation as an artist becomes over-whelming that contemporary influences become most obtrusive. One can see, for example, how derivative the vision of natural processes becomes, when under the contemplative spell of a Wallace Stevens:

> Cold and final, the imagination
> Shuts down its fabled summerhouse
> 'Two Lovers and a Beachcomber by the Real Sea'[25]

or echoing Theodore Roethke:

> Water will run by rule; the actual sun
> Will scrupulously rise and set;
> No little man lives in the exacting moon
> And is that, is that, is that.
>   Ibid.

or, in that Macleishian metaphysical stage, which represents a parting homage to the academic training she had mastered so sufficiently that it rarely affected her poetry.

> In the circus tent of a hurricane
> Designed by a drunken god
> My extravagant heart blows up again
> In a rampage of champagne-colored rain . . .
>   'Circus in Three Rings'[26]

These are not really bad poems; what is remarkable is how effortlessly, persistently, she absorbs her influences. Her develop-ment does not derive from the adoption of a specific *persona* as yet—but from that ability to find cosmic truths in the minutiae of private life. This is no peculiar feminine construct, but the gift of Emily's Transcendental heritage. Not the Emersonian variety, of course; for him the oversoul was a premise, not a discovery. But rather Thoreau's microscopic vision that the structure of the self suggests the structure of the universe, that nature is an organic externality of the soul. Such an ontology is quite apparent in a poem like 'Sculptor'.[27]

[25] *Mademoiselle*, August, 1955.
[26] *Atlantic Monthly*, August, 1955.
[27] *The Grecourt Review*, May, 1959.

> To his house the bodiless
> Come to barter endlessly
> Vision, wisdom, for bodies
> Palpable as his, and weighty.

This poem is ultimately about making poetry, not sculpture, but what must be noted is the process of capturing real, extant things, before any mythic significance is exhumed. This, of course, reflects one of the most common assumptions of modern poetry— that aesthetic reasoning is inductive, that the truth of order springs not from ideas, but from captured things—for beneath the meta-physic of the poem, one must begin with the commonplace event of Smith College girls, all tartan skirted, page-boy-bob-and-circle-pin, visiting their eccentric 'artist-in-residence', and in this artificial confrontation, a literal miracle takes place. They are moved beyond themselves, beyond their self-consciousness, even beyond culture-shopping, by the 'genuine article'.

> Until his chisel bequeaths
> Them life livelier than ours,
> A solider repose than death's.

Sylvia's images, surreal as they may appear out of context, are quite literal, reportorial descriptions of Leonard Baskin's work. She has invoked no 'wingy myth', which 'stands for' art.

Such biographical details are not essential to the poetry's life, of course—but they will repay the unborn scholar who will inevitably rediscover them, for they show us how organic a vision this poet developed.

The issues of our time which preoccupy me at the moment are the incalculable genetic effects of fallout and a documentary article on the terrifying, mad, omnipotent marriage of big business and the military in America—('Juggernaut, the Warefare State', by Fred J. Cook in a recent *Nation*). Does this in-fluence the kind of poetry I write? Yes, but in a sidelong fashion. I am not gifted with the tongue of Jeremiah, though I may be sleepless enough before my vision of the apocalypse.

My poems do not turn out to be about Hiroshima, but about a child forming itself finger by finger in the dark. They are not about the terrors of mass extinction, but about the bleakness of the moon over a yew tree in a neighboring graveyard. Not about the testaments of tortured Algerians, but about the night thoughts of a tired surgeon.

In a sense, these poems are deflections. I do not think they are an escape. For me, the real issues of our time are the issues of every time—the hurt and wonder of loving; making in all its forms, children, loaves of bread, paintings, building; and the conservation of life of all people in all places, the jeopardizing of which no abstract doubletalk of 'peace' or 'implacable foes' can excuse.

I do not think a 'headline poetry' would interest more people any more profoundly than the headlines. And unless the up-to-the-minute poem grows out of something closer to the bone than a general, shifting philanthropy and is, indeed that unicorn-thing—a real poem, it is in danger of being screwed up as rapidly as the news sheet itself.[28]

It is a rare poet who would admit the influence of an article in *The Nation*, let alone transform it into materials for the imagination.

The relationship between her perception and the sort of imagery which evolves from it is worth pursuing.

Sylvia's immediate predecessors treated nature according to the laws of their own perception, 'as things-in-themselves'. In late Stevens, for example, the poems become, not descriptions of 'things' at all, but an epistemic description of the process of poetic perception. In Sylvia's case, she at times carries the process one step further; that is to say, she overcomes the tension between the perceiver and the thing-in-itself by literally becoming the thing-in-itself. In many instances, it is nature who personifies her. As she began in awe of the ocean's breath, she gradually assumes it. In 'Private Ground'[29] for example, she begins by noticing the handy-

[28] 'Context,' *op. cit.*
[29] *Critical Quarterly*, 3, Summer, 1961.

man draining the goldfish ponds on an abandoned estate:

> They collapse like lungs, the escaped water
> Threading back, filament by filament, to the pure
> Platonic table where it lives. The baby carp
> Litter the mud like orangepeel.

Then, as the poem gains momentum, she sets the scene, Nature herself.

> I bend over this drained basin where the small fish
> Flex as the mud freezes.
> They glitter like eyes, and I collect them all.
> Morgue of old logs and old images, the lake
> Opens and shuts, accepting them among its reflections.

By the time the personal pronoun and the final metaphor are linked, she is no longer looking at the lake, but *is* the lake. This merging of the perceiver with the thing perceived is repeated even more successfully in her later work. In 'Elm',[30] for example, the elm speaks first, but the poet gradually assumes its voice, 'I have suffered the atrocity of sunsets.' While in 'Ariel',[31] title poem of her last book, the girl and her horse become both a physical and mythical unity, 'The dew that flies / Suicidal, at one with the drive / Into the red / Eye, the cauldron of morning.'

One might recognize this as Keats's 'negative capability', the poet's identification with the 'personality' of the poetic subject. Or, perhaps, as an element of mystic traditions of which she was a serious if occasional student. As the Zen poet, Bunan, states: 'I've become the Thingness / Of all the things I see'.

But moreover, within her own context, such an identification represents the poet's triumph over 'Otherness'.

. . . The state of being in love threatens to obliterate the boundaries between ego and object. . . .

---

[30] Originally published as 'The Elm Speaks', in *The New Yorker,* August 3, 1963.
[31] *The Review*, October, 1963. (See pp. 60–61 for complete text.)

*We were waked by the ticking of
bells,—the bells tick in
Amherst for a fire to tell the
firemen . . . I could hear the
buildings falling and the oil
exploding and people walking
and talking gaily, and cannons
soft as velvet from the parishes
that did not know we were burning
up . . . And so much brighter than
day was it, that I saw a cater-
pillar measure a leaf far down in
the orchard; and Vinnie kept
saying bravely, 'It's only The
Fourth of July.'*

THE BELL JAR

She published *The Bell Jar* under the pseudonym of Victoria Lucas (echoing the nationalities of both husband and father) because she apparently did not consider it a 'serious' work. What she felt, I would guess, was that it was *too* serious—that is, it recorded autobiographical data not completely absorbed and transformed by her art. Nevertheless, it remains a remarkable work in many respects.

In the first place, it is one of the few American novels to treat adolescence from a mature point of view, although the narrator is an adolescent. Secondly, it chronicles a nervous breakdown and consequent professional therapy in non-clinical language. And finally, it gives us one of the few sympathetic portraits of what happens to one who has genuinely feminist aspirations in our society, of a girl who refuses to be simply an *event* in anyone's life.

Essentially, this is the record, in a strange blend of American and British vernacular, of a female Holden Caulfield driven to self-destruction by despair with the alternatives adult life apparently offers. Except that Esther Greenwood is both more intelligent and less mannered than Holden, and her conflict the more serious one between a potential artist and society, rather than the cult of youth versus the cult of middle age. Further, Holden Caulfield, for all his charm, is a psychotic; which is to say, his world is the pure world of his own distortion, and no conflicting interpretation is allowed to obtrude upon his narration. The fascinating and terrifying technique of *The Bell Jar*, on the other hand, is the continuous conflict between the real world and the narrator's desperate reconstruction of it. It chronicles what that first flight to the ocean previewed.

We can guess from the background how her problems were clinically defined; what is more interesting is how she chose to make aesthetic use of her 'illness'—which *personae*, in fact, could successfully mediate between the world of external truth and her own more profound, if nemesic vision.

For those critics who find her work indicative of maladjustment, it might do to measure her art against the ills of the society she came to view so circumspectly. In *Mademoiselle*'s 'last word on college,'53'[32] for example, we find twenty young co-eds holding hands in a five-pointed star, testing those open-mouthed horsey grins which will serve them for every emotion they will ever acknowledge. At the topmost point of the star, Sylvia Plath, Guest-Editor, Smith '54, is labelled Number 1, and below, she speaks premonitorily for her accomplices:

> We're stargazers this season, bewitched by an atmosphere of evening blue. Foremost in the fashion constellation, we spot MLLE's own tartan, the astronomic versatility of sweaters, and men, men, men—we've even taken the shirt off their backs! . . .

This is, of course, how we are accustomed to hear our number 1 young ladies speak, and when the truth finally sifts through veils such as these, it is not likely to be kind.

In any event, it is clear she does not become sick as a consequence of *seeing* the 'awful' truth—indeed her imagination functions as a necessary counterweight to reality—it is when her vision is ignored, that it becomes only internalized and not projected, that her 'health' degenerates.

In one of her few sustained prose descriptions, Emily Dickinson

[32] *Mademoiselle*, No. 37, August 1953 (see also her interviews with poets in the same issue).

gives a classic illustration of the cost of such vision. The scene is Amherst, and a fire which subsequently razes the town is raging unnoticed behind the commotion of a Fourth of July celebration. While others sense only the celebration, Emily knows that they are literally 'burning up'. The signals for rejoicing and doomsday are the same. Only the listeners differ. The explanation which Vinnie offers to calm her is as 'true' as it is kind—but it is only the ritual truth. The clinical consequences are clear. The 'neurotic' sees herself as suspect by those less perceptive than herself, and through accumulated experiences such as the Fourth of July, becomes unable to trust any description of reality save her own. It may be that is where art begins; it is certainly where society insists that sickness begins.

It is precisely such a relationship with her world that Esther Greenwood narrates. Gradually the eccentricity of her perception, her candour, her fastidiousness, isolate her from the 'real world'— her mother, her fiancé, her peers, her job with *Mademoiselle*. The bell jar descends, isolating her in the vacuum of her own ego— 'The silence depressed me. It wasn't the silence of silence. It was my own silence . . .' She is closeted with nothing save her own fierce irony—what remains remarkable is her resistance to simple praise or blame—she is determined to record her very inability to communicate. And in her hands, the crisis of adolescent identity is given both a rare dignity and perspective. In the following scene, her fiancé, ironically enough a pre-med, takes her to the university hospital, and then back to what he must conceive as his laboratory.

As soon as the baby was born the people in the room divided up into two groups, the nurses tying a metal dog-tag on the baby's wrist and swabbing its eyes with cotton on the end of a stick and wrapping it up and putting it in a canvas-sided cot, while the doctor and Will started sewing up the woman's cut with a needle and a long thread.

I think somebody said, 'It's a boy, Mrs. Tomolillo,' but the woman didn't answer or raise her head.

'Well, how was it?' Buddy asked with a satisfied expression as we walked across the green quadrangle to his room.

'Wonderful,' I said. 'I could see something like that every day.'

I didn't feel up to asking him if there were any other ways to have babies. For some reason the most important thing to me was actually seeing the baby come out of you yourself and making sure it was yours. I thought if you had to have all that pain anyway you might just as well stay awake.

I had always imagined myself hitching up on to my elbows on the delivery table after it was all over—dead white, of course, with no make-up and from the awful ordeal, but smiling and radiant, with my hair down to my waist, and reaching out for my first little squirmy child and saying its name, whatever it was.

'Why was it covered with flour?' I asked then, to keep the conversation going, and Buddy told me about the waxy stuff that guarded the baby's skin.

When we were back in Buddy's room, which reminded me of nothing so much as a monk's cell, with its bare walls and bare bed and bare floor and the desk loaded with Gray's *Anatomy* and other thick gruesome books, Buddy lit a candle and uncorked a bottle of Dubonnet. Then we lay down side by side on the bed and Buddy sipped his wine while I read aloud 'somewhere I have never travelled' and other poems from a book I'd brought.

Buddy said he figured there must be something in poetry if a girl like me spent all her days over it, so each time we met I read him some poetry and explained to him what I found in it. It was Buddy's idea. He always arranged our week-ends so we'd never regret wasting our time in any way. Buddy's father was a teacher, and I think Buddy could have been a teacher as well, he was always trying to explain things to me and introduce me to new knowledge.

Suddenly, after I finished a poem, he said, 'Esther, have you ever seen a man?'

The way he said it I knew he didn't mean a regular man or a man in general, I knew he meant a man naked.

'No,' I said. 'Only statues.'

'Well, don't you think you would like to see me?'

38

I didn't know what to say. My mother and my grandmother had started hinting around to me a lot lately about what a fine, clean boy Buddy Willard was, coming from such a fine, clean family, and how everybody at church thought he was a model person, so kind to his parents and to older people, as well as so athletic and so handsome and so intelligent.

All I'd heard about, really, was how fine and clean Buddy was and how he was the kind of person a girl should stay fine and clean for. So I didn't really see the harm in anything Buddy would think up to do.

'Well, all right, I guess so,' I said.

I stared at Buddy while he unzipped his chino pants and took them off and laid them on a chair and then took off his underpants that were made of something like nylon fishnet.

'They're cool,' he explained, 'and my mother says they wash easily.'

Then he just stood there in front of me and I kept on staring at him. The only think I could think of was turkey neck and turkey gizzards, and I felt very depressed.

Buddy seemed hurt I didn't say anything. 'I think you ought to get used to me like this,' he said. 'Now let me see you.'

But undressing in front of Buddy suddenly appealed to me about as much as having my Posture Picture taken at college, where you have to stand naked in front of a camera, knowing all the time that a picture of you stark naked, both full view and side view, is going into the college gym files to be marked A B C or D depending on how straight you are.

'Oh, some other time,' I said.

'All right.' Buddy got dressed again . . .[33]

The detachment[34] that birth and Buddy's exhibit inspires, gradually loses its ironic edge and becomes self-loathing, suicidal. Eventually, she can no longer read or write, and is reduced to contemplating her senior honours thesis on 'twin images' in *Finnegans Wake*. In

---

[33] *The Bell Jar*, Heinemann, London, 1962, pp. 69–71.
[34] There is in Sylvia, as in most writers affected by the Transcendental heritage, a strong Calvinist strain, a religious asceticism which reappears in an aesthetic guise. In this context, the male is idealized as the woman once was in our literature, and falls, as she did, when he neglects his authoritative role for a 'common' impulse.

one climactic scene, she throws all her wardrobe, her body's thesaurus, piece by piece from the roof of a New York hotel. In another, only elemental instinct saves her.

> I thought I would swim out until I was too tired to swim back. As I paddled on, my heartbeat boomed like a dull motor in my ears.
> I am I am I am.[35]

Finally, after several abortive attempts to take her life, she swallows a bottle of sleeping pills and lies down in the basement crawl space of her family home to die. After several days she is found, saved, and institutionalized. It is in this context that we see her suspicion has become paranoiac, her vision schizophrenic. Yet just how undescriptive such labels are is clearly shown in her own undiagnostic analysis.

> The negro wheeled the food cart into the patients' dining-room. The Psychiatric Ward at the hospital was very small— just two corridors in an L-shape, lined with rooms, and an alcove of beds behind the OT shop, where I was, and a little area with a table and a few seats by a window in the corner of the L, which was our lounge and dining-room.
> Usually, it was a shrunken old white man that brought our food, but today it was a negro. The negro was with a woman in blue stiletto heels, and she was telling him what to do. The negro kept grinning and chuckling in a silly way.
> Then he carried a tray over to our table with three lidded tin tureens on it, and started banging the tureens down. The woman left the room, locking the door behind her. All the time the negro was banging down the tureens and then the dented silver and the thick, white china plates, he gawped at us with big, rolling eyes.
> I could tell we were his first crazy people.
> Nobody at the table made a move to take the lids off the tin tureens, and the nurse stood back to see if any of us would take the lids off before she came to do it. Usually Mrs. Tomolillo had taken the lids off and dished out everybody's food like a

[35] *Ibid.,* p. 167.

little mother, but then they sent her home, and nobody seemed to want to take her place.

I was starving, so I lifted the lid off the first bowl.

'That's very nice of you, Esther,' the nurse said pleasantly. 'Would you like to take some beans and pass them round to the others?'

I dished myself out a helping of green string beans and turned to pass the tureen to the enormous red-headed woman at my right. This was the first time the red-headed woman had been allowed up to the table. I had seen her once, at the very end of the L-shaped corridor, standing in front of an open door with bars on the square, inset window.

She had been yelling and laughing in a rude way and slapping her thighs at the passing doctors, and the white-jacketed attendant who took care of the people in that end of the ward was leaning against the hall radiator, laughing himself sick.

The red-headed woman snatched the tureen from me and upended it on her plate. Beans mountained up in front of her and scattered over on to her lap and on to the floor like stiff, green straws.

'Oh, Mrs. Mole!' the nurse said in a sad voice, 'I think you better eat in your room today.'

And she returned most of the beans to the tureen and gave it to the person next to Mrs. Mole and led Mrs. Mole off. All the way down the hall to her room, Mrs. Mole kept turning round and making leering faces at us, and ugly oinking noises.

The negro had come back and was starting to collect the empty plates of people who hadn't dished out any beans yet.

'We're not done,' I told him. 'You can just wait.'

'Mah, mah!' The negro widened his eyes in mock wonder. He glanced round. The nurse had not yet returned from locking up Mrs. Mole. The negro made me an insolent bow. 'Miss Mucky-Muck,' he said under his breath.

I lifted the lid off the second tureen and uncovered a wedge of macaroni, stone-cold and stuck together in a gluey paste. The third and last tureen was chock-full of baked beans.

Now I knew perfectly well you didn't serve two kinds of beans together at a meal. Beans and carrots, or beans and peas,

41

maybe, but never beans and beans. The negro was just trying to see how much we would take.

The nurse came back, and the negro edged off at a distance. I ate as much as I could of the baked beans. Then I rose from the table, passing round to the side where the nurse couldn't see me below the waist, and behind the negro, who was clearing the dirty plates. I drew my foot back and gave him a sharp, hard kick on the calf of the leg.

The negro leapt away with a yelp and rolled his eyes at me. 'Oh Miz, oh Miz,' he moaned, rubbing his leg. 'You shouldn't of done that, you shouldn't, you reely shouldn't.'

'That's what *you* get,' I said, and stared him in the eye. . . .[36]

Curiously enough, the aesthetic detachment which isolated her in the outside world confers on her, within the asylum, a peculiar source of strength. Surrounded by the insane and perverse, shorn of worldly hypocrisy, her self-pity is expanded to empathy. As she is able to become tolerant of her 'peers', she is able to finally sympathize with herself. Indeed, the suicide of a fellow inmate marks the point of her return to the world. Her ability to feel remorse and responsibility for another's death, is the sign that she has ceased to be so fascinated with her own.

Gradually, she is allowed to leave the sanitorium for forays into the 'real' world—a triumphal trip to Margaret Sanger, for example—and a slapstick deflowering at the hands of Irwin, 'a full professor at 26, with the pale, hairless body of a boy genius . . .' In the end, she is given her formal release.

The eyes and faces all turned themselves to me, and guiding myself by them as by a magical thread, I stepped into the room.[37]

It is a pat ending. Yet, all the clichés of the emancipated woman are salvaged in the end by her wry humour, recalling George Sand's remark, 'A woman can become a man, but never a gentleman', or perhaps Emily's more ambiguous '*All men say "what" to me / I thought it but a fashion*.' Yet, either as a novel or a case history, *The Bell Jar* is abortive. Indeed, as a hopeful premise plotted on the curve of her life, it is ironically tragic. Nevertheless,

[36] *Ibid.*, pp. 190–93.
[37] *Ibid.*, p. 258.

it can be valued as a poet's notebook, a holding action of the imagination against the tyranny of both fantasy and flat fact. For this novel was written not to regain her psychic balance, but to transform the opacity of language, the tyrannous headlines, into her own medium.

SCHOLARSHIP GIRL MISSING, MOTHER WORRIED . . .
SLEEPING PILLS FEARED MISSING WITH GIRL . . .
Police Sgt. Bill Hindley says: It doesn't look good . . .
GIRL FOUND ALIVE![38]

Indeed, all the characters in the book are finally reduced to the verbal equivalencies which express their various approaches to life—her mother to shorthand, her suitor to Gray's *Anatomy*, her professor to *Finnegans Wake*, her psychiatrist to professional jargon, her father to his epitaph, herself to her own epigrammatic wit, inhumanly equal to every situation. The characters stagnate in their own limited language as the narrator develops her own. The topic sentences of each lead paragraph are curiously condensed and isolated, implying that if they were compiled vertically, we would have an associative free verse poem, and not a novel at all. The prose of this book is the testing ground for the poems which will outlast it. And the book ends how and where it does, I would guess, not because she is cured, but because her talent has matured.

> *What soft, cherubic creatures*
> *The gentlewomen are!*
> *One would as soon assault a plush*
> *Or violate a star.*

LESBOS

To explain her poetry in terms of feminism is as inadequate as describing her illness as schizophrenic, yet it is impossible to ignore the thrust towards the *persona* of the 'new woman' which emerges from *The Bell Jar*. She remains among the few woman writers in recent memory to link the grand theme of womanhood

[38] *Ibid.*, p. 210–11ff.

with the destiny of modern civilization. The lucubrations of a Mary McCarthy, a Simone de Beauvoir remain merely officious by comparison.

The problem is that while we have granted the woman a measure of sophistication and sympathy in our fiction (although for the last truly sympathetic portraits, we must go back to Joyce and Lawrence) we have been loath to permit her genuine despair. Somehow, while male protagonists can wallow forever in the absurdity of their existence, those female characters who partake of a universal scepticism usually turn out to be nothing more than morose bitches whose rejection of the world is considered presumptuous.[39]

Emily remains the exemplar of the tradition. We can understand her hurt because it involves the traditional feminine burden of being ignored or rejected; and after all, she bears it with singular good grace. But by now, Emily's 'Bright Absentee', her 'dim companion', 'old nail in the breast', appears in Sylvia's work much more ambiguously as that lover/husband, brother/confessor, father/muse. The difference, of course, is that Sylvia is doing the rejecting this time, and it is difficult not to take her inability to accept love as an effrontery. Her indictment is clear, systematic as it is lyrical.

The conflicts are charted: the co-ed and the recluse; the mother and the mistress; the wife and the poetess. What begins as an affinity for the New England spinster tradition evolves a domestic fury; *Mademoiselle*'s very own Prufrock:

> You have one baby, I have two.
> I should sit on a rock off Cornwall and comb my hair.
> I should wear tiger pants, I should have an affair.
> We should meet in another life, we should meet in the air,
> Me and you.
>
> Meanwhile there's a stink of fat and baby crap.
>
> 'Lesbos'[40]

[39] To take but one example, there is not a single woman in all of Saul Bellow's work whose search for identity is viewed compassionately, while every vice of his male introspectives is given some genuine imperative. I believe this attitude is generally indicative of serious writing since the war, but I don't pretend to be able to account for it here.

[44] *The Review*, October, 1963. (See pp. 255–7 for complete text.)

What begins as a Baudelairian lament for the father,

> . . . father—your hound-bitch, daughter, friend.
> 'Electra on the Azalea Path'[41]

becomes an epiphany for her own kind.

> . . . Toad stone! Sister Bitch! Sweet Neighbor!
> 'Eavesdropper'[42]

What begins as ironic detachment in *The Bell Jar* becomes an active vengeance in 'Stings'.

> I stand in a column
>
> Of winged, unmiraculous women,
> Honey drudgers.
> I am no drudge
> Though for years I have eaten dust
> And dried plates with my dense hair.[43]

What begins as the paradox of sex and marriage becomes nothing less than the conflict between art and life.

> Perfection is terrible, it cannot have children.
> 'The Munich Mannequins'[44]

> The thought of a baby
> Stealer of cells, stealer of beauty
> She would rather be dead than fat.
> Dead and perfect, like Nefertit.
> 'The Fearful'[45]

What begins as the jealousy of another's birth becomes the jealousy of death itself. What begins as an embarrassing curiosity has become an awful certainty, or more briefly—Electra becomes Clytemnestra.

[41] *Op. cit.*
[42] *Poetry*, August, 1963.
[43] *London Magazine 3*, April, 1963.
[44] *Ariel*, Faber and Faber, 1962, pp. 74–75.
[45] *The Observer*, February 17, 1963.

> . . . And at his next step
> I shall unloose
>
> I shall unloose—
> From the smalled jeweled
> Doll he guards like a heart—
>
> The Lioness,
> The shriek in the bath,
> The cloak of holes.
>
> 'Purdah'[46]

> *My life had stood a loaded gun . . .*
> *None stir a second time*
> *On who I lay a yellow eye*
> *Or an emphatic thumb.*

WITCHBURNING

She is a very different woman in the last long year of her life. Photographs at the time indicate she has lost all resemblance to the Smith girl who won the *Mademoiselle* fiction contest. She is deliberately dowdy, hyper-English, very much the mother and established poetess. She has moved beyond the *persona* of the 'new woman'. 'Deflection' is how she chose to describe the confrontation between experience and art.

It is with the same calculated indifference, and at a period of similarly repressed crisis, that Emily Dickinson begins to dress 'all in white'. It is simply a modern reversal of style on Sylvia's part to accentuate her sense of specialness with severe hair and Victorian puffiness, as 'the magician's girl who does not flinch'.[47]

'*I am one of the lingering bad ones*,' Emily says in faintly

[46] *Poetry*, August, 1963. (See pp. 258–9 for complete text.)
[47] 'The Bee Meeting', *London Magazine*, April, 1963.

disguised self-assertion, for the Transcendentalists saw acknowledged sin as a means to grace.[48] With Sylvia, the paradox is in-
verted. Grace, the workings of the elect in our time, ultimately
turns us back to the nature of evil. Emily chose to pose as an angel
to emphasize her witchcraft; Sylvia adopts witchcraft to approach
heavenly perfection. Or in Emily's words:

> 'Twas a divine insanity
> The sorrow to be sane
> Should I again experience,
> 'Tis antidote to turn
> To tones of solid witchcraft.
> Magicians be asleep
> But magic hath an element
> Like Deity to keep!

Sylvia suggests the same vision through a Janus-mask:

> Only the Devil can eat the devil out.
> In the month of red leaves I climb to a bed of fire.
> . . .
> My ankles brighten. Brightness ascends my thighs.
> I am lost, I am lost, in the robes of all this light.
>
> 'Witch Burning'[49]

In these poems, while the witch replaces the bitch, so to speak,
she remains aware of the cost of such ennobling. As she interjects
laconically in the above poem; 'it is easy to blame the dark'. Yet,
more importantly, the adoption of the witch, the avenger, signi-
fies a further intensification of technique. Compare the last lines,
for example, of 'Main Street Midnight',[50]

> Rats' teeth gut the city
> Shaken by the owl cry.

---

[48] See R. W. Emerson's 'Uriel' for the most radical statement of this doctrine; i.e.
'Evil will bless, and ice will burn.'
[49] 'Witch Burning', *The Texas Quarterly*, Winter, 1960.
[50] *The Spectator*, February 13, 1959.

with those of 'Watercolour of Grantchester Meadows[51] a year later:

> How in such mild air
> The owl shall stoop from his turret, the rat cry out.

Or more dramatically, look at 'Facelift':[52]

> Now she is done for, the dewlapped lady
> I watched settle, line by line, in my mirror—
> Old sock-face, sagged on a darning egg.
> They've trapped her in some laboratory jar.
> Let her die there, or wither incessantly for the next fifty years,
> Nodding and rocking and fingering her thin hair.
> Mother to myself, I wake swaddled in gauze,
> Pink and smooth as a baby . . .

and then at 'Getting There',[53] one of the last poems:

> > I shall bury the wounded like pupas,
> > I shall count and bury the dead.
> > Let their souls writhe in a dew,
> > Incense in my track.
> > The carriages rock, they are cradles.
> > And I stepping from this skin
> > Of old bandages, boredoms, old faces
> >
> > Step to you from the black car of Lethe,
> > Pure as a baby.

There is a new swift, breathless tone—which Emily would recognize as 'gem tactics'—in these later poems. With the same imagery and to the same music, she is stepping out of the cocoon of a disgruntled feminism; even the vehicle of witchcraft, the self-conscious sleight-of-hand is absorbed. The terms of her private war have been escalated.

She is becoming the myth of herself.

[51] *The New Yorker*, May 28, 1960.
[52] *Poetry*, March, 1962.
[53] *Encounter*, October, 1963.

My life closed twice before its close.

EDGE

The last poems are written with an intensity and rapidity which cause her friends to fear for her; they remain one of the most astonishing creative outbursts of our generation. I believe they will be recognized as a breakthrough in modern poetry—perhaps even more importantly, as a break of poetry *from* the modern—for she not only rewedded imagist technique to the narrative line, but demonstrated that our present division of poetry into the 'academic' and 'beat'—'cooked and uncooked' in Robert Lowell's words—is historically arbitrary. She showed us that the poet can still deal with the most mystical elements of existence without sacrificing any precision of craftsmanship. In the last poems, there is not the slightest gap between theory and realization, between myth and the concrete particular—they utterly escape the self-consciousness of craft. Her experience and her art are again indivisible, as they were when she lived by the sea.

> You have a hole, it's a poultice.
> You have an eye, it's an image.
> My boy, it's your last resort.
> Will you marry it, marry it, marry it.
>   'The Applicant'[54]

Metrically, the accomplishment is deceptively simple. The final poems recall Emily's hymn meters as their syllabic plainsong intensifies the apocalyptic imagery.

> O heart, such disorganization!
> The stars are flashing like terrible numerals.
> A B C, her eyelids say.
>   'An Appearance'[55]

[54] *London Magazine,* January, 1963.
[55] *Times Literary Supplement,* January 20, 1966. (See p. 254 for complete text.)

The 'larger, weary breath' is named finally in 'Death & Co.';[56]

> Two, of course there are two.
> It seems perfectly natural now . . .

and the 'Other' returns in his several guises; as the lover in 'The Other';[57]

> You come in late, wiping your lips . . .
>
> . . . how you insert yourself
>
> Between myself and myself!

as the husband in 'The Jailor';[58]

> My night sweats grease the breakfast plate.
> The same placard of blue fog is wheeled into position . . .
>
> . . . What would the dark
> Do without fevers to eat?
> What would the light
> Do without eyes to knife, what would he
> Do, do, do without me?

and finally, as the father in 'Daddy'.[59]

> You do not do, you do not do
> Any more, black shoe
> In which I have lived like a foot
> For thirty years, poor and white,
> Barely daring to breath or Achoo!
>
> Daddy, I have had to kill you.

We must constantly be attuned to the shifts in *personae*—whether she speaks as the poor, plain bright girl of *The Bell Jar,* or the archetypal Jew of 'Daddy'—for this movement is the dynamic principle of her art. It is essential to both biographical fact and the measure of her poetry to see these shifts in role as a poet's search for the most authoritative voice possible. She is not

[56] *Encounter*, October, 1963.
[57] *Ibid.*
[58] *Ibid.*
[59] *Ibid.* (See pp. 231–33 for complete text.)

relating herself to history or to any systematic philosophy in these last poems, any more than she related herself to nature in her early work. She is using history, like nature, to explain herself. It is the Transcendental vision that history is within ourselves, and that history is the flux of Compensation.

*

'The Fifty-ninth Bear, is certainly not her best work,[60] but we can value it like *The Bell Jar* as an excursion into prose to test her experience against language. The story is devastatingly straightforward. Norton and his wife Sadie are driving through the North Woods on the last day of their camping vacation. Sadie, nervous with travel and herself, invents a game of counting bears to break the monotony. Like children identifying licence plates, they bet ten dollars on the number of bears they will see by the end of the day.

Sadie takes fifty-nine, and gradually their relationship is obliterated by her obsession to realize her chosen number. At one point, Sadie crashes down a slope into a thicket, camera swinging wildly from her neck, in the hope of getting a shot of an elk. The elk and its image elude her; she laments that it was probably too dark for a picture anyway. Her husband, totally insular now, sympathizes with the animals his wife is tracking down, identifying with the natural processes she is disturbing. For the rest of the day she exhausts him, wanting to see *everything*, and finally, fifty-eight bears later, low on gas, they make camp by a lake, eat and retire to their tent. They are awoken by number fifty-nine, naturally; *Her* Bear, amok in their garbage. Norton goes out to confront him:

> The darkness fisted and struck. The light went out. The moon went out in a cloud. A hot nausea flamed through his heart and bowels. He struggled among petals, waxy white and splotched with red, tasting the thick, sweet honey that filled his throat. As from a rapidly receding planet, he heard Sadie's cry, whether of terror or triumph, he could not tell . . .[61]

[60] None of her short stories seem to me as effective as most of her poetry or *The Bell Jar*, though they deal with similar themes.
[61] 'The Fifty-ninth Bear', *London Magazine*, February, 1961.

Sadie's menagerie is complete at the expense of Norton and his commonplace natural impulses; the completed image conquers inchoate nature. 'I have done it again'[62] as Lady Lazarus says. Yet we know in the awful consequences of her triumph, that, 'If he were I, he would do what I did.'[63]

> *Love is anterior to life,*
> *Posterior to death,*
> *Initial of creation, and*
> *The exponent of breath.*

WORDS

Hers is extremist poetry, to be sure, and as such, we cannot tell how well it will wear. But one thing is certain; if the literature of this decade has focused on the Apocalyptic vision, in both its prophetic and parodic forms, then this poetry is the definitive— exhaustive—statement of that vision.

It must be left to others to fit the development of her *personae* more precisely against the details of her private life, as clinical/biographical information and more poetry, possibly, becomes available. But they should be careful about delimiting her art in either psychological or historical terms. In this regard, I am not sure that 'confessional' is the appropriate term for the late poems, even though her concerns frequently parallel those of Lowell and Sexton.[64] For there seems to me to be a definite effort to move *beyond* the anguish of the self in these poems, towards the establishment of a new, more impersonal, editorial, even pro-

---

[62] 'Lady Lazarus', *Encounter*, October, 1963.

[63] 'The Hanging Man', *Ariel*.

[64] The greatest single influence on Sylvia Plath's work may have been overlooked since it is so obvious—Ted Hughes. I do not refer to the poems obviously written on the same occasion (his 'View of a Pig', and her 'Sow' for example) but without suggesting any specific causal connection, I would draw attention to the poetic point of view and image building of such poems by Hughes as :'The Hawk in the Rain', 'Incompatibilities', 'Childbirth' and 'Cleopatra to the Asp'. While it may seem gratuitous in this context, I still want to note that Hughes's work has developed extraordinarily since this time, and from an American point of view at least, he has become the most accomplished contemporary British poet.

phetic voice. While the 'self' still remains at the centre of the poem, it is nonetheless a different self, one more powerful, less biographically identifiable; a voice at one remove from the crises it invokes. [I am reminded here of a student who, after a lecture on Plath, told me with no little scorn; 'the only difference between artists and people like me is that artists watch themselves die, while we're dead before we know it'.]

Are we surprised that such fierce talent could develop in Wellesley, Massachusetts and Cambridge, England? Had she been incarcerated, exiled, undiscovered, executed, we could understand her as a part of the extreme twentieth-century violence which most Anglo-American poets have been personally spared. We might then see her as heir to Mayakovsky, Rimbaud, Lorca, Rilke, more than Emily Dickinson or Wallace Stevens. Yet this is the very point. For in absorbing, personalizing the socio-political catastrophes of the century, she reminds us that they are ultimately metaphors of the terrifying human mind. Sylvia Plath is, above all, a poet of the cold-war; not that conflict of pseudo-ideologies, but of the private guerrilla warfare we carry out against each other every day. Remember the conflagration behind the Fourth of July!

In the very last poems, death is pre-eminent but strangely unoppressive. Love and Death, all rivals, are resolved within the irreversability of experience.

> Words dry and riderless,
> The indefatigable hoof-taps.
> While
> From the bottom of the pool, fixed stars
> Govern a life.
> 'Words'[65]

Yet death, through the art which prefigures and triumphs over it, is finally confronted in a way even Freud could not imagine.

[65] *Ariel*, p. 86. [This was the last poem she wrote.]

Originally, the ego includes everything, later it detaches from itself the external world. The ego-feeling we are aware of now is thus only a shrunken vestige of a far more *extensive feeling*—a feeling which embraced the universe and expressed an inseparable connection of the ego with the external world. If we may suppose that this primary ego-feeling has been preserved in the minds of many people . . . it would co-exist like a sort of counterpart with the narrower and more sharply outlined ego—feeling or maturity, and the ideational content belonging to it would be precisely the notion of limitless extension and oneness with the universe . . . 'oceanic' . . . I can imagine that the oceanic feeling could become connected with religion later on . . .[66, 67]

That art may have become the modern 'religion' is not the interesting question here. It is rather the way this strange girl, so totally in awe of herself, experimented with the voices available to her. At its height, her poetry expresses that 'extensive feeling' which Freud claims we lose as the cost of enduring and is regained only in pathological guises. *The state of being in love threatens to obliterate the boundaries between ego and object.* . . . She rejected that warning; in the final poems there is no boundary between life and death, mind and artifact. The ultimate *persona* is that of transcendence, and for the cost of that vision, Emily remains the better psychologist:

> *Ah, brig, good-night*
> *To crew and you;*
> *The ocean's heart too smooth, too blue,*
> *To break for you.*

[66] Freud, *op. cit.*

[67] Wittgenstein again . . . 'Freud has not given a scientific explanation of the ancient myth. What he has done is propound a new myth. The attractiveness of the suggestion, for instance, that all anxiety is a repetition of the anxiety of the birth trauma, is just the attractiveness of a mythology. "It is the outcome of something that happened long ago." Almost like referring to a totem . . . it may be an immense relief if it can be shown that one's life has the pattern rather of a tragedy—the tragic working out and repetition of a pattern which was determined by the primal scene.

'There is of course the difficulty of determining *what scene is the primal scene*—whether it is the scene which the patient recognizes as such, or whether it is the one whose recollection effects the cure. In practice these criteria are mingled together.' [*Conversations on Freud, op. cit.*] My italics.

Sylvia Plath evolved in poetic voice from the precocious girl, to the disturbed modern woman, to the vengeful magician, to—*Ariel*—God's Lioness. She ends a long way from the 'wingy myths' she first rejected. Like Emily, she becomes the Spirit's apprentice. Not God himself;

> Oh God, I am not like you
> In your vacuous black,
> Stars stuck all over, bright stupid confetti.
> Eternity bores me,
> I never wanted it.
>
> 'Years'[68]

but rather Pythia, Cassandra, the Whore of Babylon—harbingers of the apocalypse—those whose words defy both divinity and congregation.

If, through her art, Emily practised valour in the dark of a hopelessly constricted life, then Sylvia likewise demonstrates the integrity possible in a life hopelessly overblown. Both heroines of the peripheral, they conquer the 'incalculable malice of the everyday',[69] and precisely an existence is what they pay.

> They thought death was worth it, but I
> Have a self to recover, a queen.
> Is she dead, is she sleeping?
> Where has she been,
> With her lion-red-body, her wings of glass?
>
> Now she is flying
> More terrible than she ever was, red
> Scar in the sky, red comet
> Over the engine that killed her——
> The mausoleum, the wax house.
>
> 'Stings'[70]

---

[68] *London Magazine*, April, 1963.
[69] See 'Three Women', excerpted in the Appendix.
[70] *London Magazine*, April, 1963.

SYLVIA PLATH

A. ALVAREZ

What follows was originally written as a memorial broadcast which went out on the BBC Third Programme very shortly after Sylvia Plath's death in 1963. It was designed partly as a tribute and partly as an attempt to show how those strange last poems might be read. Clearly, their newness made some kind of explanation, or hints, seem necessary. The British Council had interviewed her and taped her reading some of the last poems not long before she died. I based my broadcast on these tapes, and planned it as little more than a running commentary. So inevitably it lacks the formal poise of a proper essay. And because it was written so close to her death—a time of great turmoil and confusion—it is far rougher than anything I would do today. But perhaps that roughness is a genuine part of the thing; it seems impossible now, without entirely recasting it, to polish it up much or amplify the many points that are made too briefly. I don't even believe that more elegance would be appropriate.

At the time, it seemed more important to try to define the extraordinary originality of her later poems—what they were doing and how they were doing it—than to dwell on the tragic circumstances of her death. I still believe that that is the right priority.

The broadcast was later published in The Review *and seemed, as a result, to acquire some kind of underground critical currency. But in the process, some of the closing remarks have been misunderstood. So I have added a final note to try to get the emphasis right.*

She was a tall, spindly girl with waist-length sandy hair, which she usually wore in a bun, and that curious, advertisement-trained, transatlantic air of anxious pleasantness. But this was merely a nervous social manner; under it, she was ruthless about her perceptions, wary and very individual.

She was born in 1932. Her parents were both teachers and both of German origin: her mother Austrian, her father pure Prussian; he died when she was nine. They lived in Boston, Massachusetts: 'I went to public school,' she wrote, 'genuinely public. Everybody went.'[1] Hers was Wellesley High School. From there she went to Smith College, remorselessly winning all the prizes. In 1955 she got a Fulbright Scholarship to Newnham College, Cambridge. Whilst there she met Ted Hughes, who at that point had published almost nothing; they were married in 1956, on Bloomsday. They went to America, where she taught at Smith for a year. In 1959 they returned to England and settled there for good—first in London, then in Devon. By this time she had become a full-time exile and used to refer to herself as an English poet. In 1960 her first child, Frieda, was born and her first book, *The Colossus*, was published. Two years later she had a son, Nicholas. In the middle of January, 1963, she published her first novel, *The Bell Jar*, using a pseudonym, Victoria Lucas, partly, she told me, because she didn't consider it a serious work—though it was more serious and achieved than she admitted, and got quite good reviews—and partly because she thought too many people would be hurt by it—which was probably true. She died one month later, on the 11th of February, 1963.

Her first poem came out in the *Boston Traveller*, when she was eight-and-a-half. I have no idea what these earliest poems were like, though their subject-matter appears to have been conventional enough: 'Birds, bees, spring, fall,' she said in an interview,

> —all those subjects which are absolute gifts to the person who doesn't have any interior experience to write about.[2]

Clearly the poems were very precocious, like everything she did in her school and college days. She seemed effortlessly good at things: she was a prize scholar as well as a prize poet; and later, when she married, she was good at having children and keeping a house clean, cooking, making honey, even at riding horses. There was a ruthless efficiency in all she did which left no room for mistakes or uncertainties.

---

[1] From 'The All-Round Image', a talk prepared for the BBC Third Programme.
[2] From an interview and reading of poems made by her for the British Council.

Poetry, however, is not made by efficiency—least of all Sylvia Plath's poetry. Instead, her extraordinary general competence was, I think, made necessary by what made her write: an underlying sense of violent unease. It took a great deal of efficiency to cope with that, to keep it in check. And when the efficiency finally failed, her world collapsed.

But she was disciplined in art, as in everything else. For a first volume, by someone still in her twenties, *The Colossus* is exceptionally accomplished. A poem like 'The Ghost's Leave-taking' is fairly typical. It exhibits her broad and flexible range of language, in which the unexpected, right word comes so easily:

> . . . the waking head rubbishes out of the draggled lot
> Of sulphurous dreamscapes and obscure lunar conundrums

and her ability to make startling images out of humdrum objects:

> The oracular ghost who dwindles on pin-legs
> To a knot of laundry, with a classic bunch of sheets
> Upraised, as a hand, emblematic of farewell.

But that last line is also typical of the book's weakness: certainly it's beautiful, but also peculiarly careful, held in check, a bit ornate and rhetorical. Throughout *The Colossus* she is using her art to keep the disturbance, out of which she made her verse, at a distance. It is as though she had not yet come to grips with her subject as an artist. She has Style, but not properly her own style. You can trace the influence of Ted Hughes, and there are also poems which sound like Theodore Roethke's—including the long 'Poem for a Birthday', which stands last in the book and attempts, I think, to deal with a subject which later possessed her: her nervous breakdown and near suicide at the age of nineteen. It was this which also made the climax and main subject of her novel.

Most of the poems in *The Colossus* were written during the first three years of her marriage, from 1956 to 1959. The *real* poems began in 1960, after the birth of her daughter, Frieda. It is as though the child were a proof of her identity, as though it liberated her into her real self. I think this guess is borne out by the fact that her most creative period followed the birth of her son, two years later. This triggered off an extraordinary outburst: for two or three months, right up to her death, she was writing one, or two, sometimes three poems a day, seven days a week. She said, in a note written for the BBC:

'These new poems of mine have one thing in common. They were all written at about four in the morning—that still blue, almost eternal hour before the baby's cry, before the glassy music of the milkman, settling his bottles'.[3]

A poem like 'Poppies in October' is simpler, much more direct, than those in *The Colossus*. The unexpectedness is still there, both in the language—

. . . a sky

Palely and flamily
Igniting its carbon monoxides,

and the images—

. . . the woman in the ambulance
Whose red heart blooms through her coat so astoundingly—

But that leaping, arching imagination is no longer baroque, no longer a gesture on the surface of the poem. It is part of what she is actually saying. The poem is about the unexpectedness of the poppies, their gratuitous beauty in her own frozen life.

This change of tone and access of strength is partly, as she said herself, a technical development:

'May I say this: that the ones I've read are very recent, and I have found myself having to read them aloud to myself. Now this is something I didn't do. For example, my first book, *The Colossus*—I can't read any of the poems aloud now. I didn't write them to be read aloud. In fact, they quite privately bore me. Now these very recent ones—I've got to say them. I speak them to myself. Whatever lucidity they may have comes from the fact that I say them aloud.'[4]

[3] From the introductory notes to 'New Poems', a reading prepared for the BBC Third Programme but never broadcast.
[4] From an interview and reading of poems made by her for the British Council.

The difference, in short, is between finger-count and ear-count; one measures the rhythm by rules, the other catches the movement by the inner disturbance it creates. And she could only 'write poems out loud' when she had discovered her own speaking voice; that is, her own identity.

The second main difference between this and her earlier verse is in the direct relevance of the experience. In 'The Ghost's Leave-taking' the subject is nominally very personal—it's about the way dreams stay with you when you first wake up—but the effect is predominantly of very brilliant scene-setting. In 'Poppies in October', on the other hand, what starts as a description finishes as a way of defining her own state of mind. This, I think, is the key to the later poems; the more vivid and imaginative the details are, the more resolutely she turns them inwards. The more objective they seem, the more subjective they, in fact, become. Take, for example, a poem about her favourite horse, 'Ariel':

> Stasis in darkness.
> Then the substanceless blue
> Pour of tor and distances.

> God's lioness,
> How one we grow,
> Pivot of heels and knees!—The furrow

> Splits and passes, sister to
> The brown arc
> Of the neck I cannot catch,

> Nigger-eye
> Berries cast dark
> Hooks——

> Black sweet blood mouthfuls,
> Shadows.
> Something else

Hauls me through air——
Thighs, hair;
Flakes from my heels.

White
Godiva, I unpeel——
Dead hands, dead stringencies.

And now I
Foam to wheat, a glitter of seas.
The child's cry

Melts in the wall.
And I
Am the arrow,

The dew that flies
Suicidal, at one with the drive
Into the red

Eye, the cauldron of morning.

The difficulty with this poem lies in separating one element from
another. Yet that is also its theme; the rider is one with the horse,
the horse is one with the furrowed earth, and the dew on the
furrow is one with the rider. The movement of the imagery, like
that of the perceptions, is circular. There is also another peculiarity:
although the poem is nominally about riding a horse, it is curiously
'substanceless'—to use her own word. You are made to *feel* the
horse's physical presence, but not to see it. The detail is all inward.
It is as though the horse itself were an emotional state. So finally
the poem is not just about the stallion 'Ariel'; it is about what
happens when the 'statis in darkness' ceases to be static, when the
potential violence of the animal is unleashed. And also the violence of the rider.

In a way, most of her later poems are about just that: about the unleashing of power, about tapping the roots of her own inner violence. There is, of course, nothing so very extraordinary about that. I think that this, in general, is the direction all the best contemporary poetry is taking. She, certainly, did not claim to be original in the kind of writing she was doing:

'I've been very excited by what I feel is the new breakthrough that came with, say, Robert Lowell's *Life Studies*. This intense breakthrough into very serious, very personal emotional experience, which I feel has been partly taboo. Robert Lowell's poems about his experiences in a mental hospital, for example, interest me very much. These peculiar private and taboo subjects I feel have been explored in recent American poetry—I think particularly of the poetess Anne Sexton, who writes also about her experiences as a mother; as a mother who's had a nervous breakdown, as an extremely emotional and feeling young woman. And her poems are wonderfully craftsmanlike poems, and yet they have a kind of emotional and psychological depth which I think is something perhaps quite new and exciting.'[5]

Robert Lowell and Anne Sexton make pretty distinguished company, but I think Sylvia Plath took further than either of them her analysis of the intolerable and the 'taboo'. And she did it in a wholly original way. For example, her poem 'Fever 103°', which she described in this way:

'This poem is about two kinds of fire—the fires of hell, which merely agonize, and the fires of heaven, which purify. During the poem, the first sort of fire suffers itself into the second.[6]

Reading it for the first time, it sounds as though it were just free association on a theme: the theme that illness and pain are cumbersome and intolerable, but that if they go on long enough they cancel themselves out and the purity of death takes over. But the progress is not in fact haphazard. Death is there from the start:

[5] From an interview and reading of poems made by her for the British Council.
[6] From the introductory notes to 'New Poems', a reading prepared for the BBC Third Programme but never broadcast.

'dull, fat Cerberus . . . wheezes at the gate' right from the beginning. What the poem does is to work away at this idea of a heavy, mundane death until it is purified of all extraneous matter and only the essential bodilessness remains. At the same time this movement is also that of a personal catharsis. She is clarifying not only an abstract death, but also her feelings about it, from the cluttered and insufferable to the pure and acceptable. Her method is to let image breed image until, in some curious way, they also breed statements, conclusions:

> They will not rise,
>
> But trundle round the globe
> Choking the aged and the meek,
> The weak
>
> Hothouse baby in its crib,
> The ghastly orchid
> Hanging its hanging garden in the air,
>
> Devilish leopard!
> Radiation turned it white
> And killed it in an hour.
>
> Greasing the bodies of adulterers
> Like Hiroshima ash and eating in.
> The sin. The sin.

The baby becomes the orchid, the spotted orchid the leopard, the beast of prey the adulteress; by which time the fever has become a kind of atomic radiation (perhaps she was remembering the film *Hiroshima mon amour*, where adultery, radiation and expiation were also joined inextricably together). The idea of the individual and the world purged of sin is established, and the poem is free to move on to the realm of purification.

Now, the movement is complicated. Often in these last poems it seems unnecessarily so. The images came so easily to her that sometimes they confuse each other until the poems choke in the obscurity of their own inventiveness. But they never suffer from the final insoluble obscurity of private references—as, say, Pound's do in the *Pisan Cantos*. The reasons for Sylvia Plath's images are always there, though sometimes you have to work hard to find them. She is, in short, always in intelligent control of her feelings. Her work bears out her theories:

> I think my poems come immediately out of the sensuous and emotional experiences I have, but I must say I cannot sympathise with these cries from the heart that are informed by nothing except a needle or a knife or whatever it is. I believe that one should be able to control and manipulate experiences, even the most terrifying—like madness, being tortured, this kind of experience—and one should be able to manipulate these experiencies with an informed and intelligent mind. I think that personal experience shouldn't be a kind of shut box and mirror-looking narcissistic experience. I believe it should be generally relevant, to such things as Hiroshima and Dachau, and so on.

It seems to me that it was only by her determination both to face her most inward and terrifying experiences and to use her intelligence in doing so—so as not to be overwhelmed by them—that she managed to write these extraordinary last poems, which are at once deeply autobiographical and yet detached, generally relevant.

'Lady Lazarus' is a stage further on from 'Fever 103°'; its subject is the total purification of achieved death. It is also far more intimately concerned with the drift of Sylvia Plath's life. The deaths of Lady Lazarus correspond to her own crises: the first just after her father died, the second when she had her nervous breakdown, the third perhaps a presentiment of the death that was shortly to come. Maybe this closeness of the subject helped make the poem so direct. The details don't clog each other: they are swept forward by the current of immediate feeling, marshalled by it and ordered. But what is remarkable about the poem is the objectivity with which she handles such personal material. She is not just talking about her own private suffering. Instead, it is the very closeness of her pain which gives it a general meaning; through it she assumes the suffering of all the modern victims. Above all, she becomes an imaginary Jew. I think this is a vitally important element in her work. For two reasons. First, because anyone whose subject is suffering has a ready-made modern example of hell on earth in the concentration camps. And what matters in them is not so much the physical torture—since sadism is general and perennial—but the way modern, as it were industrial, techniques can be used to destroy utterly the human identity. Individual suffering can be heroic provided it leaves the person who suffers a sense of his own individuality—provided, that is, there is an illusion of choice remaining to him. But when suffering is mass-produced, men and women become as equal and identityless as objects on an assembly line, and nothing remains—certainly no values, no humanity. This anonymity of pain, which makes all dignity impossible, was Sylvia Plath's subject. Second, she seemed convinced, in these last poems, that the root of her suffering was the death of her father, whom she loved, who abandoned her, and who dragged her after him into death. And in her fantasies her father was pure German, pure Aryan, pure anti-semite.

It all comes together in the most powerful of her last poems, 'Daddy' (see pp. 231–233), about which she wrote the following bleak note:

> The poem is spoken by a girl with an Electra complex. Her father died while she thought he was God. Her case is complicated by the fact that her father was also a Nazi and her mother very possibly part Jewish. In the daughter the two strains marry and paralyse each other—she has to act out the awful little allegory once over before she is free of it.[7]

'Lady Lazarus' ends with a final, defensive, desperate assertion of omnipotence:

> Out of the ash
> I rise with my red hair
> And I eat men like air.

Not even that defence is left her in 'Daddy'; instead, she goes right down to the deep spring of her sickness and describes it

[7] From the introductory notes to 'New Poems', a reading prepared for the BBC Third Programme but never broadcast.

purely. What comes through most powerfully, I think, is the terrible *unforgivingness* of her verse, the continual sense not so much of violence—although there is a good deal of that—as of violent resentment that this should have been done to *her*. What she does in the poem is, with a weird detachment, to turn the violence against herself so as to show that she can equal her oppressors with her self-inflicted oppression. And this is the strategy of the concentration camps. When suffering is there whatever you do, by inflicting it upon yourself you achieve your identity, you set yourself free.

Yet the tone of the poem, like its psychological mechanisms, is not single or simple, and she uses a great deal of skill to keep it complex. Basically, her trick is to tell this horror story in a verse form as insistently jaunty and ritualistic as a nursery rhyme. And this helps her to maintain towards all the protagonists—her father, her husband and herself—a note of hard and sardonic anger, as though she were almost amused that her own suffering should be so extreme, so grotesque. The technical psychoanalytic term for this kind of insistent gaiety to protect you from what, if faced nakedly, would be insufferable, is 'manic defence'. But what, in a neurotic, is a means of avoiding reality can become, for an artist, a source of creative strength, a way of handling the unhandleable, and presenting the situation in all its fullness. When she first read me the poem a few days after she wrote it, she called it a piece of 'light verse'. It obviously isn't, yet equally obviously it also isn't the racking personal confession that a mere description or précis of it might make it sound.

Yet neither is it unchangingly vindictive or angry. The whole poem works on one single, returning note and rhyme, echoing from start to finish:

> You do not do, you do not do . . .
> . . . I used to pray to recover you.
> Ach, du . . .

There is a kind of cooing tenderness in this which complicates the other, more savage note of resentment. It brings in an element of pity, less for herself and her own suffering than for the person who made her suffer. Despite everything, 'Daddy' is a love poem.

When Sylvia Plath died I wrote an epitaph on her in *The Observer*, at the end of which I said, 'The loss to literature is inestimable.' But someone pointed out to me that this wasn't quite true. The achievement of her final style is to make poetry and death inseparable. The one could not exist without the other. And this is right. In a curious way, the poems read as though they were written posthumously. It needed not only great intelligence and insight to handle the material of them, it also took a kind of bravery. Poetry of this order is a murderous art.

Postscript, 1966.

These final remarks seem to have caused some confusion. I was not in any sense meaning to imply that breakdown or suicide is a validation of what I now call Extremist poetry. No amount of personal horror will make a good poet out of a bad one. Rather, the opposite: to know from evidence outside the poetry that a man has suffered a great deal will throw into high relief just how much he lacks as an artist.

I was also not in any sense meaning to imply that a breakdown or suicide is the necessary corollary or result of Extremist work. Obviously, the poet is not obliged to prove in his life that what he writes about is genuine. After all, he is a poet by virtue of his ability to create an imaginative world which has an objective existence apart from him. The poetry is its own proof. Indeed, the chances are that the more hip the art, the squarer the life of the artist who creates it. A genuinely hip life leaves little time for art.

But I did mean to imply that this kind of writing involves an element of risk. The Extremist artist sets out deliberately to explore the roots of his emotions, the obscurest springs of his personality, maybe even the sickness he feels himself to be prey to, 'giving himself over to it', as I have written elsewhere, 'for the sake of the range and intensity of his art'.[8] It is precisely here that the risk lies. I do not personally believe in the classical Freudian argument that art is therapeutic, that the artist is relieved of his fantasies by expressing them. On the contrary, the weird logic of art seems to be that the act of formal expression merely makes the dredged-up material more readily available to the artist. So

[8] *Under Pressure*, Penguin, 1965, p. 185.

the result of handling it in his art may well be that he finds himself living it out. Keats is the prime example of this devious mechanism: the poems of his great period—from the second Hyperion onwards—are all about death. Apparently, this great creative outburst was triggered off by nursing his brother Tom through his final illness. But if Tom's death were the cause, Keats's own may have been the ultimate effect. He had, that is, pushed death so much to the foreground of his consciousness that it became unavoidable; having written the poems there was nothing left for him to do except die.

I think much the same happened with Sylvia Plath. The very source of her creative energy was, it turned out, her self-destructiveness. But it was, precisely, a source of living energy, of her imaginative, creative power. So, though death itself may have been a side-issue, it was also an unavoidable risk in writing her kind of poem. My own impression of the circumstances surrounding her eventual death is that she gambled, not much caring whether she won or lost; and she lost. Had she won, the power of those last poems would have been in no way altered or falsified, and she would have been free to go on to other work. That she didn't is the real tragedy.

SYLVIA PLATH AND
CONFESSIONAL POETRY

M. L. ROSENTHAL

On July 30, 1965, the Third Programme of the British Broad-casting Corporation carried a discussion of confessional poetry by a number of poets and critics. It was notable that, while the poems assigned for discussion included two that were genuinely confessional in the special sense I have chosen to develop, the others were so only peripherally. Lowell's 'Skunk Hour' and Sylvia Plath's 'Lady Lazarus' were true examples because they put the speaker himself at the centre of the poem in such a way as to make his psychological vulnerability and shame an embodiment of his civilization. At its lowest point of morale, Lowell's poem presents him as for the moment a *voyeur* suffering from a sickness of will and spirit that makes him, literally, lower than the skunks that take over the poem at the end. Sylvia Plath's poem presents the author in the midst of what proved to be her final, and finally successful, suicide attempt. She sees herself as a skilled suicide-artist whose self-loathing the sadistic and voyeurist audience, easily envisioned as the Nazi-tending aspects of the civilization, appreciates all too well. It is perhaps begging the question to suggest that a genuine confessional poem has to be superbly successful artistically if it is to achieve this fusion of the private and the culturally symbolic, but it must at any rate be far more highly charged than the usual poem.

In Sylvia Plath's 'Lady Lazarus', as in 'Skunk Hour', the slow release of transforming energy, after the self-mocking 'I've done it again' with which the poem begins, builds up in a rocking movement that becomes more powerful as the poem proceeds. At the beginning the speaker is not only mocking but describing herself literally. At the end, having pushed into the depths of her hatred of the whole matrix of family, cannibalistic erotic love, and society that she is destroying symbolically by destroying herself, she promises herself a rebirth. The rebirth is couched as a threat: she will rise in her demonic fury from the grave; she is a witch who 'eats men'.

'Lady Lazarus', like many of the other poems of the volume *Ariel* (1965), is written out of a strange kind of terror, the calm centre of hysteria, the triumphant surge of affirmative projection that comes with a clear perception of despair by an energetically creative spirit. 'These new poems of mine,' wrote Sylvia Plath in an unpublished typescript, 'have one thing in common. They were all written at about four in the morning—that still, blue, almost eternal hour before cockcrow, before the baby's cry, before the glassy music of the milkman, settling his bottles.' That is, at any rate, the symbolic scene of their creation. Some of her comments on the particular poems in the same typescript (prepared for a radio broadcast that was never delivered) give a comparable impression of her sense of an ordered setting or consciousness of motivating elements within which the paradoxically doughty terror of the poems is framed. Of 'Lady Lazarus': 'The speaker is a woman who has the great and terrible gift of being reborn. The only trouble is, she has to die first. She is the phoenix, the libertarian spirit, what you will. She is also just a good, plain, very resourceful woman.' Of 'Death & Co.' (to be discussed shortly): 'This poem . . . is about the double or schizophrenic nature of death—the marmoreal coldness of Blake's death mask, say, hand in glove with the fearful softness of worms, water and the other katabolists. I imagine these two aspects of death as two men, two business friends, who have come to call.' Of 'Daddy': 'Here is a poem spoken by a girl with an Electra complex. Her father died while she thought he was God. Her case is complicated by the fact that her father was also a Nazi and her mother very possibly part Jewish. In the daughter the two strains marry and paralyse each other—she has to act out the awful little allegory once over before she is free of it.' In each of these descriptions we see the confessional being given external order by an artist's balancing of the elements involved, even though the active element in the poems is the suicidal urge and purpose in which they are caught up. In no instance does the poet confine her account of the poem to the interpretation of a purely idiosyncratic psychological state.

Sylvia Plath's range of technical resources was narrower than Robert Lowell's, and so, apparently, was her capacity for intellectual objectivity. As a highly organized woman, intensely absorbed by her children and by the emotional problems of her marriage—'a good, plain, very resourceful woman', as she says—the path she took as a poet was perhaps predictable. She chose, if that is the word, what seems to me the one alternative advance position to Lowell's along the dangerous confessional way, that of literally committing her own predicaments in the interests of her art until the one was so involved in the other that no return was possible. It was the old romantic fallacy, if you will, of confusing motive and art, or the real with the ideal. But in this instance the conception has no real meaning because the long, escalating drive towards suicide and the period of extraordinary creativity (comparable in its way to the brief, miraculous period of Keats's most fruitful writing) actually coincided, or were at least two functions of the same process. The commitment was violent, excluding other possibilities—although the poems themselves, because of their artistic character by which private obsession and disorientation become normalized as they are organized into a structure outside themselves, have many doors opening to other worlds. The poems of *Ariel*, written in 1962, were an extraordinary change from the careful, highly promising, but seldom exciting work of *The Colossus* (1960). Contemplation of the meaning of this change can easily arouse fear, for it suggests the dangers of the real thing, as opposed to the safer titillations of what usually passes for artistic and intellectual imagination. *The Colossus* does show some flashes of the long-standing imminence in Sylvia Plath of her final kind of awareness. We see it there, for instance, in one macabre line of her 'Two Views of a Cadaver Room', with its grisly echo of 'Prufrock':

In their jars the snail-nosed babies moon and glow.

We see it, in fact, in the whole of this poem, which is divided

71

into two sections. The first is about a girl's visit to a dissecting room, where she sees 'white-smocked boys' working on four cadavers, 'black as burnt turkey', and where her friend (one of these boys) hands her 'the cut-out heart like a cracked heirloom'— a gross love-token that seems to foreshadow the morbidity of the lover hinted at in 'Lady Lazarus'. The second section describes a Brueghel painting of a war scene, but with a romantic love-scene painted in the lower right-hand corner showing two lovers absorbed in one another and 'deaf to the fiddle in the hands of the death's-head shadowing their song'. The attempt to relate by simple juxtaposition a shocking personal experience of the brutal facts of death to the general theme of war represented in Brueghel's 'Panorama of smoke and slaughter' and of a 'carrion army' and to the transcendent character of art points to Sylvia Plath's major preoccupations just a short time later. So does her attempt in 'Suicide Off Egg Rock' to reconstruct exactly how the suicide of the poem felt at the moment when he drowned himself (with all the signs of a cheaply commercialized civilization behind him —the sights on the public beach, the gas tanks and factory stacks in the near distance—as well as the normal sights of children, dogs, gulls, and the breaking waves) and how it was with him afterwards when his body was an inert object.

Sylvia Plath was a true 'literalist of the imagination'. When we use the word 'vision' about her poems, it is in a concrete and not a philosophically general sense.[1] We must place one other sad earlier poem side by side with the two I have mentioned. It is 'The Disquieting Muses',[2] which gives us a literal report of her 'muses'. These were the 'three ladies' whom from childhood she would see 'nodding by night around my bed mouthless, eyeless, with stitched bald head'.

> Day now, night now, at head, side, feet,
> They stand their vigil in gowns of stone,
> Faces blank as the day I was born,
> Their shadows long in the setting sun
> That never brightens or goes down. . . .

[1] This quality is what gives a piece like 'Daddy' a dramatic and political force that is a triumph of active symbolism.
[2] *The Colossus.*

After her death, her husband, Ted Hughes, said in a memorial note that in her later poems 'there is a strange muse, bald, white, and wild, in her "hood of bone", floating over a landscape like that of the primitive painters, a burningly luminous vision of a Paradise. A Paradise which is at the same time eerily frightening, an unalterably spot-lit vision of death.'[3]

The evolution of her muse is one sign of the growth and clarification, within a brief span of months, of Sylvia Plath's peculiar awareness of the burden of her life in the whole context of modern existence. In 'Ariel', the title-poem of her second book, in which 'Lady Lazarus' appeared as well, we see how the exhilaration of swift movement on horseback—or the mere *idea* of it— suggests to her every other kind of ecstatic movement and life-awareness. Just for that very reason, the mood suddenly becomes a desolate realization of the plunge into death that is going on:

> And now I
> Foam to wheat, a glitter of seas,
> The child's cry
>
> Melts in the wall.
> And I
> Am the arrow,
>
> The dew that flies
> Suicidal, at one with the drive
> Into the red
>
> Eye, the cauldron of morning.

The difference between the early flash of ironic knowledge at sight of the 'snail-nosed babies' that so excitingly 'moon and glow' in their jars and the beautiful unfolding in 'Ariel' is very great. It lies in the author's mastery of the dynamics of a poem and in her shedding of self-consciousness after the limited success of her first book. 'She was truly driven,' wrote Lowell, in a letter to me, 'but with the mercy of great opportunities.'

I was struck, in a conversation with Sylvia Plath in 1960, with

[3] *Poetry Book Society Bulletin* (London), No. 44, February, 1965, p. 1.

her absolute certainty about the transcendence of this kind to be achieved through Lowell's methods, if only one were dauntless enough and gifted enough. Lowell writes in the same letter: 'Maybe, it's an irrelevant accident that she actually carried out the death she predicted . . . but somehow her death is part of the imaginative risk. In the best poems, one is torn by saying, "This is so true and lived that most other poetry seems like an exercise," and then one can back off and admire the dazzling technique and invention. Perfect control, like the control of a skier who avoids every death-trap until reaching the final drop.' I am reminded of the passage in Pasternak's memoirs on the suicides of the Russian poets, and of the career of Hart Crane and its relation to his *Voyages*. Lowell is the master who has survived the 'imaginative risk' both in his life and in his art.

How do we relate his remarks to a poem like 'Ariel'? I would point first to its emotional conception. In a single leap of feeling, it identifies sexual elation (in the full sense of the richest kind of encompassment of life) with its opposite, death's nothingness. As with Keats, the more intensely we pursue the exquisite essence, the more swiftly and surely we stare into the eye of mortality. And then I would point to the specifics of what Lowell calls Sylvia Plath's 'perfect control'. These have to do with the rapid exploration and compression of her motifs; with the functional use of rhyme and stanza which are yet ravishing to the ear; with the pulling up short of any tendencies to overexpand, falsify, and comment.

She was, as she says in 'Lady Lazarus', 'only thirty' when she threw herself into that last burst of writing that culminated in *Ariel* and in her death, now (as in the case of Hart Crane's poems and his suicide) forever inseparable. We shall never be able to sort out clearly the unresolved, unbearably exposed suggestibility and agitation of these poems from the purely aesthetic energy that shaped the best of them. Reading 'Daddy' or 'Fever 103°', you would say that if a poet is sensitive enough to the age and brave enough to face it directly it will kill him through the excitation of his awareness alone. Sometimes, as I have suggested in discussing 'Lady Lazarus', Sylvia Plath could not distinguish between herself and the facts of, say, Auschwitz and Hiroshima. She was victim, killer, and the place and process of horror all at once.[4]

This is not the whole picture. Though Sylvia Plath may become a legend, we ought not to indulge in oversimplification. Some of her last poems ('Poppies in October', for instance) are cries of joy despite some grimmer notes. There is rhythmic experimentation looking to the future, in particular with an adaptation of Whitman's characteristic line:

> By the roots of my hair some god got hold of me.
> I sizzled in his blue volts like a desert prophet.
>
> 'The Hanging Man'

> The tulips are too red in the first place, they hurt me. . . .
> Their redness talks to my wound, it corresponds.
> They are subtle: they seem to float, though they weigh me down,
> Upsetting me with their sudden tongues, and their colour,
> A dozen red lead sinkers round my neck.
>
> 'Tulips'

The buoyant Whitman line and the energetic impression of external forces and sense-impacts invading the private self and taking it uncontrollably in new directions of awareness should remind us that a poem is an aesthetic projection of the psychological motives behind it, perhaps, but is not the same thing as those motives. Artistically, these poems had a destiny not defined by their author's private life and suicide. Apart from the fact that they were all 'written at four in the morning', she noted, they were intended 'for the ear, not the eye'; they were 'poems written out loud'. In 'Ariel' alone, despite its tragic dimension, the leap into absolute mastery of phrasing and of the dynamics of poetic movement must be considered an important kind of affirmation. (But there are poems too that are hard to penetrate in their morbid secretiveness, or that make a weirdly incantatory black magic against unspecified persons and situations. These were not resolved by artistic process, and often seem to call for biographical rather than poetic explanations.)

Under all the other motifs of Sylvia Plath's work, however, is

---

[4] See her novel *The Bell Jar* (published under a pseudonym in 1963 and under her own name in 1966) for the light it throws on a personality like her own.

the confusion of terror at death with fascination by it. The visions of the speaker as already dead are so vivid that they become yearnings towards that condition. In a later poem like 'Death & Co.', what I have called her mastery of dynamics enables her to escape the almost inert heaviness of 'The Disquieting Muses'. 'Death & Co.' is one of several nearly perfect embodiments of this deeply compulsive motif of hers. In it, as in 'The Disquieting Muses', there is a literal vision, this time of the two faces of death: the face of the condor and the face of the revolting but irresistible lover. (These two faces are foreshadowed in 'Two Views of a Cadaver Room', already discussed, by the lover who hands the girl the heart of a corpse and by the romantic lover in the Brueghel painting.) The faces are seen in relation to a projection of herself as dead, as part of a possibly beautiful series of patterned objects though a series in which she, as her *living* self, no longer exists. The tone shifts from the literalness of almost naturalistic description to passionate contempt to incantation and then to a single death-knell effect. The pictorial shifts, meanwhile, are comparable in variety to those that might be contrived with a motion-picture camera. They move from a disgusted imagery of death the predator and connoisseur of the beauty of dead babies to an equally disgusted yet erotic picture of him as the self-centred would-be lover 'masturbating a glitter', and at last to such a vision of the speaker's own death as I have already mentioned:

> I do not stir.
> The frost makes a flower,
> The dew makes a star,
> The dead bell,
> The dead bell.

> Somebody's done for.

Thinking of this pitifully brief life (1932–1963) and career, it is hard not to ask whether the fine cultivation of poetic sensibility is after all worth the candle. The answer is yes, for reasons that I hope we all know. Yet it seems important to keep raising the question anyway.

SYLVIA PLATH: 'And I Have No Face, I Have Wanted to Efface Myself . . .'

RICHARD HOWARD

The first review I ever wrote of a book of poems was of *her* first book of poems, that breviary of estrangement (the rhymes are all slant, the end-stop avoided like a reproach), *The Colossus* (1961; all the poems in it were completed by 1959), and in my account—

> her eye is sharp and her wits responsive to what she sees. She prefers, though, to make you *hear* what she sees, the texture of her language affording a kind of analogue for the experience she presents . . . Event is reproduced in the aural imagery: 'a racket of echoes. . . . Tacking in moon-blued crooks from the black stone-built town . . . Gave way to fields and the incessant seethe of grasses.'[1] Once in a while this concern for texture as the dramatization of experience blurs the poem's movement, but in most cases what catches in the ear is governed, checked, and we grasp what it is she wishes us to know because of the way we hear it—

my *audition*, then, of these well-behaved,[2] shapely poems by a *summa cum laude* graduate of Smith who had worked as a guest editor of *Mademoiselle* and won a Fulbright to Newnham, the wife of Ted Hughes and the mother of two children, I missed a lot—I had no premonition of what was coming. Perhaps I glimpsed, though, what was *going*, what was being discarded, or stepped over, or fended off; for once I had identified the girl who speaks in 'The Manor Garden':

[1] 'Hardcastle Crags', *The Colossus*.
[2] The quality of their good conduct is fixed by her later account of her vocation: 'I feel like a very efficient tool or weapon used and in demand from moment to moment . . .

The fountains are dry and the roses over.
Incense of death. Your day approaches . . .

Hours of blankness. Some hard stars
Already yellow the heavens . . .

The small birds converge, converge . . .

as an Oracle at the world's funnelling centre, as the Lady of
Situations who acknowledged herself the victorious victim of
paralysis, the world round about locked in a process of corresponding necrosis ('the crow *settles* her garments'):

Sylvia Plath's burden is, throughout, the disaster inscribed
within the surface of landscape (if she is a 'nature poet' it is not
because she runs ahead down the path and holds out her hand):
she makes us push through the weeds with her every step of
the way, and occasionally snaps a bramble back in the most
unladylike manner:

Grub-white mulberries redden among leaves.
I'll go out and sit in white like they do,
Doing nothing. July's juice rounds their nubs . . .

Berries redden. A body of whiteness
Rots, and smells of rot under its headstone
Though the body walk out in clean linen:[3]

her poems, though there are no people in them, are instinct
with Presences, which best arrive of themselves through the
accurate evocation of their site. She has a genius for the *genius
loci* . . .

once I saw that much, once I saw that the spirit of place, for her,
was *her* spirit in *that* place: 'mist-shrouded sun focusing all the
white and silent distances that poured from every point of the
compass, hill after pale hill, to stall at my feet', why then I could
see more—my notice ended so:

[3] 'Moonrise', *The Colossus*.

78

The last poem in *The Colossus*, 'The Stones', is what I take to be a new departure. Here there is more than the Pythoness' expectancy as she broods over a broken landscape: here is a vividly human voice, speaking from 'the city of spare parts', 'the city where men are mended'. I look forward to hearing more about that.

And indeed I was—we all were—to hear a great deal more about that, more in her novel or narrative of renewal *The Bell Jar* (1963), where the same note is struck that *I* had been so struck by in 'Stones':

> There ought, I thought, to be a ritual for being born
> twice-patched, retreaded and approved for the road.[4]

and more in her second, posthumous book of poems *Ariel* (1965—Sylvia Plath took her life, or rather left us her death, in 1963).

Of course when I spoke of 'The Stones' as a departure, I did not intend the word in all the drastic sense it has come to have in Sylvia Plath's case. Still, the valedictory was there, and the words certainly drastic:

>   . . . I entered
> The stomach of indifference, the wordless cupboard.
>
> The mother of pestles diminished me.
> I became a still pebble.

The conflict, or at least the confrontation between what I should designate the lithic impulse—the desire, the need to reduce the demands of life to the unquestioning acceptance of a stone, 'taciturn and separate . . . in a quarry of silences'—and the impulse to live on, accommodating the rewards as well as the wrecks of existence so that 'the vase, reconstructed, houses/the elusive rose': such was the dilemma I glimpsed as a departure at the end of *The Colossus*, and whatever it was I missed then of the true bent, or actually the breach, of Sylvia Plath, what I *did* make out is interestingly ratified by Mr. Hughes's notes on the order of her poems:

---

[4] There is more to it than surviving another suicide attempt. 'We are all,' said Wordsworth, the least suicidal of poets, 'we are all children of a second birth.'

'The Stones' was the last poem she wrote in America. The immediate source of it was a series of poems she began as a deliberate exercise in experimental improvisation on set themes. She had never in her life improvised. The powers that compelled her to write so slowly had always been stronger than she was. But quite suddenly she found herself free to let herself drop, rather than inch over bridges of concepts.

Yet now that we have the whole thing together, the two books of poems and the novel—their interdisciplinary relevance, by the way, is suggested by conferring, as the old books used to say, such a quotation as this from the novel:

> Wherever I sat . . . I would be sitting under the same glass bell jar, stewing in my own sour air and listening to the old brag of my heart. I am, I am, I am . . .

with these lines from 'Suicide Off Egg Rock':

> Sun struck the water like a damnation.
> No pit of shadow to crawl into,
> And his blood beating the old tattoo
> I am, I am, I am . . .

—now that we can see Sylvia Plath's life, as she kept meaning us to, from the vantage of her death, we must not make too great a disjunction between the 'conceptual' and the 'immanent', the bridged and the engulfed in her utterance. It was all one effort—as Mr. Hughes says perfectly: 'she faced a task in herself, and her poetry is the record of her progress in the task . . . The poems are chapters in a mythology'—and it was all one quest, as Sylvia Plath says imperfectly (that is, with the abiding awareness of imperfection), in an uncollected poem:

> With luck . . . I shall
> Patch together a content
>
> Of sorts. Miracles occur,
> If you care to call these spasmodic
> Tricks of radiance miracles.
> 'Black Rook in Rainy Weather'

Her entire body of work can be understood best as a transaction—out of silence, into the dark—with otherness: call it death, or The Stone, or as she came to call it, 'statis in darkness' ('Ariel'), 'great Stasis' ('Years'), in the first book such negotiations taking the form of a dialogue ('your voices lay siege . . . promising sure harborage'), which is to say *taking a form*; while in the later poems she is speaking from a point of identification with stasis which is complete, resolved, irreversible ('the cold dead center / Where spilt lives congeal and stiffen to history')—she is on the other side, within the Deathly Paradise, so that it is the triumph of her final style to make expression and extinction indivisible ('I like black statements').

We say that a particularized self is original—not in the paltry sense of being new, but in the deeper sense of being old: original in the sense which deals with origins—when that self acknowledges it begins somewhere and lives its own life and, being as we also say individual, lives no other life, which is to say, dies:

> . . . It is Adam's side,
> This earth I rise from, and I in agony.
> I cannot undo myself . . .
>
> It is so small
> The place I am getting to, why are there these obstacles—
>
> The body of this woman . . .
>
> An animal
> Insane for the destination . . .
> 'Getting There'

In the experience of the original individual self, then, it is true as Freud says that the aim of all life is death: the effort of the mortal self is to reduce stimuli to an equilibrium, to cancel out tension, to return to the inanimate condition. The urge to restore an earlier state of things; to impose, indeed, a *statics*, is indeed an expression of the *conservative* nature of organic life, of the inertia inherent in it ('my bones hold a stillness'). These urges towards

81

homeostasis, these impulses to cancel out, to level off ('How she longed for winter then!— / Scrupulously austere in its order / Of white and black / Ice and rock'),[5] to 'stall'—*stalling* indeed is one of Sylvia Plath's favourite words: 'distances that poured from every point of the compass to *stall* at my feet': 'desolation, *stalled* in paint, spares the little country in the corner'; 'hammers hoisted, wheels *stalled*'; another favourite is *stilled*, as in 'these *stilled* suburbs', 'air *stilled*, silvered', 'I became a *still* pebble'; both words being derived, like the series clustering around the Latin *stolidus*, from an earlier root meaning 'to be rigid'—all these yearnings towards deadlock, towards stasis, then, are indeed beyond the pleasure principle; they tend rather to that great kingdom of alienation, of *otherness* we call ecstasy (standing outside oneself) which is not a matter of moving around but of being encircled, of being the centre of an orbit, of being transfigured, *standing still*:

> . . . till there you stood,
>
> Fixed vortex on the far
> Tip, riveting stones, air,
> All of it, together.
> > 'Man in Black'

Not movement but ecstasy, then; not pleasure but—joy. We shall best realize the goal and the gain of Sylvia Plath's poetry if we reckon with Joy as Nietzsche accounts for it:

> . . . All that suffers wants to live, longing for what is farther, higher, brighter. 'I want heirs'—thus speaks all that suffers: 'I want children, I do not want *myself.*'
> Joy it is that wants *itself*—the ring's will strives in it . . .
> Joy, however, does not want heirs, or children—joy wants itself, wants eternity, wants everything eternally the same.

And we shall best recognize the vestal responsibilities of the woman occupied by such joy if we invoke the demonstrated responsibilities of other women—such heroic initiates as Pauline Réage and Doris Lessing; it is in the cause of a sacramental joy

---

[5] 'Spinster'.

that *Histoire d'O* and *To Room Nineteen* survey the entire sweep of a spiritual evolution, an ascesis whose inevitable conclusion—after everything else has been endured—is the body's destruction. With a like submission, a like dedication:

> My heart under your foot, sister of a stone . . .

> Father, bridegroom, in this Easter egg
> Under the coronal of sugar roses

> The queen bee marries the winter of your year.
> 'The Beekeeper's Daughter'

Sylvia Plath enters upon her apprenticeship to otherness, to ecstasy: more ceremonious than Lessing, more ingenuous than Réage, but like them prepared to obey a tragic ontogeny ('I am ready for enormity'), she sloughs off—we see her divest herself of —mere personality like the cloud

> . . . that distils a mirror to reflect its own slow
> Effacement at the wind's hand,
> 'Morning Song'

in order to achieve the ecstatic identity conferred by Joy. Throughout her first book, there are recorded many impediments to this nuptial occasion. Often the very instances which are meant to provide the means, the measures of acceding to stillness, refuse to enter into a dialogue with the postulant. Though she submits herself to the ordeal, the process refuses to *take*, and the would-be victim is left with only the impenetrable surface of existence:

> Sun's brass, the moon's steely patinas,
> The leaden slag of the world—
> 'Departure'

On other more fortunate occasions, the initiation proceeds, through trials by trituration, drowning, petrifaction, calcination, all manner of murderous espousals:

> Stars grinding, crumb by crumb,
> Our own grist down to its bony face.
> 'All the Dead Dears'

But even when the universal processes are willing to do their part, some unready revulsion in the bride-apparent spoils everything, and as so often in *The Colossus*, the spell breaks

> . . . The whole landscape
> Loomed absolute as the antique world was
> Once, in its earliest sway . . .
> Enough to snuff the quick
> Of her small heat out, but before the weight
> Of stones and hills of stones could break
> Her down to mere quartz grit in that stony light
> She turned back.
>
> 'Hardcastle Crags'

There is darkness ('my hours are married to shadow'), there is silence ('I saw their mouths going up and down without a sound, as if they were sitting on the deck of a departing ship, stranding me in the middle of a huge silence'[6]), there is stupefaction ('the no-color void in some secret part of her, that long, blind, doorless and windowless corridor of pain was waiting to open up and shut her in again')—all the conditions, one might assume, for the wedding between the self—'the profane grail, the dreaming skull'—and the system, between the victim and the vortex. But no—joy cannot be willed, it can only be surrendered to, gained when it has been given over:

> I tire, imagining white Niagaras
> Build up from a rock root, as fountains build
> Against the weighty image of their fall.
>
> 'Moonrise'

That is why the poems in this first book, as the quotations from the novel, are all confessions of failure, records of estrangement, even boasts of betrayal 'in this province of the stuck record', Sylvia Plath laments, she is excluded from that true stillness which is at the centre ('it seemed / a sly world's hinges had

[6] The kinetic image of withdrawal is reworked so strikingly in *The Bell Jar* that it is worth noting here: 'it's like watching Paris from an express caboose heading in the opposite direction—every second the city gets smaller and smaller, only you feel it's really you getting smaller and smaller and lonelier and lonelier, rushing away at about a million miles an hour . . .'

swung / shut against me. All held still'—all, that is, except her own awareness, circling even yet in the stream of mere animal perpetuation,

> The stream that hustles us
> Neither nourishes nor heals
> 'The Burnt-Out Spa'

The exhaustion before its term of the lithic impulse, as I have called it, the impoverishment of the effort to escape effort ('the stars are no nearer . . . and all things sink / into a soft caul of forgetfulness . . . This is not death, it is something safer') is the worry of *The Colossus*, and we may take the aporia of the title poem as the correct centrepiece of these poems that implore the broken earth for rest:

> I shall never get you put together entirely,
> Pieced, glued, and properly jointed . . .
> Thirty years now I have labored
> To dredge the silt from your throat.
> I am none the wiser.

Landscape and weather have failed her, have refused to take her into their stony certainty ('clearly the genius of plenitude', she observes wryly, 'houses himself elsewhere'), and in two poems of supplication, the most poignant in this first book, Sylvia Plath begs the Rock Maidens—the Mothers, the Sisters, the Fates, the Muses, the Lorelei: her names are many for the Medusa-figure that will release her from the bonds of life ('my mendings itch') into the barrow of death ('by day, only the topsoil heaves. / Down there one is alone'). In the first of these, 'The Disquieting Muses', she acknowledges the gradual take-over of her being by these 'muses unhired by you, dear mother . . . these three ladies nodding by night around my bed, / Mouthless, eyeless, with stitched bald head.' The changeable earth is stanza by stanza renounced, the mortal mother is occulted, 'and I faced my travelling companions'. A little guilty still as the last two lines suggest, her loyalties to life dividing her a little from the nodal peace she seeks, Sylvia Plath accounts for her situation, says plainly enough (though I for one failed to hear her) where she is, fixed fast:

85

Day now, night now, at head, side, feet,
They stand their vigil in gowns of stone,
Faces blank as the day I was born,
Their shadows long in the setting sun
That never brightens or goes down.
And this is the kingdom you bore me to,
Mother, mother. But no frown of mine
Will betray the company I keep.

And in the second poem of petition, 'The Lorelei' (which in my first review I took for mere stage properties, though now I see— she has helped me, made me see—the *auto sacramental* which employed such devices, ritual objects in the passion of achieved death), the prayer goes up to the overpowering yet elusive forces for which she is not, palpably, ready—'it is no night to drown in'. Except for John Ashbery's early poem 'Illustration', I know of nothing that echoes farther into that undiscovered country of suicide as yet felt to be unearned, unmerited. Deterred, recalled, Sylvia Plath pleads to make the journey for which she is unready ('all the gods know is destinations'), though so eager:

Your voices lay siege. You lodge
On the pitched reefs of nightmare,

Promising sure harborage;
By day, descant from borders
Of hebetude, from the ledge

Also of high windows. Worse
Even than your maddening
Song, your silence. At the source

Of your ice-hearted calling—
Drunkenness of the great depths.
O river, I see drifting

Deep in your flux of silver
Those great goddesses of peace.
Stone, stone, ferry me down there.

So much has been said about *Ariel*, and its success—or at least its cessation—has been so vividly acknowledged, that it would be politic to agree with Sylvia Plath, or with Ted Hughes's account of her, in dismissing everything prior to 'The Stones' as juvenilia, produced in the days before she became herself. But as I hope I have shown, it was not herself she became, but totally Other, so that she (or the poems—it is all one now) looked back on 'herself' as not yet having become anything at all. The poems we know were written first in *Ariel* still admit an uncertainty:

> I am exhausted, I am exhausted—
> Pillar of white in a blackout of knives
> > 'The Bee Meeting'

—but one soon to be resolved. 'Your first gift,' she says to death in 'The Rival', 'is making stone out of everything.' And in most of these poems, we have the sense that the fierce calm sisters apostrophized in 'The Lorelei' have done their work for her, and that she has come to that place to which she asked to be ferried: the last poem in the book, 'Words', is that poem of Nietzschean Joy which dispenses with heirs, with children, which wants itself, wants eternity, wants everything eternally the same:

> Words dry and riderless,
> The indefatigable hoof-taps.
> While
> From the bottom of the pool, fixed stars
> Govern a life.

No longer a postulant, she has been accepted in that 'country far away as health', and we may take all these terrible statements as the spousal-verses of the marriage arranged so long ago: 'the soul is a bride / in a still place.' There is no pathos in the accents of these final poems, only a certain pride, the pride of an utter and ultimate surrender (like the pride of O, naked and chained in her owl mask, as she asks Sir Stephen for death); 'Tulips', for example, is a poem of total purification—not even the rhythms any longer resist the run of utterance from what Sylvia Plath called her 'silent centre':

87

My body is a pebble . . . they tend it as water
Tends to the pebbles it must run over, smoothing them
    gently . . .
I am a nun now, I've never been so pure.

I didn't want any flowers, I only wanted
To lie with my hands turned up and be utterly empty.
How free it is, you have no idea how free—
The peacefulness is so big it dazes you,
And it asks nothing . . .
It is what the dead close on, finally.

Deliver me from the body of this death! That is the great sacramental cry of our culture, and in these unquestioning last poems
of Sylvia Plath's, it is to death that the words are addressed, and
what she is delivered of, as of a child, is the world itself, to which,
in her mystical marriage, she has given birth:

Let it not come by the mail, finger by finger.
Let it not come by word of mouth, I should be sixty
By the time the whole of it was delivered, and too numb
    to use it.
Only let down the veil, the veil, the veil . . .

There would be a nobility then, there would be a birthday.
And the knife not carve, but enter

Pure and clean as the cry of a baby,
And the universe slide from my side.
                                                    'A Birthday Present'

88

PART II

SEA-IMAGERY IN THE WORK OF
SYLVIA PLATH

EDWARD LUCIE-SMITH

Since Sylvia Plath's reputation was to a large extent created by her second and posthumous volume of poems, *Ariel*, and since it is clear, even to a casual reader, that there is a marked change of style between the poems in this and those to be found in her first book, *The Colossus*, there has been an understandable tendency to think of her literary career as something which was broken into two distinct halves. I believe that this view of her work is a false one, and that she was really a writer of exceptional and persistent unity. The accidents of publication have in fact seen to it that a whole segment of her work is largely missing—the middle-period poems. These have only so far been brought together in a small, limited-edition booklet, *Uncollected Poems*, published under my own imprint, Turret Books. It is these poems which to some extent provide the key to her development as a writer. Sylvia Plath herself was inclined to reject them, as she felt that they had been transcended by later work. But they are still poems of exceptional quality and interest, and they show a marked advance on *The Colossus*, while at the same time pointing forward to the poet's late style.

One of the easiest ways to prove this continuity of development is by looking at a particular kind of imagery which occurs again and again in Sylvia Plath's poetry—the imagery of the sea. One can guess how much the sea and the sea-shore meant to her from one of the most powerful scenes in her autobiographical novel, *The Bell Jar*. The heroine sits on the shore, trying to summon up the resolution for a suicide by drowning. The episode ends like this:

I shivered.

The stones lay lumpish and cold under my bare feet. I thought longingly of the black shoes on the beach. A wave drew back, like a hand, then advanced and touched my foot.

The drench seemed to come off the sea-floor itself, where blind white fish ferried themselves by their own light through the great polar cold. I saw sharks' teeth and whales' earbones littered about down there like gravestones.

I waited, as if the sea could make my decision for me.

A second wave collapsed over my feet, lipped with white froth, and the chill gripped my ankles with a mortal ache.

My flesh winced, in cowardice, from such a death.

I picked up my pocket-book and started back over the cold stones to where my shoes kept their vigil in the violet light.

The tone, and style of this are instantly recognizable to anyone who has read the poetry. So, too, is the notion that the sea is simultaneously menacing yet peaceful—a solution, even if a harsh one, to the problems of life. Here is another version of these feelings, as expressed in the rather literary early poem 'Lorelei', which concludes thus:

> At the source
>
> Of your ice-hearted calling—
> Drunkenness of the great depths.
> O river, I see drifting
>
> Deep in your flux of silver
> Those great goddesses of peace.
> Stone, stone, ferry me down there.

And the very next poem in *The Colossus* is still mulling over the same ideas, in a style which perhaps owes something to Robert Lowell. 'Point Shirley' speaks of the place where the poet's grandmother used to live:

> Steadily the sea
> Eats at Point Shirley. She died blessed,
> And I come by
> Bones, bones only, pawed and tossed,
> A dog-faced sea.
> The sun sinks under Boston, bloody red.

In this passage, the mature writer is already fleetingly visible. The conjunction of 'bones' and the 'dog-faced sea' has something of the strength and crispness of the writing in *Ariel*.

In a third poem, 'Suicide Off Egg Rock', Sylvia Plath comes closest of all to finding a poetic equivalent to the scene from *The Bell Jar* which I've already quoted. The poem begins thus:

> Behind him the hotdogs split and drizzled
> On the public grills, and the ochreous salt flats,
> Gas tanks, factory stacks—that landscape
> Of imperfections his bowels were part of—
> Rippled and pulsed in the glassy updraught.
> Sun struck the water like a damnation.

It would not, I believe, be going too far to say that the sea, and more especially the idea of death by water, is the central image of the whole of this first collection. The poet returns to it obsessively, again and again:

> You defy other godhood.
> I walk dry on your kingdom's border
> Exiled to no good.
>
> Your shelled bed I remember.
> Father, this thick air is murderous.
> I would breathe water.
>
> 'Full Fathom Five'

> . . . whole crabs, dead, their soggy
> Bellies pallid and upturned,
> Perform their shambling waltzes
> On the waves' dissolving turn
> And return, losing themselves
> Bit by bit to their friendly
> Element . . .
>
> 'Mussel Hunter at Rock Harbour'

One of the subtlest identifications of the sea with death occurs in 'Man in Black', a tautly written poem which is one of the very best in a volume which is now in some danger of being under-rated. The poem describes how the man's figure moves out towards the sea:

Snuff-colored sand cliffs rise

Over a great stone spit
Bared by each falling tide,
And you, across those white

Stones, strode out in your dead
Black coat, black shoes, and your
Black hair till there you stood

Fixed vortex on the far
Tip, riveting stones, air,
All of it, together.

There are several features in this passage which anticipate the subtleties of the later work—the placing of the adjective 'dead' for example, and especially the imaginative notion of this death-figure as a 'vortex'—that is, something which sucks you in, or sucks you towards itself.

The distinction which critics usually make between the poems in *The Colossus* and those in *Ariel* is that there is something much swifter, more abrupt, more sardonic about the latter. Frequently, as in the famous poem 'Daddy', there is a kind of bitter jesting on the edge of hysteria. It is interesting to see how far these characteristics have already developed in the eleven poems which are brought together in *Uncollected Poems*. 'An Appearance', in particular, has the new style fully in being:

The smile of iceboxes annihilates me.

Such blue currents in the veins of my loved one!
I heard her great heart purr.

From her lips ampersands and percent signs
Exit like kisses.
It is Monday in her mind: morals

Launder and present themselves.

94

One might hazard a guess, in fact, that this is pretty much contemporary with some of the work in *Ariel*.

In *Uncollected Poems*, the obsession with the sea is unabated. In 'Blackberrying', for example, the poet describes how she suddenly comes upon it, after following a sheep-path:

> A last hook brings me
> To the hills' northern face, and the face is orange rock
> That looks out on nothing, nothing but a great space
> Of white and pewter lights, and a din like silversmiths
> Beating and beating at an intractable metal.

In another poem, significantly entitled 'A Life', she concludes:

> The future is a grey seagull
> Tattling in its cat-voice of departure, departure.
> Age and terror, like nurses, attend her,
> And a drowned man, complaining of the great cold,
> Crawls up out of the sea.

Again, in 'Finisterre', the poet speaks of:

> Souls, rolled in the doom-noise of the sea.

The poems which go to make up *Ariel* duly continue the use of sea and water-imagery, though other symbols have now come to join this one, and perhaps manage to take precedence over it. The watery death-wish has not changed at all, however, as perhaps the specimens that follow will serve to show:

> A disturbance in mirrors,
> The sea shattering its grey one—
> 'The Couriers'

> My bones hold a stillness, the far
> Fields melt my heart.

> They threaten
> To let me through to a heaven
> Starless and fatherless, a dark water.
> 'Sheep in Fog'

The second time I meant
To last it out and not come back at all.
I rocked shut

As a seashell.
'Lady Lazarus'

The water I taste is warm and salt, like the sea,
And comes from a country far away as health.
'Tulips'

This is the sea, then, this great abeyance.
'Berck-Plage'

In a pit of rock
The sea sucks obsessively,
One hollow the whole sea's pivot:
'Contusion'

From the bottom of the pool, fixed stars
Govern a life.
'Words'

It is interesting to see how the new symbols in *Ariel* link up with this long-established one. The book, for example, has many references to the moon—'bare', 'merciless', with a light that is 'cold and planetary'; a thing 'beautiful but annihilating', a creature who 'abases her subjects'. At one point the poet tells us that:

. . . the moon, for its ivory powder, scours the sea.

The connections are so obvious as to need little stressing.

Another important set of symbols in *Ariel* is connected with the idea of 'the black man who / Bit my pretty red heart in two'. The black man is also symbolized as the 'black shoe / In which I have lived like a foot'.[1] In the second section of 'Berck-Plage', the poet says:

[1] 'Daddy'.

96

This black boot has no mercy for anybody.
Why should it, it is the hearse of a dead foot,

The high, dead, toeless foot of this priest
Who plumbs the well of his book . . .

All of these are references to the poet's father, of whom she says:

I was seven, I knew nothing.
The world occurred.
You had one leg, and a Prussian mind.

. . .
I remember a blue eye,
A briefcase of tangerines.
This was a man, then!
Death opened, like a black tree, blackly.

'Little Fugue'

But surely we have met the 'black man' before—in the pages of
The Colossus? Fairly clearly, he must also be the 'Man in Black' in
the poem of that title which I have already quoted. This hypo-
thesis is strengthened by the fact that we seem to find him again,
still walking towards the sea, in the first section of 'Berck-Plage':

The lines of the eye, scalded by these bald surfaces,

Boomerang like anchored elastics, hurting the owner.
Is it any wonder he puts on dark glasses?

Is it any wonder he affects a black cassock?
Here he comes now, among the mackerel gatherers

Who wall up their backs against him.
They are handling the black and green lozenges like
the parts of a body

The sea, that crystallized these;
Creeps away, many-snaked, with a long hiss of distress.

As one studies the relationship of the 'black man' image to the sea-imagery, it rapidly becomes plain that the sea-imagery itself has certain striking peculiarities. For example, the sea is usually thought of as hostile, and sometimes, contrary to tradition, it is thought of as male. 'Full Fathom Five', by its very title ('Full fathom five / Thy father lies . . .') makes the connection between the ocean and the hated father. Where the sea is not hostile, as I have already noted, it represents nothingness, oblivion, abeyance—things which the poet both seeks for and fears. She does not venture into it or on to it, but watches from the shore. 'Daddy' is a striking poem—perhaps the most striking Sylvia Plath ever wrote—but its theme of ritual killing, of total exorcism —does not ring quite true to the rest of her work.

Indeed, it seems apparent that one of the reasons why that work makes such a tremendous impact on the reader is through its cunning, obsessional harping on a comparatively limited number of themes and situations (almost the only major one which I have not discussed here is that to do with conception and the birth of children). These themes and situations exist as plainly in the early poems as they do in the later. Most of them are unresolved.

It is my analysis of these which leads me to feel very grave doubts about the theory which has been put forward (notably by A. Alvarez) that Sylvia Plath was an 'extremist' artist, or even one who was forced into genius by the extremity of her situation. The more closely one studies her work, the less convincing becomes the theory of a dramatic 'break', which is, I think, an essential part of Alvarez's view of it. There is no question that Sylvia Plath developed considerably as a poet. She was the very opposite of an idle writer—she was extremely ambitious, and she took a close interest in her craft. The basic themes, the basic materials of her poetry (some of them almost too frightening for anyone to confront) were there from the very beginning—it was simply that she learned to deal with them more truthfully, more incisively and more orginally. If extremism was involved, I suspect it was involuntary—something planted a long time beforehand in the psychic mechanism. In *The Colossus* she is struggling, for the most part, with precisely the same problems that she confronted in *Ariel*, and the development between the two books (a fairly continuous one as I have tried to show) must be attributed to something other than merely the problems themselves. In this respect at least, the already powerful Plath legend seems to be at variance with the facts.

THE WORLD AS ICON
On Sylvia Plath's themes

ANNETTE LAVERS

Many critics and poets have commented on Sylvia Plath's last poems. They have chiefly stressed the impact of her poetry, which galvanizes the reader like 'a keen, cold gust of reality, as though somebody had knocked out a window pane on a brilliant night', as Robert Penn Warren put it. Yet an essential character of Sylvia Plath's world seems to have been overlooked, as I gradually came to realize when I attempted to translate poems from *Ariel* and other late poems. I found that the only way in which I could hope to understand the more difficult poems was first to collect the themes and images which occurred most frequently, and then to elucidate their meaning, their significance and their interrelation. My attention was attracted by the recurrence of certain images, as well as by the fact that many poems, obscure individually, became less so when read in conjunction with others containing similar themes and images. My method was to isolate various sequences where images were relatively easy to interpret within the context. I could then attempt to attribute these newly-discovered meanings to the same images in more obscure texts, the justification of this process being the resulting intelligibility of such texts. An attempt to account for these poems intellectually does not of course replace an aesthetic assessment; it rather leads to it and facilitates it: for it becomes far easier afterwards to distinguish between the poems in which the various images coalesce harmoniously and those which could be better described as repertoires of themes. But it must be stated that even in the latter case Sylvia Plath's poetry stands on its remarkable formal merits alone; some poems may not 'make any sense' at first, but they always, and immediately, make poetic sense.

I also believed such an attempt possible because I felt that, however hermetic this poetry might be (sometimes because of biographical references), it contained nothing gratuitous. But such an approach could not perhaps have been adopted, had not the last poems formed a remarkably homogeneous corpus. This is explained by the circumstances of composition of the later poems. Sylvia Plath herself has described in an interview how many of these last poems were written at short intervals, sometimes several on the same day, many in the same surroundings and in similar circumstances.

An unexpected truth is then reached: for all the freshness of perception they reveal, the poems are essentially emblematic. They derive their meaning, both profound and sometimes literal, from an underlying code, in which objects and their qualities are endowed with stable significations, and hierarchized. It is indeed only because such a pre-ordained scheme (probably unconscious to a great extent) existed that such a large output, of such quality, was made possible. The reader cannot but perceive such a system, however dimly, and has to adopt it while he reads; for without such a feat of identification—sometimes difficult because of the highly personal interpretation Sylvia Plath put on certain objects already accepted, with other meanings, as current symbols —many poems remain impenetrable, or at least lose most of their harmonics.

This code is extremely rigid, inasmuch as an object, once charged with a given signification, never forfeits it: the moon, the snow, the colour black, always have the same function. But the attitude of the poet can vary, and thus introduce some ambiguity: the colour red, the colour blue, can play different parts in various contexts. The child as theme and the child as subject appear in very different guises. But such differences are minimal, and we can only admire the inexhaustible freshness of inspiration which allowed infinite variations on such fixed themes.

Recognition of this fact also sheds light on what Sylvia Plath was attempting to do in her poetry. She was not trying to render each experience by means uniquely suited to it, but rather to dominate such experiences by making them fit (sometimes with difficulty) within a previously adopted framework, which automatically results in their being integrated in a scale of values. Indeed, there is evidence, from those poems which seem more directly biographical in inspiration, that the same could be said about her approach to her life itself, many events having no doubt been experienced on the symbolical and mythical plane as well as on the personal, at the time they occurred. This, to some extent, applies to all of us, but without the rigidity of connotation by which the poet seems to have hoped to control the violence of her reactions.

This reduces considerably the relevance of whether some allusions are personal or not, and here the poet showed us the way in her analyses of her own poems, 'Daddy' or 'Fever 103°'; and furthermore, as we shall see, subject and object, torturer and victim are in her poetry finally indistinguishable, merely lending the depth of their existence to all-powerful entities and symbols.[1] This is not to say that biographical details are of no importance; but it should be realized that Sylvia Plath was, both consciously and unconsciously, constantly trying to establish the distanciation without which there can be no art. Thus the obscurity of some poems never springs from the fact that we do not know what personal experiences were their immediate cause (even when it is plain that there were such experiences), but from our inability to grasp the central structure according to which the clusters of images are arranged. Were the poet's private mythology more flexible, definitive impossibility to understand would follow; fortunately, this is not the case, and even poems like 'The Jailor', or 'The Other', which are written in a kind of symbolical shorthand, can eventually be made to yield their wealth of overtones.

[1] The theme of adultery, for instance, seems to transcend all possible biographical sources; if sometimes the writer takes up the position of the victim, at other times she assumes that of the guilty one, guilty of a lover's involvement with her baby or her father, or death itself:

> All day. . . .
> I dream of someone else entirely.
> And he, for this subversion,
> Hurts me, he
> With his armoury of fakery
> 'The Jailor'

Sylvia Plath's effort to achieve a necessary distanciation in her life and her art is also revealed in a fund of cultural imagery, which is greater than appears at first sight: classical reminiscences, references to historical events, contemporary allusions, numerous Christian anecdotes and symbols, philosophical concepts, legends (such as that of the vampire) and superstitions (such as that of the cracked glass as a portent of death). But the subject of the poems is never anything but an individual experience. The starting point can be a sensation ('Cut', 'Contusion'), an action (going to the cellar in 'Nick and the Candlestick'), an abstraction brought to mind by a given circumstance ('Kindness'), or, very often and in a way which affords us a glimpse into the working of her poetic self, an object which is used as a peg for a fluid symbolism ('Balloons', or the whole sequence of the bee poems). The primary object of experience is then explored at leisure, and all its symbolic potentialities reviewed, only to organize themselves finally according to familiar categories, with man firmly in the centre. Nature, reality, the world, are only in appearance interrogated as potential sources of meaning; for this meaning has been chosen once and for all, and henceforth they will only be used for their expressive possibilities. The mood is never collective; although the poet projects her private experience on a wide background, the speaking voice remains individual. Nor does this distanciating generalization ever imply that the subject of the poems is intellectual; indeed, this refusal to acknowledge the intellect as a 'positive' value will be seen to have far-reaching and tragic consequences.

Within such limits, however, Sylvia Plath's particular way of experiencing life is shown to have been an interplay between the particular and the general, which finds expression in the vast range of her vocabulary and images. The juxtaposition of the sublime and the homely, the 'poetic' and the scientific (words like *carbon monoxide*, *acetylene*, *ticker-tape*, *adding machine*), is no accident: it reveals a constant and vivifying exchange between depth and surface. 'A Birthday Present', 'Stings' are, among other things, a reflexion on the ambiguous nature of the Poet, the most common and the most unusual of beings, nearest to Nature and farthest from it.

There *is* indeed in the world of Sylvia Plath, which I shall now try to outline, an intuition of a kinship between poetry and death; yet, and this is what radically separates her from the great Romantic prototypes, this intimacy with death never gives rise to positive, fundamentally religious, feelings. In spite of a certain masochistic complacency, death always appears as a terrifying conclusion. At the most, it has a kind of saving nobility which favourably contrasts with a prosaic life.

Thus we must be aware of the danger of romanticizing a poet who would have been outstanding in any circumstances; yet it is inevitable that one should start a review of themes and images with the major theme of vulnerability, for the impression derived from even a cursory reading of her poetry is that of an overall threat. The mood is virtually always negative (we shall see that even the few optimistic poems call for a significant reservation), and ranges from mere foreboding to hopeless revolt and utter despair. In such an atmosphere, clichés assume a new significance, as in the beginning of 'Totem':

> The engine is *killing* the track, the track is silver,
> It stretches into the distance. It will be *eaten* nevertheless.
>
> Its running is useless.
> At nightfall there is the beauty of *drowned* fields . . .

The living flesh is felt as essentially vulnerable, a prey to axes, doctors' needles, butchers' and surgeons' knives, poison, snakes and tentacles, acids, vampires, leeches, bats and bees, jails and brutal boots. Small animals are butchered and eaten, man's flesh can undergo the final indignity of being cut to pieces and used as an object. The poet feels her kinship with 'the aged and the meek, / The weak / Hothouse baby in its crib' ('Fever 103°'), all those whom the 'super-people', 'with torsos of steel / Winged elbows and eyeholes / awaiting masses / Of cloud to give them expression' would condemn ('Brasilia'), and whose present 'terrible faults' she feels her 'heart too small to bandage' ('Berck-Plage'). Subjects and metaphors include a cut, a contusion, the tragedy of thalidomide, fever, an accident, a wound, paralysis, a burial, animal and human sacrifice, the burning of heretics, lands devastated by wars, exter-

mination camps: her poetry is a 'garden of tortures' in which
mutilation and annihilation take nightmarishly protean forms:

> Indeterminate criminal,
> I die with variety—
> Hung, starved, burned, hooked!
>
> 'The Jailor'

On the realistic plane, there is a feeling of an almost unbelievable
luck if nothing untoward happens:

> Spidery, unsafe.
> What glove
>
> What leatheriness
> Has protected
>
> Me from that shadow—
> 'Thalidomide'

But on the psychological plane, the mind cannot but see a sign of
its own fragility in this very multiplicity of symbols. Disintegration threatens, all the more because of a past history of breakdown.
This word is here to be understood literally:

> . . . they pulled me out of the sack,
> And they stuck me together with glue
>
> 'Daddy'

Although hidden, the break is still there. And to images which
express man's effort to build up his life and happiness:

> All night, I carpenter
>
> A space for the thing I am given,
> A love
>
> Of two wet eyes and a screech.
>
> 'Thalidomide'

or:

Love, love,
I have hung our cave with roses,
With soft rugs—

The last of Victoriana.

'Nick and the Candlestick'—see also 'The Jailor'

correspond much more numerous images of anarchic forces and centrifugal destruction ('The Arrival of the Bee Box', 'Elm', 'A Birthday Present', 'Thalidomide', and in a slightly different context, in 'Fever 103°' and 'Ariel', for instance). This obsession with catastrophe is in itself the most potent force of disintegration; it sometimes takes the form of revolt and despair, and at other times of almost an infatuation with death. We shall see that it finally vitiates and destroys every foundation for hope. In some poems, she seems to show an awareness of herself as primarily self-condemned, 'the slap and the cheek, the wound and the knife', as Baudelaire put it, and in none better than 'A Birthday Present', in which the speaker is seen to impose on a mysterious event the meaning which he expects and fears, as often happens in nightmares.[2]

In this respect, two of the numerous dangers which threaten in her poems occur with a symbolic frequency. The first is the threat of stifling or strangulation, in which an obstacle stands between life and the person, finally destroying the latter: scarves, fumes, veils, placenta and umbilical cords, tentacles are found in 'Fever 103°' or 'Medusa', for instance. The second is the threat of destruction by small enemies, outside or inside the body: bats and piranhas, bees 'complicating the features' ('Stings'), 'the isolate, slow faults/That kill, that kill, that kill', the 'spider-men', 'Winding and twining their petty fetters', 'the million / Probable motes that tick the years off my life', 'the mercuric atoms that cripple', the worms on the corpse ('The Moon and the Yew Tree', 'Nick and the Candlestick', 'Gulliver', 'Lady Lazarus', 'Elm', 'A Birthday Present', etc.). Death by fumes or carbon monoxide shows how the first threat is reducible to the second, since chemical death is due to changes in the small units of the body. Typically

[2] See also 'The Jailor'—'What would he do, do, do without me?'

blood is almost always presented in a plural form, as the 'blood berries', the 'blood bells of the fuchsia' or a 'bowl of red blooms' ('Tulips', 'Years'), as if the individual was made up of smaller units endowed with a spontaneity not necessarily in agreement with the conscious self. Thus the ambiguity found in 'A Birthday Present' is echoed in 'Cut', where the thumb is called a 'saboteur', a 'kamikaze man', and the blood is an army of a million soldiers about whom can be asked:

> Whose side are they on?

The threat being interiorized means that one touch of decay can start a systematic degeneration:

> The size of a fly,
> The doom mark
> Crawls down the wall.

> The heart shuts,
> The sea slides back,
> The mirrors are sheeted.
>   'Contusion'

This is why sinful passion is represented by spotted animals or flowers: the leopard, the tiger, the calla, the orchid; here, the stain is more than the common emblem of impurity; it goes deeper, 'like Hiroshima ash and eating in', whereas in the child 'the blood blooms clean'.

Broadly speaking, we can say that the dialectic of life and death is the sole subject of the poems. The poet's existence is presented as a cosmic drama in which these two great principles are confronted, and their struggle is expressed in patterns whose structure is accordingly antithetic. The life-principle is colour, pulsating rhythm, noise, heat, radiance, expansion, emotion and communication. Death is the other pole: darkness, stasis, silence, frost, well-defined edges and the hardness of rocks, jewels, and skulls, dryness, anything self-contained and separate or which derives its positive attributes from some other source, instead of generating them freely—for death is absence, nothingness. Such is the framework on which the poems base their innumerable variations.

The natural symbol of life is 'the beautiful red' ('Letter in November'). It is the colour of blood, the life-fluid, which expresses emotion by its pulsating centre, the heart, in its turn comparable to a wound which reveals life, or to the mouth, which kisses and screams. Colour comes as 'a gift, a love gift' ('Poppies in October'), the heart 'opens and closes / Its bowl of red blooms out of sheer love of me' ('Tulips'), with essential exuberance and generosity. In several poems, flowers like tulips and poppies evoke this centre of energy: 'Their redness talks to my wound, it corresponds' ('Tulips'). But the poet's reaction to the violent affirmation of life against a neutral background of white varies according to her degree of vitality: humble thankfulness when life manifests itself in the desert of depression and daily chores ('Poppies in October'), or despair at not being able to experience its bite and burn any more ('Poppies in July'), and the consequent wish for sensations to be finally dulled (the poppies here are a conveniently dual symbol, evoking life but containing death). Most disturbing of all is the call of life when vitality is at a low ebb; for it cannot but be responded to. The individual feels unable to cope with the demands from life, the latter in turn threatens with disintegration and appears as malevolence:

> Even through the gift paper I could hear them breathe
> Lightly, through their white swaddlings, like an awful baby.

> . . . The vivid tulips eat my oxygen.

> . . . The tulips should be behind bars like dangerous animals;
> They are opening like the mouth of some great African cat . . .

Here, as in the previous poem, whiteness, the anonymous life in hospital and needle-brought unconsciousness are preferred as a refuge.

Classically, death is black and so is foreboding, which heralds it:

> Death opened, like a black tree, blackly.
>
> 'Little Fugue'

> All morning the
> Morning has been blackening . . .
>
> 'Sheep in Fog'

It can be the darkness of caves, of cellars, of winter ('Nick and the Candlestick', 'Wintering'), or the monstrous lack of consciousness, as in 'Thalidomide':

> Negro, masked like a white,

> Your dark
> Amputations crawl and appal—

But white is also an absence of colour, and is indeed the symbol of death in some civilizations. This, coupled with the other attributes of death, makes the moon the perfect symbol for it: it shines in the night, its light is borrowed, its shape regular, well-defined and self-contained, and its bald light turns everything into stone—such are the aspects which are repeatedly stressed in poems like 'Medusa', 'Elm', 'The Moon and the Yew Tree', 'Childless Woman', 'The Rival', 'The Munich Mannequins', 'Paralytic', 'Edge'. They form a constellation which obviously transcends any personal application; although certain poems do seem to have been written with someone definite in mind, their relevance for an understanding of the poet *herself* is unquestionable, and is in fact stated in 'The Moon and the Yew Tree':

> The moon is my mother

and:

> I live here,

which has obviously a double meaning, and in 'Elm', where pursuer and pursued are as confused as they are in 'A Birthday Present', and the word 'caught' can be understood in two different and complementary ways:

> The moon also is merciless: she would drag me
> Cruelly, being barren.
> Her radiance scathes me. Or perhaps I have caught her.

> I let her go. I let her go
> Diminished and flat, as after radical surgery.
> How your bad dreams possess and endow me.

'Flat' is often used, as in 'Tulips', to express a superficial contact with life, when shapes seem two-dimensional as they do in moon-light. As the last quotation shows, it also points to childlessness—rather as an elected state than when due to sterility—a state both ridiculous ('The Rival') and guilty, since it makes passion its own end:

> The blood flood is the flood of love,
>
> The absolute sacrifice.
> It means: no more idols but me,
>
> Me and you.
> 'The Munich Mannequins'[3]

The moon is also a suitable symbol for sterility because of its circular shape, the most perfect of all, and because it rules the flux of menstrual blood. In the latter, death is in the midst of life, which is cut from its rightful end, according to Sylvia Plath (the association blood/sterile diamond is also found in Mallarmé):

> Perfection is terrible, it cannot have children.
> Cold as snow breath, it tamps the womb
>
> Where the yew trees blow like hydras
> The tree of life and the tree of life
>
> Unloosing their moons, month after month, to no purpose.
> 'The Munich Mannequins'

or in 'Childless Woman':

> The womb
> Rattles its pod, the moon
> Discharges itself from the tree with nowhere to go.
> . . . Uttering nothing but blood.

The significance of this cycle of poems devoted to what Beaudelaire called 'the cold majesty of sterile womanhood' clearly appears in 'Berck-Plage', where a hearse is described with a startlingly evocative simile:

[3] The 'sulphurous loveliness' of the mannequins, in the same poem, remind us of other poems of destructive passion; and in 'Lesbos', it is the sameness which is the perverting element.

> . . . a beautiful woman,
> A crest of breasts, eyelids and lips
> Storming the hilltop.

Death is essentially the beautiful, bad mother of fairy-tales; it has tentacles, 'it petrifies the will' ('Elm').

The feeling of guilt for a self-seeking life is so strong that it sometimes involves the notion of children. Thus in 'The Night Dances', the subject of which seems to be an attempt to oppose something to the dissolving power of infinite space and of eternity in order to establish and vindicate the power of life, the beauty of the sleeping child, all pinkness and light, is cited, but immediately this is shown as valueless, for children are a worthless extension of the self:

> Their flesh bears no relation.
> Cold folds of ego, the calla,
> And the tiger, embellishing itself—
> Spots, and a spread of hot petals.

And in 'Edge' the dead woman has claimed them back:

> She has folded
> Them back into her body as petals
> Of a rose close when the garden
> Stiffens . . .

This very important theme, with its cluster of associations, allows us, better than any other, to get an insight into the working of the poet's mind and methods. She uses what the child-psychologist Piaget has called transductive thought, a syncretic approach in which qualities are associated, not substances or concepts. Thus, once we have realized what the moon symbolizes, we can easily recognize the same connotation every time some attribute of the moon is used to qualify some object or event. This leads to underlying associations and derived meanings which can be extremely cryptic if one is not aware of their derivation. Here is an example:

> Perfection is terrible, it cannot have children.
> Cold as a snow breath, it tamps the womb
> Where the yew trees blow like hydras . . .

Others will be seen later.

Words like 'pearl', 'silver' or 'ivory', which can be used to describe moonlight, always announce some untoward event or indicate a condemnatory judgment, as in 'A Birthday Present', 'The Munich Mannequins', 'Childless Woman', 'Totem', 'Contusion', the 'sticky pearls' on 'Lady Lazarus', etc. Thus again with snow, which is cold, white, made of regular units, and melts to nothing, thus revealing its kinship with absence, death, as in 'Night Dances' or 'Wintering'. In this light, an antithesis which was startling at first seems perfectly normal: the Munich Mannequins are

> Intolerable, without mind.
> *The snow drops its pieces of darkness,*[4]
>
> Nobody's about.

Frost is a touch of death, and the dew reminds one of snow-flakes; the silver track left by a snail reminds one of the frost: thus in a poem on untoward portents:

> The word of a snail on the plate of a leaf . . .
>
> Frost on a leaf . . .
>   'The Couriers'

and more explicitly in 'Death & Co.':

> The frost makes a flower,
> The dew makes a star,
>
> The dead bell,
> The dead bell.
>
> Somebody's done for.

(see also 'Poppies in October', 'Nick and the Candlestick', etc.)

The moon is also 'bald and wild', and 'bald' is another word laden with negative connotations, as in 'The Munich Mannequins', and the 'bald and shiny suit' of the self in 'Totem'. Bald light and glare can mean the inhuman, as in 'The Hanging Man', the coldness of science, and the proximity of death.

[4] My italics.

The candle, as in 'Nick and the Candlestick' and 'Berck-Plage', symbolizes the warmth and fragility of personal life.

In 'Medusa', where the victim feels 'overexposed, like an X-ray', we find the telling phrase 'cobra light', and 'cobra' is again found (because, of course, of another link with the image of tentacles) in 'Totem'.

The image of the snake is pregnant with yet a third association: the sibilant sounds which are another, and remarkable, part of the same vast constellation, especially when associated with the vowel 'i'. These are truly, for the poet, 'the sounds of poison', as she says in 'Elm'. For instance:

> There is no mercy in the glitter of cleavers,
> The butcher's guillotine that whispers: 'How's this, how's this?'
> > 'Totem'

> > Acetic acid in a sealed tin
> > > 'The Couriers'

> > > . . . your wishes
> > Hiss at my sins
> > > 'Medusa'

> Or shall I bring you the sound of poisons?
> This is rain now, this big hush.
> And this is the fruit of it: tin-white, like arsenic.

and

> Its snaky acids kiss.
> > 'Elm'

> > And the snow, marshalling its brilliant cutlery
> > Mass after mass, saying Shh!
> > Shh! these are chess people you play with,
> > Still figures of ivory
> > > 'The Swarm'[5]

[5] A friend of the poet, on reading this, pointed out very relevantly that her own name ominously fitted within this untoward cluster of concepts, images and sounds: her married name 'Sylvia Hughes' is full of hissing sounds and calls 'silver' to mind, and Plath is a German name which, correctly pronounced, sounds like the French feminine epithet, *plate*, 'flat'. Such facts can hardly have escaped a mind and an ear as sensitive to words and emblematic associations as hers.

Moonlight turns everything into stone, and death, in a phrase of Malraux's which Sylvia Plath almost re-invents, 'turns life into destiny'. She writes in 'Berck-Plage' about a dead man:

> This is what it is to be complete. It is horrible.
>
> How far he is now, his actions
>
> Around him like livingroom furniture, like a décor.

And in 'Edge':

> The woman is perfected.
> Her dead
>
> Body wears the smile of accomplishment . . .

Events seem necessary once they have occurred, although this may be only a fatal illusion, and this is of tragic import when it concerns someone who found fascination in death. Thus, about the dead woman in 'Edge':

> The illusion of a Greek necessity
>
> Flows in the scrolls of her toga . . .

and in 'Death & Co.', where the repose of death assumes the same deceptive character:

> He tells me how sweet
> The babies look in their hospital
> Icebox, a simple
>
> Frill at the neck,
> Then the flutings of their Ionian
> Death-gowns,
> Then two little feet.

This also happens about the past, into which the present continually turns itself:

> . . . spilt lives congeal and stiffen to history.
> 'A Birthday Present'

In a poem built on the contrast between life kindled by love and the things which endure but are dead, the sharp and well-defined holly leaves evoke the latter:

> This is my property.
> Two times a day
> I pace it, sniffing
> The barbarous holly with its viridian
> Scallops, pure iron,
>
> And the well of old corpses.
> I love them.
> I love them like history.

And by a typical condensation similar to 'cobra light', the holly leaves are in another, and probably later, poem, used by themselves to signify the same petrifying quality of passing time:

> They enter as animals[6] from the outer
> Space of holly where spikes
> Are not the thoughts I turn on, like a Yogi,
> But greenness, darkness so pure
> They freeze and are.
>   'Years'

Most of Sylvia Plath's ideas seem to have needed to be translated into her personal and specific poetic language in order to become integrated to her mental universe. Of course, a general congruence between object and concept determines the adoption of a symbol; but once this is done, the concrete qualities of these symbols react in their turn on the messages and opinions they embody. Thus the antithesis whose aspects have just been studied explains to a great extent the poet's opinions on religion, the deity and the metaphysical structure of the world, on the intellect and art, on daily life and on the self.

Religion, especially as it appears in tender images of mother and child, seems to offer a refuge against the bald and wild moon, as in 'The Moon and the Yew Tree' or 'Mary's Song'; but the poet belongs outside, with the latter. And besides, the symbols of

[6] A contrasting symbol—see below, about the child.

possible intimations of a transcendent reality behind the world, clouds, are always depicted as far and high, and indifferent:

> . . . Clouds are flowering
> Blue and mystical over the face of the stars.
> Inside the church, the saints will be all blue,
> Floating on their delicate feet over the cold pews,
> Their hands and faces stiff with holiness.

('The Moon and the Yew Tree': see also 'Gulliver', 'Little Fugue', etc.)

The stiffness has a special meaning here, and so has the blue colour, blue having a very ambiguous value in this code, as we shall see. Its negative aspect is obvious when it is associated with she cobra, as in 'Totem':

> Shall the hood of the cobra appal me—
> The loneliness of its eye, the eye of the mountains
>
> Through which the sky eternally threads itself?

Here the infinity of space and time reveals its participation in the nature of death, and is felt as an enemy. In this sense, one can say about these poems what Rimbaud wrote in *A Season in Hell*, that during his mystical attempt he 'rejected from the sky azure, which is blackness'. The wastes of space are usually dark and starry; they seem at first impressive, but they are no different from the cellar of 'Wintering', full of

> appalling objects—
> Black asininity. Decay.

In this cellar the bees have to feed, during the winter, on Tate and Lyle, the ersatz of flowers, 'the refined snow', and are indeed surrounded by snow, into which they can only bury their dead. The dark reveals itself as mindlessness, 'dead boredom' ('Nick and the Candlestick'), 'black amnesias' ('Night Dances'), whose triumph over transient life is all the more unbearable. Against this, the poet reacts with revolt and a refusal to submit:

O God, I am not like you
In your vacuous black,
Stars struck all over, bright stupid confetti.
Eternity bores me,
I never wanted it . . .

And you, great Stasis—
What is so great in that!
                                'Years'

Whereas 'the world is blood-hot and personal', death, although
multiplied by the terror of the many individuals it catches, is
anonymity, 'the one death with its many sticks' ('Totem').

Hence the revolt against the deity, which is shown in 'Totem'
as a bloodthirsty pagan idol, grimacing like a skull, and at the
same time mobile like a scarecrow, and ridiculous and counter-
feit, like it. Revolt also against the priest who represents it; and
the images used in 'Daddy', which form a link between those of
'Totem' and those of 'Berck-Plage', show that there is probably
also in this a Freudian element of revolt against the father. In
'Berck-Plage', the lines:

This black boot has no mercy for anybody.
Why should it, it is the hearse of a dead foot,

The high, dead, toeless foot of this priest
Who plumbs the well of his book . . .

recall the beginning and the 10th stanza of 'Daddy', and in the
latter poem the father is described as

Not God but a swastika
So black no sky could squeak through.

This image is found again, more diffuse and mobile, in the black
spider whose arms sweep the infinite—which is therefore a net, a
trap, also—and which evokes both death and the divine totem, as
is shown by the word *stick*:

I am mad, calls the spider, waving its many arms.

And in truth it is terrible,
Multiplied in the eyes of the flies.

They buzz like blue children
In nets of the infinite,

Roped in at the end by the one
Death with its many sticks.

'Totem'

All this, of course, can apply not only to Christianity, but to all idealistic and spiritualistic philosophies, and produces all the more anxiety because a definite attraction is felt for them; and this attraction agrees with the fundamentally symbolical nature of Sylvia Plath's poetry.

In *Three Women*, the Secretary comments on God's male world:

The faceless faces of important men.

It is these men I mind:
They are so jealous of anything that is not flat!

They are jealous gods

That would have the whole world flat because they are.
I see the Father conversing with the Son.
Such flatness cannot but be holy.
'Let us make heaven,' they say.
'Let us flatten and launder the grossness from these souls'.

But in 'Totem' we read about the dead hare:

Let us eat it like Plato's afterbirth,
Let us eat it like Christ.

and with irony and revolt, but also hopeless belief:

These are the people that were important—

But elsewhere are to be found equally revealing remarks, such as, in 'Mary's Song':

> The Sunday lamb cracks in its fat,
> The fat
> Sacrifices its opacity . . .

The idea of sacrifice as the central notion of religion has deeply impressed the poet; sacrifice either of the heretics, or of the most precious and most innocent; the golden child in the poem above, the tortured Christ in 'Elm', or his suicidal 'awful God-bit' in 'Years'. Because of an identification in which the sadism attributed to the deity is fused with a masochistic drive, the idea of redemption actually has death as a consequence, as appears in 'Brasilia':

> O you who eat
>
> People like light-rays, leave
> This one
> Mirror safe, unredeemed
>
> By the dove's annihilation,
> The glory,
> The power, the glory.

The fat had to sacrifice its opacity because matter, in this dualistic universe, is the inferior partner. In the incarnation, Ideas become individualized sullied beings. The poet reacts to this basic notion with a fluctuating attitude, now existentialist, when she stresses her anguished preference for the 'blood-hot and personal' world, now essentialist, as in 'Berck-Plage':

> And the soul is a bride
>
> In a still place, and the groom is red and forgetful, he is featureless.

But if actual existence can be considered a superiority, individualized existence means separateness, which has, we have seen, a negative value. Hence the desire, expressed in an open or latent manner in many poems, for a transfiguration which will dissolve the limits of the self, this same old suit 'bald and shiny, with pockets of wishes' ('Totem'). This can be achieved in orgastic ecstasy, and in the horse's gallop we find a double symbol, for the utmost experience and the pulsating rhythm of life, and for the dispersion of the individual into the 'substanceless blue' ('Ariel', 'Years', 'Words', 'Elm').

But 'Fever 103°' indicates that guilt feelings and a desire for expiation and purification may have determined this choice of a metaphysical framework. Their origin was probably multiple and ancient; this appears when comparing 'Daddy' and 'Little Fugue':

> I am guilty of nothing (. . .)

> I was seven, I knew nothing.
> The world occurred.

with the end of 'Getting There' (see also 'The Jailor' and *Three Women*).

In 'Fever 103°', the identification of the individual, who repudiates the multiple and deceptive embodiments of the Unique in her life, with a God whom 'the world hurts' is achieved through a transfiguration. And gold, a symbol for whatever is most precious, often associated with the child or with love (as in 'Letter in November'), also evokes images of sacrifice, as in 'Mary's Song':

>   . . . On the high
> Precipice
> That emptied one man into space,
> The ovens glowed like heavens, incandescent.

> It is a heart,
> This holocaust I walk in.

It is remarkable that in this universe ideas are never felt to be life-giving; intellect is therefore no help:

> This is the light of the mind, cold and planetary.
> The trees of the mind are black. The light is blue.

('The Moon and the Yew Tree'; see also 'Nick and the Candlestick'.)

This anti-intellectualism can only cause depression, since every enduring reality is thereby interpreted as participating in the nature of death. Knowledge is therefore condemned: in *Three Women* the male world is

> . . . flatness from which ideas, destruction
> Bulldozers, guillotines, white chambers of shrieks proceed,
> Endlessly proceed . . .;

the surgeon lives among cut-up bodies in 'Berck-Plage', he is 'one mirrory eye' and surrounded by 'glittering things'. We find in these similes, as in the 'bald and shiny suit' and the 'folding mirror' of the self ('Totem') another clue. Shine, glitter, mirrors, which are or cause reflections, like the moon, are always used in a derogatory manner. And this in turn has a bearing on the status of another symbol, that of the smile.

It is sometimes used to signify tenderness, a gentle and un-alloyedly positive feeling; but it soon becomes a negative sign, because it is commonly used without sincerity, in order to re-assure oneself or the others that everything is all right, as in 'Lady Lazarus': 'Soon (. . .) the flesh (. . .) will be at home on me,/And I a smiling woman', or in 'Berck-Plage'

> Why is it so quiet, what are they hiding?
> I have two legs, and I move smilingly.

Henceforth, coupled with glitter, it symbolizes deceit, the Maya, the illusion to which all the comforting manifestations of life are shown to belong in the end. Thus can be seen the link between images such as the following ones, all expressing distrust:

> A ring of gold with the sun in it?
> Lies. Lies and a grief.
> > 'The Couriers'

> Tremulous breath at the end of my line,
> Curve of water, upleaping
> To my water rod, dazzling and grateful,
> Touching and sucking!
> > 'Medusa'

and above all 'Death & Co.', the subject of which is the terrible awakening whereby what seemed the supreme embodiment of animation and life reveals its profound kinship with death:

> Two, of course there are two.
> It seems perfectly natural now—
> The one who never looks up . . . and who
> . . . does not smile or smoke.[7]

On the contrary,

> The other does that.[8]
> His hair long and plausive.
> Bastard
> Masturbating a glitter,
> He wants to be loved.

Or again, in 'The Jailor'

> What have I eaten?
> Lies and smiles.

It is only normal, and highly significant, if in spite of all this the ever-changing face of the mirror is still used as a symbol for life which is preferred to fixity; the shattered mirror is then a metaphor for death. Thus in 'The Couriers', a poem on all the sinister portents:

> A disturbance in mirrors,
> The sea shattering its grey one—

or in 'Brasilia': 'O you (. . .) leave This one mirror safe', in 'Contusion': 'The mirrors are sheeted', or in 'Thalidomide':

> The glass cracks across,
> The image
>
> Flees and aborts like dropped mercury.[9]

---

[7] In connection with this, the 'blue and red jewels' of kindness, which smoke in the windows, and in *Three Women* that of tenderness which heals and unites, blurring harsh outlines, will be remembered. These 'blue and red jewels' are probably sleeping-pills (see 'Insomniac' in *Uncollected Poems*, and *The Bell Jar*).

[8] The poem 'The Other' is a repertoire of all the attributes of death.

[9] This last image is even clearer in 'Nick and the Candlestick'; see other centrifugal images in 'Fever 103°', or 'Ariel'.

and above all in 'Words', this being one of the two constellations of images on which the poem is built—the second will be commented on shortly:

> The sap
> Wells like tears, like the
> Water striving
> To re-establish its mirror
> Over the rock
>
> That drops and turns,
> A white skull,
> Eaten by weedy greens.

But this effort is doomed to failure, for

> From the bottom of the pool, fixed stars
> Govern a life.

Evil and nothingness are ubiquitous in Sylvia Plath's poetry. Her positive themes are therefore presented against a negative background, with an undertone of frightened defiance, as being capable of holding death and failure at bay. We shall see that even in those poems which at first sight appear untouched by menace or the obsession of death, the choice of details and adjectives betrays an underlying defensiveness, and implicit contrast. And this can be said even with regard to the few poems on the subject of children, for all other positive themes contain possibilities of degeneration and disillusion.

The child is, in principle, the fountainhead of all life and hope. His self is not yet 'bald and shiny', he is 'vague as fog', and 'Trawling (his) dark as owls do' ('You're'): a vagueness imbued with infinite possibilities, before which the parents are humbled: 'your nakedness / Shadows our safety' ('Morning Song'). He is akin to the elements, the sea, the wind, the clouds 'with no strings attached and no reflections' (as written elsewhere, in 'Gulliver'). The poet acknowledges the freedom of her own child:

> I'm no more your mother
> Than the cloud that distils a mirror to reflect its own slow
> Effacement at the wind's hand.
>
> 'Morning Song'

In the child, innocence, which for the adult can only be obtained in forgetfulness and annihilation, as in 'Getting There', 'Tulips', 'Fever 103°', is miraculously combined with individuality:

A clean slate with your own face on.
'You're'

In the face of disintegration and universal dissolution in a deceptive glitter, he is a *plenum*, the fixed point on which the envious spaces lean ('Nick and the Candlestick'), heavy and precious as gold, a divine redeemer. This is expressed in 'Morning Song' and 'You're' by an accumulation of metaphors—a poem in *The Colossus*, about pregnancy, is actually called 'Metaphors'—with rippling consonants which seek to convey this close texture, this compactness, fullness and rightness: 'a well-done sum', 'a creel of eels, all ripples'. He is like the tremendously compact and potent germ of a future universe, the absolute beginning of some ancient mythologies.

This is not to say that the image of the child never appears in poems whose general tone is one of foreboding and even despair; several have already been quoted. Even in a poem like 'Balloons', where the image, already encountered in 'Morning Song', recalls 'oval animal souls', the balloons are opposed to 'dead furniture'; in 'Nick and the Candlestick' the child is like a faltering candle in a frozen cave full of murderous fishes.[10]

Furthermore, the obvious justification of one's existence which the child brings is not always potent enough to appease the guilt of the egotist, as appears in the poems on the childless woman or those which show the dead children as appendages to the dead woman. In 'Fever 103°', guilt actually evokes the image of a 'spotted', dying child, whereas in 'Nick and the Candlestick', the blood bloomed clean in him. We might say, to summarize, that as a subject the child is positive, but that as a theme it is often combined with others which greatly diminish this positive value, and can even make it completely negative; the child-theme is then used to reinforce guilt, fear and despair.

Much the same could be said about another theme, that of the lulling comfort of everyday life. Kindness supplies another

[10] The image of the candle is again found in 'Berck-Plage' as a symbol of threatened life.

'necessary fluid', a 'poultice', and busies itself 'sweetly picking up pieces'. Love, in its beginnings, evoked 'a green in the air' which 'cushioned lovingly' the poet. And so does daily life. In the parody of the marriage ceremony which is found in 'The Applicant', the doll-like wife is in the same way guaranteed to supply whatever environment is wished for:

> You have a hole, it's a poultice.
> You have an eye, it's an image.

A task like honey-making can supply many such symbols for a poet who is capable of reading life on two levels at once; thus about the hive:

> With excessive love I enamelled it
> Thinking 'Sweetness, sweetness'.
> 'Stings'

But what happens when interest wanes and the endless stream of life-symbols dries up? The environment of daily life, when evoked like an incantation in such circumstances, is no more than 'dead furniture', fragmented and powerless:

> I survive the while,
> Arranging my morning,
> These are my fingers, this my baby.
> 'Little Fugue'

and in 'Tulips', the mood of which is the lowered vitality which makes the individual unable to cope with life:

They have swabbed me clear of my loving associations. . .

I watched my teaset, my bureaus of linen, my books
Sink out of sight, and the water went over my head.

And in the latter poem the mood is characteristically ambiguous, and the nun-like purity which follows this abandonment of all everyday associations is far from totally disagreeable. For the dullness and monotony of this life can offset its utility, especially when it is contrasted with a more vital experience; kindness and its 'cup of tea wreathed in steam' is strangely out of key with 'blood jet', poetry. And cooking, often the symbol of this daily life, after supplying a delightful metaphor for the child successfully brought into the world:

> O high-riser, my little loaf.
>
>   'You're'

can elsewhere be resented as a degrading drudgery which can make one unworthy of a revelation. The mysterious envoy in 'A Birthday Present' is made to wonder:

> Is this the one I am to appear for,
> Is this the elect one. . .?
>
> Measuring the flour, cutting off the surplus,
> Adhering to rules, to rules, to rules.
>
> Is this the one for the annunciation?
> My god, what a laugh![11]

In the cycle of the bee-poems, the hive often appears as a symbol of the hierarchy within the individual, the ancient queen 'poor and bare and unqueenly and even shameful', 'her long body rubbed of its plush' and the workers, 'unmiraculous women, honey-drudgers' ('Stings'); and the latter are felt to be malevolent, dangerous in their vast numbers. The poet expresses her kinship with the queen, the 'lost self to recover', in terms which recall poems of relevation such as 'A Birthday Present', or 'The Hanging Man':

> I am no drudge
> Though for years I have eaten dust
> And dried plates with my dense hair.
>
> And seen my strangeness evaporate,
>
> Blue dew from dangerous skin.
> Will they hate me,
> Those women who only scurry (. . .)?

[11] See also 'The Applicant': 'it can cook, it can sew . . .'

The poem ends with an image of fierce redness (which recalls that of 'Lady Lazarus' and the 'scar' in 'A Birthday Present'), and its 'final, defensive, desperate assertion of omnipotence', as A. Alvarez expressed it:

> Now she is flying
> More terrible than she ever was, red
> Scar in the sky, red comet
> Over the engine that killed her—
> The mausoleum, the wax house.

—the honey-machine, which is of course used by another of her own selves.

To the maimed self, therefore, daily life cannot give back wholeness, only crutches, a frequent symbol ('Berck-Plage', 'The Applicant'). And death can actually be welcome, since it frees one from this useless lumber, useless, yet irreversibly acquired, for man is the prey of an 'adding-machine'. The self, in 'Totem', is described as made of

> Notions and tickets, short circuits and folding mirrors

and Lady Lazarus exclaims:

> What a trash
> To annihilate each decade.

> What a million filaments.

images which recall Baudelaire's famous poems entitled 'Spleen', in which the self is similarly cumbered with things which no longer have meaning. This 'reification' which alienates the living self (and is a frequent theme in Existentialist literature) fits in the neo-platonic schema outlined above, whereby degeneration into matter is the sign of an irreversible degradation. The proliferation of *things, things* ('Berck-Plage') is used in Ionesco's plays to the same purpose. The tired person can surrender to the Welfare State-like atmosphere of hospital, which divests him from individuality and responsibility, and the style of 'The Applicant' achieves a kind of Kafkaesque bureaucratic lyricism. And 'things' are another aspect of death: in 'Berck-Plage' the dead furniture turns into nothing, like the corpse; the visible is an illusion, and the invisible alone matters.

We have seen that purification can be achieved in death, in which the scattered personality is seen as gradually withdrawing towards its vital centre and abandoning its tainted externals, as in 'Fever 103°', in 'Tulips' and in 'Paralytic':

> I smile, a buddha, all
> Wants, desire
> Falling from me like rings
> Hugging their lights.

Echoes are often used as a symbol of these externals, since they are a degradation of sound, a repetition travelling away from the original event. Thus in 'Words', in which emotion, animation, life, were contrasted with the unchangeably bare skull and the fixed stars, a second constellation of images confirms the meaning of the first: the words are 'Axes / After whose stroke the wood rings', while echoes travel off from the centre. But the words by themselves are powerless once the central intention which informed them has gone—and the horse-symbol makes us think that the poet is here thinking of love in particular:

> Years later I
> Encounter them on the road—
>
> Words dry and riderless,
> The indefatigable hoof-taps.[12]

If poetry and death can denounce the illusion of a comfortable life, cannot love bring about the same realization? This does seem to be the meaning of a line in a poem whose subject is the resurrection due to the irruption of love in a frozen life, 'Letter in November':

> O love, O celibate.

Here the solitude elsewhere brought about by ebbing life is savoured for its own sake because, like the dying person, he who is in love

---

[12] See also' old echoes' in 'Nick and the Candlestick' and *Three Women*.

> Drunk on its own scents
> Asks nothing of life.

and is momentarily free from all 'loving associations' and 'little smiling hooks'.

Yet, and as might be expected, love is the supremely ambiguous theme. To begin with, some poems, like 'Daddy' or 'Medusa', whatever their actual personal associations, present love as something to be achieved in the teeth of opposition, in spite of the past, or of terrific obstacles, as in 'Getting There'. The ten-yearly rhythm of death offsets the pulsation of life. It is true that 'Lady Lazarus' ends on a note of defiance, and 'Daddy' on the successful nailing down of the vampire, the undead, followed by compassion and a purified feeling for this other man, badly known, who was the vampire's victim:

> Daddy, you can lie back now.

But elsewhere this forced marriage appears as a certain immolation:
> Death opened, like a black tree, blackly.

> I survive the while . . .
> The clouds are a marriage dress, of that pallor.
> 'Little Fugue'

We therefore understand the ambiguity of a revelation such as that in 'A Birthday Present', where love is hoped for, but the parcel is suspected to contain death instead. Yet it is still wished for passionately, as in 'Elm', and can alone metamorphose a frozen world as in 'Letter in November':

> Love, the world
> Suddenly turns, turns colour . . .

It fills the 'Arctic' with images of spring, 'a green in the air, soft, delectable'. But this applies only to love in its beginnings, for it rapidly turns into red passion which can prove too much to bear and, in addition, being a world to itself, brings guilt.

Even more tellingly, however, the ecstasy of love, which is suggested by the gallop of a horse, is always evoked in a strangely passionless manner, which leads one to suggest that a blue and transparent transfiguration is preferred to a more personal feeling, as being psychologically safer. In 'Ariel' the horse is indeed pulsation conquered on 'stasis in darkness'; but it leads not to a fever of blood but to a pearly ecstasy:

> I foam to wheat, a glitter of seas

and a happily suicidal wish. We deal here with a sublimation, the idea of love rather than actual love. The 'substanceless blue' is that of the mystical clouds 'with no strings attached', the light of the prophets and of the superhuman 'Brasilians' who eat people like light-rays. Love is therefore subject to three forms of degradation and disappearance: the petrification of daily life and meaningless forms, the dissolution into glitter, the transfiguration which depersonalizes both object and subject. There is in fact no place here for adult relationships: in *Three Women* the Girl is unmarried, the Secretary has a bloodless relationship with her husband, although she finds at the end that she has become 'a wife'; but the Wife herself never says anything at all about the father of her child—this male baby is her only 'lover'.

Nor does the awareness of her difference and of her gifts seem to have given the poet much reassurance—certainly nothing comparable to the notion of giving birth to a child. The lack of any trace of a feeling of achievement seems, on the evidence of the poems alone, to be explained by the fact that, although the poetic urge flows irrepressibly, this generosity is suicidal, it is in the nature of a wound:

> The blood jet is poetry
> There is no stopping it.

So, although a divine visitation is wished for in the midst of everyday life, and although the poet cannot help feeling some pride and some nobility in her calling, she always conceives it as another of those numerous disintegrating factors which threaten her, and incomparably the most potent and terrifying. In fact, it is in this connection only that we can detect a genuine feeling of the divine, and a religious attitude which is on the contrary conspicuously absent in all mentions of a conventional deity.

This seems at least one of the possible interpretations of 'The Hanging Man'.[13] This in itself is evidence of great purity in poetic feeling; but if we turn to the part in which the poet can feel himself to be to some extent responsible for her art, dominating poetry as a craft, instead of being dominated by it, there is merely disenchantment, and especially when looking back on the achieved poem, always inferior in its very achievement to the ideal one. This seems to be the subject of 'The Night Dances'; in this poem, we can see that the uniqueness of the living flesh is placed, in her scale of values, *a priori* above the cold, impersonal 'mathematics' of poems. The child is elemental like the clouds, the poem is an artefact, whose beauty and regularity remind one of snowflakes, which will melt to nothing. Perhaps we are here given the rare sight of an exceptionally gifted poet who did not believe enough in poetry.

But in addition there seems to have been, in her particular case, another disturbing factor: a profound uncertainty about the possibility of reconciling womanhood and intellect, whether the origin of this is to be sought in long-standing sociological or psychological causes, or in the special circumstances which preceded the writing of the last poems. Among the latter was the birth of her son, which, we are told, was followed by a great burst of creativity; if so, this may have been the sign of a release from a guilt associated with her vocation. The 'Childless Woman' utters 'nothing but blood'—a revealing use of words which clearly shows the alternative between dead words and living beings. This particular factor supplies the meaning of the 'monologue for three voices', *Three Women*, which is a repertoire of all the images and themes which we have outlined. In this story of three women who recall the discovery of their pregnancy, have their confinements at the same time and resume their interrupted life, the familiar metaphorical structure is buttressed by a narrative which confirms its meaning; for the fate of the three characters is in poetic conformity with their outlook. The Wife is 'slow as the world', 'very patient', 'ready' and 'smiling'. She feels at one

[13] Another, and complementary one, is an evocation of the wakefulness and increased mental activity which accompany some types of anxious depression. See the same image in 'The Other' ('smilingly, blue lightning . . .'). See also 'Insomniac'.

with the life-giving earth, and her pregnancy is knowledge. The Secretary suddenly feels her life in a male world as 'a death in the bare trees, a deprivation'; she is afraid of having 'caught' the male disease of flatness, and feels guilty of being found wanting. The Girl is 'not ready', resents her pregnancy, accuses the men of it, and wishes she had aborted. The Wife has a son, marvels at him and prepares to cushion him from all threats:

> I shall meditate upon normality . . .

> I do not will him to be exceptional.
> It is the exception that interests the devil . . .
> I will him to be common . . .

The Secretary has a still-born baby, the sex of which we do not know; but although this agrees with the atmosphere of sterility which surrounded her pregnancy, she feels her faith in life's possibilities restored at the end and prepares for a future child. But the college girl, who felt a child as a threat to her individuality, has a daughter, very much alive, whom she abandons. First she feels like 'a wound walking out of hospital', then forgets and enjoys her death-like intellectual existence anew:

> My black gown is a little funeral:
> It shows that I am serious.
> The books I carry wedge into my side.[14]

She rejoices in having no attachments but, her old wound now a dream, she still wonders:

> What is it I miss?
> Shall I ever find it, whatever it is?

She is, therefore, further from nature than the less intellectual Secretary, who could voice her torment:

> I see myself as a shadow, neither man nor woman,
> Neither a woman, happy to be like a man, nor a man
> Blunt and flat enough to feel no lack.
>   I feel a lack.

[14] Whereas the mother was all roundness like the hills. Cf. in this connection the cycle of the bees where the 'square baby' of the hive is a symbol of death.

That the Wife's symbiotic relationship with her baby son may not be very healthy is nowhere suggested (the only fear is that this state cannot endure very long); and even less that life and mind are not, for most people, irreconcilable enemies. Even individuality is resented, in Sylvia Plath's universe, and is associated by the Secretary with the lipstick she puts on again when she regretfully leaves the elemental world of the lying-in hospital.

To conclude, we can say that the symbolic net which Sylvia Plath casts on the world of perception has above all a personal value, and that we must consent to a partial identification with her if we are to enjoy her poems to the full, and even to understand them. Ultimately, however, her work stands on stylistic merits alone. And it is remarkable that the devices she uses, although we can to some extent list and classify them, are almost as varied as the thematic content is rigid. The ease of composition to which she has testified in connection with her last poems shows that the unconscious processing of her material was formal as well as thematic, for the felicitous rhythmic and phonetic inventions, which perfectly render the finest intentions are innumerable. Let us mention only a few: among the dramatic and unexpected cuts which are such a striking feature of her poems, some are particularly evocative. In 'Cut', they perfectly express the highly complex reaction of the speaker, a mixture of fear, breathless fascination and narcissistic tenderness for her own body, and a heightening of the intensity of perception conveyed by the clinically precise description in the opening lines. In 'Ariel', the cuts convey the final ecstasy and 'volatilization', and in 'Fever 103°', admirably suggest the feeling of ascension and forgetfulness of all earthly involvements, an effect very similar to that of the beginning in Baudelaire's 'Elévation'. The impression of calm finality and despair is due to the rhythmic chiasmus in 'Edge', and that of egoistic narcissism in 'Childless Woman', to the repetition of the same word at the end of a line and the beginning of the next. The particularly knotty texture of the lines in poems like 'Medusa' or 'Berck-Plage' suggests a concentration of loathing.

Generally speaking, the cuts tend to induce a strong narrative tension, chiefly due to a counterpoint between grammatical and rhythmic structure, and sometimes, when the rhythm becomes obsessively marked, or in the last line of a five-line stanza, there is a feeling of foreboding very similar to many piano accompaniments of romantic ballads such as Schubert's, as in, for instance, 'The Arrival of the Bee Box'.

Apart from the thematic value of sibilants, which we have discussed above, the same freedom is observed in the sounds as in the rhythm. We might just detect an embryonic thematic function in a few others, such as the fullness and gaiety of the child's world in 'a creel of eels, all ripples', the vagueness of 'oval animal souls', or 'trawling your dark as owls do', the gaping chasm of death in 'the flesh the grave cave ate', or 'your dark amputations crawl and appal', or the hollowness of deceit in

> Lies and smiles. (. . .)
> And he, for this subversion,
> Hurts me, he
> With his armoury of fakery.

The general tone is very rarely purely elegiac, since we have seen that the effort to dominate experience and the fear of fighting a losing battle result in most poems being built on a feeling of duality and antagonism. Stylistically, this ambivalence results in a Laforguian juxtaposition of the sublime and the homely, of compassion and hatred. It is noticeable that, just as the first line often states boldly the subject and the dominant tone of the poem, the last line is often markedly prosaic, at variance with the prevailing rhythm, as if there was, at the end of each of these efforts to shape experience into patterns and thus dominate it, a loss of faith and a return to a shapeless and hopeless existence, a feeling of the uselessness of effort.[15] Yet the fact that we are always strongly aware of an individual voice speaking to us, even from the midst of despair, is a testimony to the poet's achievement. This must be remembered when we notice the dolorist accent of many poems, and when we face what seems almost a masochistic infatuation with death, in 'A Birthday Present', 'Elm' or 'Lady Lazarus', and a rather repellent familiarity with its gruesome

[15] See 'The Rival', 'Sheep in Fog', 'Little Fugue' and, in a slightly different way, 'The Arrival of the Bee Box' and 'The Hanging Man'.

aspect. For this passivity is necessarily that of the poet, who must experience reality with the utmost intensity even if he must be broken in the process—an attitude erected into a dogma by Rimbaud and the Surrealists; and as a French philosopher said,[16] the masochist experiences himself not so much as the victim as the battlefield. The poet must re-enact in his life the struggle between anarchy and order, and it is doubtless a silent but profound awareness of this duty which accounts, in Sylvia Plath's poems, for the essential ambiguity of the themes and the protean presence of death.

[16] Georges Blin: *D'un certain consentement à la Douleur*, in *Fontaine*, Juin, 1945.

THE POETRY OF SYLVIA PLATH
A Technical Analysis

JOHN FREDERICK NIMS

What I offer is something in the way of a technical analysis of the poetry of Sylvia Plath. Amid much high talk of culture and poesis and metaphysics, I come, many will think, in a humble capacity: a sort of podiatrist among the brain surgeons, clutching my little bag of timeworn axioms from Michelangelo and Goethe and Valéry, now and then grabbing and brandishing one defiantly. 'The artist who is not also a craftsman is no good'—Goethe. 'Trifles make perfection, and perfection is no trifle'—Michelangelo.

It is true that Sylvia Plath was struck by a lightning from the spirit. But it is also true that she had spent much of her life forging speech of a metal to conduct the lightning without being instantly fused. There is little that can be said about how to get struck by lightning but a good deal that can be said about how to forge a resistant metal.

We might begin by saying to young writers: Forget *Ariel* for a while; study *The Colossus*. Notice all the stanza-forms, all the uses of rhythm and rhyme; notice how the images are chosen and related; how deliberately sound is used. It is no accident, for instance, that there are seven identical drab *a*'s in '. . . salt flats,/ Gas tanks, factory stacks—that landscape . . .'?[1] Remember that *The Bell Jar* tells us she 'wrote page after page of villanelles and sonnets', and this in one semester of one class. Perhaps for writers this is the gist of the Plath case: without the drudgery of *The Colossus*, the triumph of *Ariel* is unthinkable.[2]

[1] 'Suicide Off Egg Rock'.
[2] Since writing this, I have found that Peter Davison has made much the same point in 'Inhabited by a Cry: The Last Poetry of Sylvia Plath' (*Atlantic*, August, 1966, pp. 76–77). He too considers *The Colossus* 'advanced exercises'; and says of *Ariel* . . . 'these poems

As a teacher, I speak from experience. How many poets are there on the hairy campuses of the land we love? Maybe 50,000? 200,000? More, certainly, than at any time in the history of the world. Being a 'poet' is the young folk's thing these days: they get that look and slap down on paper the holy thoughts no elder ever thought, and troop around in their poet-clothes, non-conforming exactly like the milling thousands in their peer-group, and, man, it's beautiful! Only they don't work much. Spontaneity, they think, that's where it's at. Write it like it is. Cries from the heart. But Sylvia Plath, in some prefatory remarks for a recording dismissed such indulgence with acidity:

'I think my poems come immediately out of the sensuous and emotional experiences I have, but I must say I *cannot* sympathize with these cries from the heart that are informed by nothing except, you know, a needle or a knife, or whatever it is. I believe one should be able to control and manipulate experiences, even the most terrifying, like madness, like being tortured . . . and should be able to manipulate these experiences with an informed and intelligent mind . . .'[3]

Control, manipulate, informed, intelligent, mind—these are the key words, for our present purpose. It does not follow that a poem never 'comes' easily (though this is rare); but it comes only along circuits laboriously prepared, generally for years in advance.

My plan is to discuss the work of a good contemporary poet in terms of those things which have made up the physical body of poetry in all times and places, and which indeed never change. Things which could be illustrated from any of the great poets of our tradition: Sappho, Catullus, the Archpoet, Bernart de Ventadorn, Villon, San Juan de la Cruz, Goethe, Leopardi, Valéry, Rilke, or the English poets we presumably know better. One of the more frivolous ways of judging poetry is in terms of contemporary significance. Looking at the works of the ten

---

would never have come into being without the long, deliberate, technical training that preceded them. We can only perform with true spontaneity what we have first learned to do by habit.'

[3] *The Poet Speaks*, Argo Record Co. No. RG 455, London. Sylvia Plath reads 'Lazy Lazarus', 'Daddy', and 'Fever 103°', as well as commentary. Other readers are Ted Hughes, Peter Porter and Thom Gunn. (Recorded, October 30, 1962.)—Ed.

poets I mention, I am struck by how timeless, how uncontemporary, their essential quality is. San Juan de la Cruz refers at most once to the exciting events of his day. A poet long ago loved a girl for the same reasons we still do:

ἔρατόν τε βᾶμα
κἀμάρυκμα λάμπρον ἴδην προσώπω

or perhaps because, in a metaphor,

sa beutatz alugora
bel jorn e clarzis noih negra . . .

As she grows old the lament is still 'Quelle fus, quelle devenue!' Any might have brooded with the confessional Archpoet, 'In amaritudine loquor meae menti,' or stared upon skies that were 'Gestaltenreiche, bald Gestaltenlose', or found the night 'Dolce e chiara . . . e senza vento.' No matter what the language, this is really where it's at.

Poetry, if it is anything, is a real voice in a real body in a real world. The world does not change as much as we think; and the body, with its voice-producing mechanisms, changes probably not at all. The timeless excellence of Sylvia Plath lies in what she has in common with such poets as I have mentioned (though I am not saying that she is of their rank): the sense of language and of metaphor; the throat-produced sounds of her poetry; the physical rhythms that invigorate it.

Metaphor (I use the word here to include simile and all metaphoric ways of seeing) was for Aristotle 'by far the greatest thing . . . which alone cannot be learned; it is the sign of genius'. Some contemporary theorists are against it, although to reject metaphor is not only to enervate poetry but to do violence to the human mind.

The qualities of a good metaphor would seem to be two: when A is compared to B, B is a thing at first sight surprisingly (and delightfully or shockingly) remote from A; and B is a thing at least as common, as available, as A. Or probably more common, since the purpose of metaphor is to see more clearly.

Sylvia Plath seems to me more brilliant at metaphor than others popularly grouped with her as confessional poets.

In her two books almost all of the metaphors are on target, having the excellences I mentioned (and often a third I can only suggest now: A is not only like B in one salient respect, but also picks up a supercharge of meanings proper to B but impregnating A also, as in the *smile-hook* image below). In *The Colossus* we find 'The pears fatten like little buddhas'; a corpse is 'black as burnt turkey'; 'Sun struck the water like a damnation' and 'Everything glittered like blank paper'; dead moles are 'shapeless as flung gloves . . . blue suede' and they have 'corkscrew noses'; a dead snake lies 'inert as a shoelace' and the maggots are 'thin as pins'; burnt wood has the 'char of karakul'. In *Ariel*, it is said of a newborn baby that 'Love set you going like a fat gold watch', and of its voice, 'The clear vowels rise like balloons'. Family smiles in a photograph 'catch onto my skin, little smiling hooks'. The snow of Napoleon's retreat is 'marshalling its brilliant cutlery'; a swarm of bees is 'A flying hedgehog, all prickles'.

She also shows a total control of the figures she uses. This is a matter of attention and tact: how soon can one drop a metaphor, or dissolve it for another? Bad writers sometimes superimpose images so carelessly that we get an amateur's double exposure, with grotesque or comic results. Even good writers nod.

Sylvia Plath shows a more conscientious commitment to her images. 'Hardcastle Crags' begins:

> Flintlike, her feet struck
> Such a racket of echoes from the steely street,
> . . . that she heard the quick air ignite
> Its tinder and shake
>
> A firework of echoes . . .

'Flintlike', she begins; therefore the street is 'steely' and the air a 'tinder' that can 'ignite' a 'firework'. Four stanzas later she is 'a pinch of flame', and in the last stanza there is 'Enough to snuff the quick / Of her small heat out'. Beginning as flint, she ends as 'mere quartz grit'. In 'The Colossus', an early sketch for 'Daddy', imagery of a fallen statue is sustained throughout. This knitting or girdering of images is everywhere in *Ariel*: the underwater or water imagery in 'Tulips' is only one of the more obvious examples. 'Getting There' is all metaphor; 'Daddy', 'Lady Lazarus' and 'Fever 103°' are richly and consistently figurative.

The sound of words—any page of Sylvia Plath shows her pre-occupation with it. *The Colossus* shows a concern almost excessive, unless we see it as a preparation for *Ariel*. Sound is an element of poetry tricky to talk about, sense and nonsense here being so close together, and the line between so fine and wavering. The chapter on words in Herbert Read's *English Prose Style* makes sense: he believes that 'vocal appropriateness' is 'perhaps the most important aspect of the problem of style as determined by the choice of words'. Precise meaning is not enough; words have a body as well as a mind, and sometimes the body matters more. Many poets would agree with Valéry that the poet's 'inner labor consists less of seeking words from his ideas than of seeking ideas for his words and paramount rhythms'. Many would not agree: Look, they feel, I can't be bothered with these trifles when I've got these Important Things to Say. Rather like the hurdler complaining that the hurdles interfere with his stride.

Words are more expressive when they are somehow like what they mean: fast or slow or gruff or shrill, or produced by mouth and lip movements that mimic the dynamics of rejection, say, or the prolonging of a caress. That is why Catullus has given probably the best kiss in literature in his 'Illo purpureo ore suaviata', in which not only are lip movements appropriate, but, in Latin prosody, the two round *o*'s coming together fuse as one. These are effects beyond mere onomatopoeia—which we can find too in Miss Plath when it is called for, as in 'Night Shift', perhaps an exercise in the manner of 'Swarte smekyd smethes'. Her factory has less clangor, a more 'muted boom':

> though the sound
> Shook the ground with its pounding.

There is much deliberately ugly sound in 'Night Shift', especially in the way words re-echo noises from a preceding word: 'A metal detonating / Native, evidently . . . indefatigable fact'. More interesting than such onomatopoeia are those words whose sound is an analogy for, a little charade of, their meaning: *smudge* is smudgy to say: *globe* is a roundness in the mouth; *sling* hisses and then lets go. The thousands of hours Sylvia Plath spent with her thesaurus must have considered words as embodiments. And considered what happens when they go together: poets have a tendency to stay in the same key of sound, to set up patterns in it, so that what they write has a more unified and tougher texture than casual speech. Speech is a tweedy fabric; verse is a twill. Or poets work to avoid repeating a sound, when the repetition is meaningless, or meaninglessly ugly.

Look at any page of *The Colossus*, and you see expressive repetitions and patterns: 'greased machines', 'gristly-bristled', 'wingy myths', 'cuddly mother', 'clumped like bulbs', 'lambs jam the sheepfold'. In 'Mushrooms', 'Our toes, our noses / Take hold on the loam . . . Soft fists insist on / heaving the needles . . .'

Generally we can see a reason for such effects: in 'clumped like bulbs' and 'lambs jam' the sound itself is clumped or jammed.

Often Sylvia Plath repeats a sound several times: 'Drinking vinegar from tin cups'. Now we can get very arch here and talk about 'a thin metallic acidity puckering the lips'; but the most we can say sensibly is that the repetitions of the *in*-sound are sort of tinny. Tin cups do go *click* or *clink* rather than *clank* or *clunk*. If we say that the bird that 'flits nimble-winged in thickets' has his five short *i*'s to suggest quickness, we have Plato with us: he too held that the short *i* is the quickest of the vowel sounds. It is easy to find monotony dramatized in 'daylight lays its sameness on the wall', and to find a sense of unpleasant enclosure in 'This shed's fusty as a mummy's stomach'. And there are any number of lines somehow like what they mean: the great sow that is

Mire-smirched, blowzy,

Maunching thistle and knotweed on her snout-cruise . . .

'Sow'

or the texture of rocky soil in

What flinty pebbles the ploughblade upturns
As ponderable tokens . . .

in which the *ond* of *ponderable* must have encouraged the *godly* and *doddering* of the line that follows.

Sound effects in themselves are trivial, and facility with these will never write a poem. It can temper the metal, but it cannot provoke the heaven into striking. As it did strike in several of the *Ariel* poems. Sound effects here are less obtrusive than before; more subtle, more sparing, more saved for where they matter. But they are here: 'Square as a chair', 'strips of tinfoil winking,' 'starless and fatherless, a dark water'. There are many in the bee poems: 'were there not such a din in it' and 'the unintelligible syllables'. In 'Lady Lazarus' there are such things as 'the flesh / The grave cave ate'. 'Lesbos' opens with a vicious hiss.[4] But 'Nick and the Candlestick' is the real showpiece for sound:

> I am a miner. The light burns blue.
> Waxy stalactites
> Drip and thicken . . .

And what a contrast between the brilliant chill of

> Christ! they are panes of ice,
> A vice of knives . . .

and the pulpy warmth of these words to a baby:

> The blood blooms clean

> in you, ruby.

A sound-device even more compelling in *Ariel* is the kind of rhyme used. There is something really new here, though it is not easy to do anything new with a device so time-worn and so primitive. Primitive: children and simple people love it; so do composers of folk-songs authentic or pseudo. Only some of our more cerebral theorists, who write as if they had no bodies any-way, pish-tush it with prudery.

The rhymes we find in *The Colossus* are already at an advanced stage of their evolutionary history. We can assume that hundreds of earlier poems had exhausted, for the time, the poet's taste for full rhyme; it is with real surprise that we come across, in 'Snake-charmer', *breast-manifest-nest*. By preference she rhymes more atonally. The same vowel-sound but with different consonants

---

[4] 'Lesbos' is included in the U.S. edition of *Ariel* but not in the British edition. –Ed

after it: *fishes-pig-finger-history*; *worms-converge*. Different vowel-sounds but with the same final consonant: *vast-compost-must*; *knight-combat-heat* (this is her most characteristic kind of rhyme in *The Colossus*). Unaccented syllables going with accented or unaccented: *boulders-wore*; *footsoles-babel*. She considers all final vowels as rhyming with all others: *jaw-arrow-eye* (perhaps suggested by the Middle-English practice in alliteration). Or she will mate sounds that have almost anything in common: *ridgepole-tangle-inscrutable*. The ties become so very loose that it is not always clear when they are intended. *Depths-silver-there*—can these be rhymes? They occur at the end of a poem in terza rima, which has been clearly in rhyme up to this triad. In 'Suicide Off Egg Rock' the final words of the twenty-four lines each pair somewhere—in her fashion—with another, but the pairings are not immediately caught by the ear in such a list of end-words as: *drizzled, flats, landscape, of, updraught, damnation, into, tattoo, children, spindrift, wave, gallop, sandspit, blindfold, garbage, forever, eyehole, brainchamber, pages, paper, corrosive, wastage, water, ledges* (the list is interesting as diction). Rhymes like these mean more to the writer than to any reader, who will miss many of them. One feels that Sylvia Plath had an obsession with rhyme, felt poetry *had* to have it, but at times made her compliance a token one. She knows the poems rhyme, even if we do not. Should we call this 'token-rhyme'? Or 'ghost-rhyme'—since it is like a revenant never completely exorcised? Or are all these things trifles to ho-hum away? It is clear that to her they were not.

In *Ariel*, the use of rhyme is very different. In some poems it is ghostlier than ever. But more often it is obvious: rhyme at high noon. The same sound may run on from stanza to stanza, with much identical rhyme. 'Lady Lazarus' illustrates the new manner. The poem is printed in units of three lines, but the rhyme is not in her favourite terza-rima pattern. Six of the first ten lines end in an *n*-sound, followed by a sequence in long *e*, which occurs in about half of the next twenty-two lines. Then, after six more *n*'s, we have *l*'s ending eleven of fourteen lines; and then several *r*'s, leading into the six or more *air* rhymes that conclude the sequences. Almost Skeltonian: the poet seems to carry on a sound about as long as she can, although not in consecutive lines.

'Compulsive rhyme', we might call this, for it seems fair to see it as deeper than a mere literary device, and as somehow related to needs of the exacerbated psyche. Most of the poems after 'Lady Lazarus' rhyme on in this way (although the tendency is much fainter in 'Berck-Plage'). 'Lesbos' is bound together by compulsive rhyme, broken here and there by couplets that recall Eliot—and indeed this poem is her 'Portrait of a Lady', and her 'Prufrock', with even the breakers 'white and black'. In 'Daddy' the compulsion to rhyme becomes obsession. Perhaps never in the history of poetry has the device carried so electric a charge. Breathing love and hate together, it coos and derides, even more insistent at the end of the poem than at the beginning, so that form refutes what content is averring. Over half of the lines end in the *oo* sound, and of these nearly half are the one word *you*. This is rhyme with—and for!—a vengeance. The bee poems string together the same sort of compulsive rhyme: eight of the last ten lines of 'The Arrival of the Bee Box' end in long *e*. The extremely devious and intricate rhyme-work of *The Colossus*, then, has led to something almost excessively simple, something we might find monotonous if it were not so deeply significant.

All I have said about rhyme has implied something about stanza-form. She writes almost always in stanzas or stanza-like units. Often in the later poems there is no relation between rhyme-scheme and stanza-form: each goes its separate way, with a kind of schizophrenic indifference to the other. Just as her rhyme, even when barely there, *is* there, so with the stanza: even when there seems no formal reason for the unit, the poet remains faithful to its appearance on the page. Probably here, as with rhyme, we have a source of discipline that is personal and internal: it is for her, not for us. Of the 'pages of villanelles and sonnets' there is nothing in *The Colossus* except one sonnet, in nine-syllable lines. Only four of the poems are non-stanzaic, two of them barely so. There is one poem in rather free couplets. The fifty others are in stanzas of from three to nine lines. Her favourite form is terza-rima, which makes up six of the twelve poems in three-line stanzas. In some of these she adds an extra complexity to the terza-rima by having the second line short in the odd-numbered tercets, and the first and third lines short in the even-numbered ones, so that the poem seems to seesaw on the page. Among the longer stanza-forms there is much intricacy and variation; she seems to be trying out as many tight forms as possible. 'Black Rook in Rainy Weather' even follows the Provençal system of *rimas dissolutas*: each line rhymes with the corresponding lines of all the other stanzas.

In spite of several fine poems, *The Colossus* has the air of being an exercise book. *Ariel* is very different. The stanza-forms are fewer and simpler, far more loosely bound by rhyme. Before, there was one poem in two-line units; now there are nine: everything is more concise. Of the nine, none rhymes as couplets; rhyme is present, but in no regular way. Ten poems are in three-line units; two of these look rather like 'Sow' on the page, although with shorter lines. But none rhymes as terza-rima. The five-line stanzas now have no formal rhyme-scheme, although again they are rhyme-haunted. There are only two poems in longer stanza-forms (of seven lines), and one nine-line poem about pregnancy (nine-ness: an earlier pregnancy poem had nine lines of nine syllables each).

And what of rhythm? In *The Colossus*, she seems practising in the rhythms, as well as in everything else. Up until our own time, there have been chiefly two kinds of rhythm in English. The first predominated until Chaucer; it was based on the heavy stress-accent native to our language. The line was divided into two halves with two stresses in each (sometimes emphasized by alliteration); it did not matter how many unstressed syllables there were, nor where they were (pronunciation actually limits the possibilities). We find the rhythm everywhere in early poetry:

> Whére beth théy   befóren us wéren?

exactly as we find it centuries later in E. E. Cummings:

> he sáng his dídn't   he dánced his díd

and Sylvia Plath:

> Ìncense of deáth.   Your dáy approáches.

or

145

Beásts of oásis,   a bétter tíme.

Ransom discusses it as the 'folk line' or 'dipodic line'; he finds it in Thomas Hardy

We stoód by a pónd   that wínter dáy . . .

and uses it as the basis of his own 'Bells for John Whiteside's Daughter':

There was súch speéd   in her líttle bódy . . .

In *The Colossus*, there are ten poems that read themselves naturally, if freely, in the folk line. Perhaps the best are 'Suicide Off Egg Rock' and 'Blue Moles'.

As everyone knows, the other system was brought over from the continent by Chaucer. There are still some who resent the foreign importation, although at least three-fourths of the English poetry that matters has been written in it, not without success. The line has five pulsations, and in theory if almost never in fact each is a two-syllable pulsation, with the second syllable stronger than the first. We find it in Chaucer's

Hyd, Absolom, thy giltë tresses clere . . .

exactly as in Cummings's

all ignorance toboggans into know . . .

Unfortunately it is called 'iambic pentameter'—dirty words indeed for some theorists today; and a few, like Dr. Williams, have spoken against it with more animus than intelligence. Basically, iambic is the *lub-dúbb* of the heartbeat, perhaps the first sensation that we, months before our birth, are aware of. Nothing unnatural about that as a rhythm. It has always been common in human speech. Aristotle called it the most colloquial, or speechlike, of the rhythms, the one used most naturally in speech-like poetry because most commonly heard in real speech. R. P. Blackmur once said he had listened to recordings of poetry in thirty-odd languages, and in every one except Chinese could detect the iambic base. I make this defence because the rhythm is much attacked today as unnatural. But there are still some, like Sylvia

Plath, who would as soon listen to their own heart for rhythms as take dictation from a typewriter. In *The Colossus* she has eight poems in pure iambic pentameter (in the organic, not the metronomic sense), and nearly twenty others that use it freely or in combination with other line-lengths. (Why, by the way, *pentameter*? Could it have anything to do with the physiological fact that our heart pulses five times, on an average, for every time we breathe?)

She also has fourteen poems in accentual count (this is a count, not a rhythm)—the system that organizes lines by number of syllables, with no regard for their stress or importance. This is finger-counting, more foreign to the nature of spoken English than Chaucer's imported novelty. People under the stress of emotion may speak rhythmically, but they do not count their syllables. For emotion is stress in language; it is the stresses that have to pulsate if we are to have a living rhythm. And syllabic count is made up of undifferentiated elements, whereas a stress rhythm has two forces working against each other: not so much the systole and diastole of the accents as the impassioned dialogue between speech-rhythm and meter, a dialogue full of anticipations, surprises, and sudden pacts. A tension between such polarities as make up our existence. Whereas syllabic count is brain-count: sexless. Some writers like it because it is easy; anybody can do it who has fingers and toes, or a string of beads.

However: there is something to say for exercises in the syllabic line. Once attuned to the accentual, one is easily carried away into a kind of automatic facility, so that the lines 'flow' too easily. (It is the prevalence of bad iambics of course that has led its enemies into their blanket condemnation.) Writing in syllabics can be a salutary exercise in countering the sing-song—and this is the importance of the syllabics in *The Colossus*. They tend to be the colder poems: objective, intellectual, descriptive. Passion always brings the poet back to a heart-rhythm, as in 'Witch Burning':

> My ankles brighten. Brightness ascends my thighs.
> I am lost, I am lost, in the robes of all this light.

Another advantage of syllabics is that they can be of value to the writer (if not to the reader) as an additional principle of control, a way of making it harder for himself, of checking (as Valéry thinks we should) the logorrheas of 'inspiration'. And the syllabic poem can come alive if it has a physical rhythm overriding the finger-count. What speaker of English can hear *as fifteen* the fifteen syllables of a line in 'Fern Hill', or would be bothered if Dylan Thomas skipped a couple? Yet we all hear the passionate stress-rhythm that overrides them. Something of the sort happens in Sylvia Plath's 'Mushrooms':

> Nudgers and shovers
> In spite of ourselves.
> Our kind multiplies:

> We shall by morning
> Inherit the earth.
> Our foot's in the door.

These are five-syllable lines, but what catches the ear is not so much the fiveness as the traditional swing, as old as Homer at least, of dactyls and spondees, with a rest or two.

There is only one syllabic poem in *Ariel*, and it is not one of the better poems. Syllabics seem to have served their callisthenic purpose in *The Colossus*; when the poet comes to write her important work, she dismisses them. In *Ariel*, there is almost no metrical innovation—unless we think of the comma splice and its nervous impetus. But this is more a matter of syntax than of metrics. May I suggest that the best poets are not often the metrical innovators? This they leave for the fuss-budgets. It is always easier to invent a new metrical system than to write a good poem in the existing one. New medium: new tedium—was Roethke, that devotee of the nursery rhyme, thinking of this when he wrote 'Some rare new tedium's taking shape'?

Far from making meter new, *Ariel* even marks what metrists might consider a severe regression. Apart from the syllabic 'You're', everything can be accounted for by the most basic of English rhythms. Frost says that we have 'virtually but two rhythms', strict iambic and loose iambic. These, and little else, we find in *Ariel*, often both in the same poem. The loose iambics work towards that most unfashionable of all feet, the anapest (or its mirror-image, the dactyl). Probably not since the Assyrian came down like a wolf on the fold has there been so high a proportion of anapests in an important collection of poems. Not that *Ariel*, in all the ways that really matter, is not a highly original collection. But tampering with the heartbeat of poetry is not a significant kind of originality; all one is likely to get is verbal fibrillation. In *Ariel* at least, the more original and significant the poem, the more traditional the rhythm.

The lines in *Ariel* are by no means always pentameter, although they are so enough times to surprise us. Probably they are heard as pentameter even when not printed so. One example: lines 2 to 10 of 'Lady Lazarus' can be spaced, without violence to the cadence, as

> One year in every ten / I manage it—
> A sort of walking miracle, my skin
> Bright as a Nazi lampshade, / My right foot
> A paperweight, / My face a featureless
> fine / Jew linen. / Peel off the napkin / O
> my enemy. Do I terrify?— / the nose . . .

And the poem comes back to that cadence everywhere, particularly at moments of greatest intensity:

> Soon, soon the flesh / the grave cave ate will be
> At home on me / And I a smiling woman . . .

or

> The peanut-crunching crowd / shoves in to see /them
> Unwrap me hand and foot— / the big strip tease . . .

This is much more regular than the opening of Shakespeare's Sonnet 116: 'Let me not to the marriage of true minds . . .' which has only one iambic foot in the five.

Many key lines are printed as pentameter:

> And like the cat I have nine times to die . . .
> To last it out and not come back at all . . .
> And pick the worms off me like sticky pearls . . .
> For the eyeing of my scars, there is a charge . . .

'Tulips' is more in the Fletcherian mode: more anapests, more extra syllables:

I didn't want any flowers, I only wanted
To lie with my hands turned up and be utterly empty.
How free it is, you have no idea how free—
The peacefulness is so big it dazes you . . .

and the conclusion:

> The water I taste is warm and salt, like the sea,
> And comes from a country far away as health.

The poem 'Ariel' looks more irregular, but it too never gets far
from an iambic base. Much of it could be spaced so that, metrically,
it would be no looser than Jacobean verse. 'Lesbos', which opens
like an echo of Tourneur, is even more regular:

> Where they crap and puke and cry and she can't hear.
> You say you can't stand her. / The bastard's a girl . . .
> She'll cut her throat at ten if she's mad at two.

> Even in your Zen heaven we shan't meet.

It is hard for me to see how anyone can hear lines like these and
still hold that iambic pentameter does not fit the pattern of
English or American speech. (To my ear, they are considerably
more alive than most of Dr. Williams's rather wooden verses.)
Look anywhere—the poems of *Ariel* return to a solid pentameter
base again and again. Even when they do not, they tend to remain
loose iambic, whatever the line-length:

> Obscene bikinis hide in the dunes . . .
>> 'Berck-Plage'

> Love set you going like a fat gold watch . . .
>> 'Morning Song'

>> What a thrill—
>> My thumb instead of an onion.
>> The top quite gone
>> Except for a sort of hinge . . .
>>> 'Cut'

> It is a heart,
> This holocaust I walk in,
> O golden child the world will kill and eat.
>> 'Mary's Song'

150

I quote so much because I expect incredulity. 'You mean Sylvia Plath is so *square*?' In *Ariel*, square as a chair, technically. Which is one reason the book seems so original. Except to the shallow and the jaded, mere novelty is a bore: everything changes, said Valéry, except the *avant-garde*. And while 'Make it new' is very good advice, perhaps 'Make it do' is even better. If one has the strength and the resources to. But the example of what Sylvia Plath actually achieved is more convincing than my little sermon.

In the famous and terrible 'Daddy', the iambs are varied with anapests and spondees:

> no not
> Any less the black man who
>
> Bit my pretty red heart in two.
> I was ten when they buried you.
> At twenty I tried to die
> And get back, back, back to you.
> I thought even the bones would do.

'The Bee Meeting' has longer lines of the same units. It is only in the less impressive poems, those more in the manner of *The Colossus*, that we are not likely to be caught into the rhythm: in 'Medusa', for example.

Although I have said very little about diction, numerous quotations have probably suggested the point I would make. In *The Colossus* the diction is always distinguished and elegant, but it is a written language rather than a spoken one. More literary than actual. There are lines not likely to come from a human throat:

> Haunched like a faun, he hooed
> From groves of moon-glint or fen-frost
> Until all owls in the twigged forest . . .
>
> > 'Faun'

But I open *Ariel* and have no trouble hearing:

> I have done it again,
> One year in every ten
> I manage it . . .
>
> > 'Lady Lazarus'

or

Pure, what does it mean?
'Fever 103°'

or

Somebody is shooting at something in our town . . .
'Swarm'

Not every line in *Ariel* passes this difficult voice test, but what we hear almost everywhere is a real voice in a real body in a real world. In *The Colossus*, the voice is often not vibrant; indeed, it is often not her own. Sometimes, as in 'Ouija', it is the voice of Wallace Stevens, with 'aureate poetry in tarnished modes . . . fair chronicler of every foul declension'. In 'Spinster' it is the voice of Ransom, and in 'Dark House' it is purest Roethke:

> All-mouth licks up the bushes
> And the pots of meat.
> He lives in an old well,
> A stony hole. He's to blame.
> He's a fat sort.

Dylan Thomas is present, and some others. These are marvellous exercises in imitation, and, like everything else she did, prepared her to speak for herself in *Ariel*. Perhaps a writer finds himself only through having tried to be another. 'More than half a lifetime to arrive at this freedom of speech,' said Eliot of Yeats's 1914 volume. 'It is a triumph.' Sylvia Plath did not have half a lifetime, but in a few years, in all the ways I have tried to describe, she prepared herself to endure and transmit, if only for a while, the fires of heaven.

PART III

NOTES TOWARD A BIOGRAPHY

LOIS AMES

Sylvia Plath's life has already taken on the quality of a legend. The publicity attendant to the publication of *Ariel* has made any reconstruction of her life, not to mention critical estimation of work, additionally difficult. What follows is an account of her which, however skeletal, is at least fairly accurate.

My own acquaintance with Sylvia was an early if superficial one. We attended the same high school, church and college, went to the same parties and dances. Moved by her sudden death, I found myself thinking back on times we had seemed to share, though my own experience of them was not comparable to hers.

In 1965, with the generous permission of Ted Hughes, I went to talk with people who had known Sylvia Plath at different times in her life. By and large, they proved to be open and helpful. Their descriptions of Sylvia, although not in agreement at every point, were notably similar. There was, however, often a marked contrast between recollection of her at different ages.

Sylvia had the ability to adapt quickly to a person or situation. To most people she seemed genuinely open and warm, and unusually candid; for those closest to her, however, she often proved an enigma.

Sylvia Plath's father, Otto Plath, came to the United States at fifteen from a town called Grabow in the Polish corridor. He was the author of a well-known treatise on bees, *Bumblebees*,[1] and was further distinguished for his work in ornithology, entomology, and ichthyology. He held several degrees from American universities, and was a professor of biology at Boston University where he also taught scientific German. Aurelia Schober, Sylvia's mother, was born in Boston, Massachusetts, of Austrian parents.

[1] *Bumblebees and Their Ways*, Macmillan, New York, 1934.

She met her husband while studying for a master's degree in German. After their marriage they lived in Jamaica Plain, Massachusetts.

On October 27, 1932, Sylvia Plath was born at Robinson Memorial Hospital in Boston. Her parents chose her name for its associations with the herb *salvia* and the poetic adjective *sylvan*. At her birth, Otto Plath announced: 'All I want from life from now on is a son born two and a half years to the day.' Mrs. Plath obligingly brought forth Warren Joseph on April 27, 1935. Professor Plath's colleagues toasted him as 'The man who gets what he wants when he wants it'.

Sylvia and her brother grew up in the seashore town of Winthrop, Massachusetts. Her own letters and other writings deal extensively with this period in her life. Sylvia was a 'sea child'. She collected blue mussel shells 'with the rainbowy angel's fingernail interior' and 'the purple "lucky stones" . . . with a white ring all the way around.' She treasured brown, green, blue and red glass 'nuggets', bits of painted china, and tiny shells; fashioned toys from razor clams and fairy boats; 'nursed starfish alive in jam jars of seawater and watched them grow back lost arms', dreamed of Spain on the other side of the Atlantic, and believed in mermaids. She enjoyed the sea taste of 'greeny-blue-black mackerel', codfish chowder, steamed clams, and lobsters. She often visited her maternal grandparents, also associated with the sea, who lived on the exposed ocean side of Point Shirley, in a house which looked east to the Atlantic and west to Boston. It was to their number, Ocean 1212-W, that she made her first telephone call.

On September 21, 1938, when she was five, a hurricane and tidal wave eroded the New England coast, removing landmarks, smashing houses, and beaching boats. She later recalled in a BBC talk:

> My final memory of the sea
> is of violence—a still, unhealthily
> yellow day in 1939 [sic]—the sea
> molten, steely thick, heaving at its
> leash like a broody animal, evil
> violets in its eye.

156

—one of those apocalyptic images which alternately attracted and repelled her all her life.

Otto Plath died on November 2, 1940, following a long, difficult illness, and Sylvia's life changed radically within a few months. Her mother went to work as a teacher to support her family, and, for economy, combined her household with that of her parents. She then decided to move inland, thinking that Warren's asthma and Sylvia's acute sinusitis might benefit from a drier climate. From that time, Sylvia Plath felt a constant longing for the sea.

The Plaths and Schobers moved to a modest white frame house in Wellesley, Massachusetts, a conservative upper middle-class suburb of Boston. Mr. Schober worked as *maître d'hôtel* at the Brookline Country Club where he lived during the week, returning home on his days off; Mrs. Schober assumed the care of the household; Mrs. Plath taught students in the medical secretarial training programme at Boston University.

Sylvia and Warren attended local schools and on Sunday went to the First Unitarian Society of Wellesley Hills where their mother also taught Sunday School. The family did lessons together, budgeted money at the dining-room table, and read aloud. At one of these sessions, Mrs. Plath read out Matthew Arnold's 'The Forsaken Merman'; Sylvia remembered her reaction:

> I saw the gooseflesh on my skin. I didn't know what made it. I was not cold. Had a ghost passed over? No, it was the poetry. A spark flew off Arnold and shook me, like a chill, I wanted to cry; I felt very odd. I had fallen into a new way of being happy.

She began to hide little poems in her mother's dinner napkin or beneath the butter plate. She enjoyed concocting rhymes for celebrations or for anti-celebrations:

> Liver, liver.
> makes me shiver.

At eight and a half she wrote to the *Boston Sunday Herald*:

> Dear Editor:
> I have written a short poem about
> what I see and hear on hot summer nights.

POEM

Hear the crickets chirping
In the dewy grass.
Bright little fireflies
Twinkle as they pass.

Thank you for my Good Sport pin.

Sylvia Plath (Age 8½ years.)

Her other interest, drawing in pen and ink, began early and continued through her life.* She started art lessons at an early age. Sketches, too, appeared at dinner. At about the same time 'Poem' was published, she earned a dollar prize from a newspaper contest with her 'first sample of art work': a plump lady in feathered hat and corkscrew curls, round spectacles, and a circle of fat beads. Her later pen and ink drawings were remarkably skilful and have the quality of fine block prints. Occasionally they have appeared with her articles.

In Wellesley, Sylvia went to the Marshall Livingston Perrin grammar school—named, coincidentally, for the professor with whom Mrs. Plath had studied *Faust* at Boston University. Sylvia was proud of the report cards she brought to her mother to sign. In summer she went to camp where she spent much time in the handicraft shops making beaded pot holders and leather purses which she brought home as gifts. When she was in the ninth grade, her mother taught her to type; she learned quickly and within six weeks could type proficiently. In early adolescence she was invited to attend Mrs. Ferguson's judiciously selected dancing 'Assemblies'. She joined the young people's group of the Unitarian church. Later she remembered herself in these growing years as a 'gawky mess with drab hair and bad skin', but others describe her as having been a 'lively, happy, attractive little girl'.

Her brother went to a preparatory school on scholarship. Sylvia, who remained at home, attended Gamaliel Bradford Senior High School. There her writing was encouraged by Wilbury A. Crockett who taught English and creative writing. Surprised by the girl's inventiveness, he encouraged her. The desire to write, which had seemed a random interest in the small

*See Appendix.

child, became a disciplined and compelling need for the adolescent girl. She sent forty-five pieces to *Seventeen* before the acceptance in March, 1950, of her short story, 'And Summer Will Not Come Again'. In Mr. Crockett's class, Sylvia and a friend composed a letter about the international situation which they sent to *The Christian Science Monitor*. They were paid five dollars when it was published. In August, 1950, *The Christian Science Monitor* published her poem 'Bitter Strawberries', a sardonic comment on war.

She wrote of being seventeen: 'It's the *best* age.' She played tennis, was on the girl's basketball team, was co-editor of the school newspaper, *The Bradford*, joined a high school sorority, Sub-Debs, painted decorations for class dances, went on college weekend dates, was Lady Agatha in the class play, *The Admirable Crichton*, and was described in her high school yearbook, *The Wellesleyan*:

> Warm smile . . . energetic worker . . . Bumble Boogie piano special . . . Clever with chalk and paints . . . Weekends at Williams . . . Those fully packed sandwiches . . . Future writer . . . Those rejection slips from *Seventeen* . . . Oh, for a license.

In the summer before college, she and her brother biked several miles each day to Look Out Farm in Dover where they bunched spinach and picked strawberries. All of these experiences served as material for her early poems, articles and stories. The subjects were beginning romance, lost love, adolescent humiliations, and high school sorority initiations; but each ended with a withdrawal, a bleak note, or a last wry observation from the girl protagonist, an ironic divergence from the usual adolescent conclusion.

To friends, relations, and adult observers she was a pleasant, pretty, imaginative girl who was modest about her talent and was a sure critic of her own work. In later years she was to write that she had been a 'rabid teenage pragmatist' dressed in 'a uniform—the pageboy hairdo, squeaky clean, the skirt and sweater, the "loafers", those scuffed copies of Indian moccasins' pursuing the likeness of All-Round Student which seemed so essential in the 1950's.

In September, 1950, Sylvia Plath entered Smith College on a scholarship endowed by the novelist Olive Higgins Prouty, destined to become a friend and patron. She studied with concentration, determined to keep her scholarship, taking notes-on-notes of lectures, frequently doing more work than was assigned. Writing poetry on a precise schedule, she sat with her back to whoever entered the room, as she circled words in the red leather Thesaurus which had belonged to Otto Plath. She went to lectures, concerts, plays, and joined in the traditional 'step sings' in early evening on the lawn in front of Students' Building. A friend later said: 'It was as if Sylvia couldn't wait for life to come to her . . . she rushed out to greet it, to make things happen.'

In her first year, smarting under the reprimands of upper-class students who urged her to be more sociable, she decided that she was already 'different' and would learn to live with that. She assessed her classmates' successes wryly, then berated herself for jealousy. After suffering through blind date after blind date on successive weekends of her first semester, she decided to stay in on Saturday nights and talk with a friend or go to bed early.

By her sophomore year, she had hit her stride: she earned high grades in every course, even the few she found 'painful'. Her art and creative writing courses were 'pleasures' which made her feel 'guilty' because they weren't 'work'. *Seventeen* accepted poems and stories, but she wrote to a friend, 'for the few little outward successes I may seem to have, there are acres of misgiving and self doubt'.

Apparently the lessons learned in high school and the midnight warnings of upper-class students were not completely ignored; she began teaching art as a volunteer at the People's Institute in Northampton. She was elected a sophomore prom officer. In later elections she became a member of the editorial board of *The Smith Review* and, her most prestigious office, secretary to the Honour Board which dealt with infringements of the academic honour system. As a result, at the end of the year she was chosen for 'Push', the sophomore committee which serves as escort to alumnae and seniors in the graduation weekend.

In the latter part of her freshman year she had gone to the Yale Junior Prom and now was spending weekends at Princeton and at other colleges. She went down to Cambridge to visit a Harvard medical student and once, at Boston Lying-In Hospital where she was 'sacramentally swathed to the eyes in white':

I spent the whole night there—going round from room to room with the older medical students and doctors . . . I stood two feet away to watch a baby born, and I had the queerest urge to laugh and cry when I saw the little squinted blue face grimacing out of the woman's vagina—only to see it squawk into life, cold, naked and wailing a few minutes later . . . Needless to say, my sense of the dramatic was aroused, and I went skipping excitedly down the corridors of the maternity ward like a thoroughly irresponsible Florence Nightingale.

In these months she expressed herself adamantly about the faults she was unwilling to accept in society, in her friends, and in herself. She advised a beginning writer of her own age that it was essential to 'take criticism' and to submit writing on 'neat, type-written pages'. It was during this time of awakening sexuality that the conflict between the life-styles of a poet/intellectual and that of a wife and mother became a central preoccupation: '. . . it's quite amazing how I've gone around for most of my life as in the rarefied atmosphere under a bell jar.' She took as an ideal the parents of a young man whom she was seeing frequently:

Combining a superior duo of people into a working pair, with the woman knowing all about finances, tutoring, making and keeping a rich compote of friends, entertaining and home-making, and the man full of understanding about so much of the actual world—from his vegetable gardens to the explanations of storms, roads and routes and geological formations, and to sports like skating and tennis and swimming, and to a lot of other things, that in themselves seem incomprehensible and intricate: he has assimilated them all into himself and passed them on to his children who have long since, of course, grown beyond and outward, learning and advancing so much the more. Instead of making up little fairy worlds like pink cotton wool, they investigated the world around them . . . the woods, the material phenomena of nature, winds, sand, and stars and whatnot, and so [the sons], besides being versed in Lord knows how many practical skills about all such things like the reasons behind the running of cars, and household machines and appliances, are also trained to think in the greater areas of philosophy, sociology, literature and all the rest . . . learning about the body and its functions, training to become the most intelligent and well rounded of professional men . . .

In her junior year a $150 raise in tuition forced Sylvia to move to Lawrence House, a co-operative. There she quickly made friends, but described the autumn as 'carrying griefs and travail: science course appalling . . . work at Co-op house difficult—Chaucer terrifying.' By the end of the year she had increased her list of accomplishments: she was awarded two Smith poetry prizes, and was elected not only to Alpha, the Smith College honorary society for the arts, but also to Phi Beta Kappa.

As a successful competitor in the *Mademoiselle* College Board Contest, she wrote:

After being one of the two national winners of Mademoiselle's fiction contest ($500)! last August, I felt that I was coming home again when I won a guest editorship representing Smith & took a train to NYC for a salaried month working—hatted & heeled—in Mlle's airconditioned Madison ave. offices . . . Fantastic, fabulous, and all other inadequate adjectives go to describe the four gala and chaotic weeks I worked as guest managing Ed . . . living in luxury at the Barbizon, I edited, met celebrities, was fêted and feasted by a galaxy of UN delegates, simultaneous interpreters & artists . . . an almost unbelievable merry-go-round month— this Smith Cinderella met idols: Vance Bourjaily, Paul Engle, Elizabeth Bowen—wrote article via correspondence with 5 handsome young male poet teachers.

The poets were Alastair Reid, Anthony Hecht, Richard Wilbur, George Steiner and William Binford. 'Sunday at the Mintons' had won the *Mademoiselle* fiction contest a year earlier, and in the college issue 'Mlle. finally published "Mad Girl's Lovesong"—my favorite villanelle'. That summer, *Harper's* accepted three poems, paying one hundred dollars, which Sylvia identified as 'first professional earnings'. She wrote:

All in all I felt upborne on a wave of creative, social and financial success—The 6 month crash, however, was to come—'

She had been subject to fluctuations in mood before, but this time, after returning to Wellesley for the remainder of the summer, she seemed unable to 'bounce out' of depression. Every act became difficult; eventually the smallest tasks seemed almost impossible. She attempted suicide. Her disappearance, subsequent discovery, and consequent hospitalization were well publicized. In the following months she was given psychiatric treatment and electric shock therapy. She described the experience:

A time of darkness, despair, disillusion—so black only as the inferno of the human mind can be—symbolic death, and numb shock, then the painful agony of slow rebirth and psychic regeneration . . .

By midwinter the doctors and college authorities thought she could try college again.

Now in the class of 1955, she was 'back to Lawrence House after missing a semester—facing & reconstructing the old wrecked life—new & strong'. By spring she felt 'firmly established & accepted at Smith; multitudes of dates, good friends—old and new', and went to New York City for spring vacation 'while reconquering old broncos that threw me for a loop last year'. By June she could write '. . . but exams & papers proved I hadn't lost either my repetitive or my creative intellect as I had feared . . . a semester of reconstruction ends with an infinitely more solid if less flashingly spectacular flourish than last year's'. She had been awarded another poetry prize and was elected to the presidency of Alpha.

She spent the summer of 1954 on full scholarship at Harvard summer school where she studied German. The following year Sylvia stated flatly that her 'lifelong ambition' was to be published in the *New Yorker*. She took a creative writing course with Alfred Kazin and special studies in writing with Alfred Fisher, a course which was rarely given, and then only to particularly promising students. At the same time she was writing her long paper for English honours on the double personality in Dostoevski's novels.

After several poems were published in *Harper's*, she hastened to write a friend who had congratulated her:

> . . . for the few acceptances at *Harper's* there have been at least 50 rejections! It just proves I'm pigheaded and keep sending out the stuff.

When she listed her 'prizes and writing earnings 1954–1955' they totalled $750. She had won a number of prizes, including Mount Holyoke's Irene Glascock Poetry Prize for which Marianne Moore, Wallace Fowlie and John Ciardi were judges. In June, 1955, she graduated *summa cum laude*. She looked forward to a year on a Fulbright Fellowship at Cambridge University, but 'meanwhile Spring prize money makes possible a summer of reading and writing at home in blissful meditation—God Save The Queen! . . . Those terrible freshman days, I wonder how we ever got through them'. It appeared that her earlier doubts were dissipated.

At Newnham College, Cambridge, Sylvia lived in an attic studio room decorated with bouquets of bright flowers, piles of fresh fruit from the local open markets and 'vivid postcard reprints of Picasso'. Outside were 'mottled sycamore trees, orange-tile rooftops with chimney pots around which hovered enormous black rooks'. The freedoms and traditions of the English university were equally attractive: biking to town and classes 'at least ten miles a day', cheering the royal procession in the rain, punting up the River Cam to Grantchester for 'tea, scones, and Cambridgeshire honey', arguing politics with students from every continent in the 'avant garde Café Expresso houses' and eating bindhi gusht and prawn pelavi at the Indian Taj Mahal. After joining the 'powerful' Amateur Dramatic Society, she took part in Ben Jonson's *Bartholomew Fair*. She grew 'used' to seeing her breath 'come out in frosty white puffs while taking a bath', to the college diet of 'cold mashed potatoes and ubiquitous yellow custard', to 'men making tea' and 'muddy coffee'. Although in earlier days she had never cooked without suffering a cut thumb or fire in the oven, now she proudly prepared dinners for new friends on a single gas ring.

At Christmas, she went to Paris:

going to plays, walking miles & miles along seine, through montmartre up hill to sacre coeur, listening to whores (fascinating) pick up and refuse, a whole day in tuileries playing with children and going to 'grandguignol' puppetshow, endless escargots, wine, cognac sessions, louvre & orangeries with original cezannes. All this, then new year's morning seeing sun exploding up out of incredibly azure med: living in nice, motor scootered all along riviera, to italy, matisse chapel in vence . . . so much! the whole world coming alive, banging through my eyes and fibers!

Sylvia's exploration of Europe had begun and she wrote that she wanted to 'write it all down'.

But, in the winter, there was a 'dark time'. Classes were crowded, the cold barely endurable, and, as usual, she suffered 'the flu' and sinusitis. Twice she went to the casualty ward. The first time it was for an emergency 'false alarm' appendicitis. On the second occasion, a splinter was removed from her eye while she was 'fully conscious':

I was babbling frantically about oedipus and gloucester getting new vision by losing their eyes, but me wanting, so to speak, new vision and my eyes too.

The doctor replied by adapting a quotation from Housman, 'if by chance your eye offend you, pluck it out lass and be sound'. Soon Sylvia was announcing that she could 'see fine now and all is well'.

At spring term, in letters to the States, Sylvia passionately praised her 'beautiful young supervisor in philosophy' who was 'incandescent with brilliance and creative and lovely'. Stimulated by 'this woman's lecture on d.h. lawrence's concept of the redemptive power of love in "the man who died" . . . the finest, frankest I've ever heard in my life', Sylvia designated her 'my salvation', because she seemed to prove that a woman no longer 'had to sacrifice all claims to femininity & family to be a scholar!' With renewed exuberance, Sylvia 'cut out all else so I can write mornings daily, while reading german & french on my own'.

In February at a Cambridge party which celebrated the first

issue of a new student magazine, Sylvia had met Ted Hughes whose work she respected. She was impressed by the young poet and shortly was to tell friends: 'He was very simply the only man I've ever met whom I could never boss. . . .' A short time later her Fulbright grant was renewed, and she planned for spring holidays in Paris. On her return to England, the two poets decided to join what she called, their 'life forces'. They were married on June 16 in London with Sylvia's mother as witness. When Sylvia Plath became Mrs. Edward J. Hughes, she claimed that she was also the only married woman undergraduate at Cambridge.

In the summer of 1956 the Hugheses lived on 'practically nothing', going 'with pack on back' from Paris to Madrid to the Spanish fishing village of Benidorm on the Mediterranean, where they spent five weeks writing, swimming, and sunning. They bought food from the peasant markets and lived in a large white house 'with its own fig tree and grape arbor'. Sylvia's writing was going well with Hughes's encouragement; she had begun again, at his suggestion, 'those queer blocky little sketches'. Sylvia was 'ecstatic', but she was also efficient. She began to type poems and to send out manuscripts. She reported that they both had books ready for publication, and that *The Nation*, *The Atlantic* and *Poetry* had accepted poems from them both.

By the following term they were settled in a flat overlooking Grantchester meadows. Sylvia continued reading in English at Cambridge; Ted was teaching English and drama to thirteen- and fourteen-year-olds at 'a secondary modern school'. There were problems: little money, many bills, an oven without a heat regulator, no refrigerator, and uncertainty about the future. Sylvia longed to return to America, 'land of the Cookiesheet, Central heating & Frozen Orange Juice!' She hoped that her husband would 'want to settle [in America] eventually'. Although she laughed at her 'jingoism', she had decided 'that if I want to keep on being a triple-threat woman: wife, writer & teacher (to be swapped later for motherhood, I hope) I can't be a drudge, the way housewives are forced to be here'. The problems with which she struggled seemed tangible and soluble with time, effort, and intelligence.

In the spring of 1957, the Hugheses moved to the United States. They spent the summer in 'a small gray cabin hidden in the pines' on Cape Cod at Eastham, Massachusetts. They wrote 'all morning', biked 'a couple of miles to the beach for the afternoon and read in the evening'. In the fall they moved to Northampton where Sylvia was to teach English as an instructor at Smith College. She wrote of the prospect:

> I'll be scared to death the first day, but am really excited about it: if I had a million dollar fellowship to write in Italy next year, I would refuse it: I've gotten sick of living on great grants & feel very much that need . . . of 'giving out' in some kind of work: my way, apart from writing, I know is teaching. I'll probably learn a hell of a lot more from them than they do from me, but 7 years age and reading difference between me & my pupils is enough to give me courage.

She expected to teach the writers who 'stimulated' her own writing: Lawrence, Virginia Woolf, James Joyce, Henry James and Dostoevski. That November she was awarded *Poetry*'s Bess Hokin prize.

Sylvia proved to be 'one of the two or three finest instructors ever to appear in the English department at Smith College'. As a senior colleague reported years later, her classroom performance was 'thrilling', and she was 'an astonishingly good teacher, with great warmth and generosity'.

The Hugheses, however, were not entirely satisfied with academic life. Sylvia wrote, '. . . although I loved teaching, the great conflict was with writing. I wore my eyes out on 70 student themes every other week and had no energy for writing a thing.' The decision to give up teaching was difficult and significant: Sylvia discarded a plan formed in youth to accept a less certain existence. She was painfully aware that she was disappointing some of the people who had been most helpful in college and Cambridge days, but she acted with the encouragement of those who had confidence in her creative ability.

In 1958–59, the Hugheses lived in a small cramped apartment on Beacon Hill 'on a shoestring for a year in Boston writing to see what we could do'. Their savings were supplemented by occasional income from readings and small jobs. Sylvia began to visit Robert Lowell's poetry classes at Boston University where she met George Starbuck and Anne Sexton. She renewed acquaintance with Peter Davison. Sometimes she accompanied Hughes on visits to Stanley Kunitz where she remained generally silent while the men talked.

To everyone she seemed 'neat', 'trim', 'tidy', and apparently it was difficult to penetrate her shy sociability, what a friend has called 'the social Smith façade'. Lowell recalls her as a 'distinguished, delicate, complicated person' in whom there was 'no intimation of what would come later'. He thought her 'unusually sensitive and intelligent' and characterized her poetic approach as 'controlled and modest', but he was startled by the burst of talent she later displayed.

Sylvia felt she was 'beginning to wither to one of my silent centers', and in the discouragement of repeatedly submitting the manuscript of her book of poems under ever-changing titles, she wrote:

> Nothing stinks like a pile of unpublished writing, which remark I guess shows I still don't have a pure motive (O it's-such-fun-I-just-can't-stop-who-cares-if-it's-published-or-read) about writing . . . I still want to see it finally ritualized in print.

Later she agreed that it was 'healthy' to be reminded that once publication in the *New Yorker* had seemed a distant goal.

In the spring, Ted Hughes received a Guggenheim fellowship. That summer the couple took a camping trip across the United States, and from September 9 to November 9 were residents at Yaddo. In December, 1959, they returned to England to live and work. Sylvia was pregnant with their first child. The next weeks were to be exhausting, when, coming down to London from The Beacon, the Hughes family home in Yorkshire, they hunted in the intense cold for an apartment.

On February 1, 1960, the Hugheses moved into a small flat in a London building which was being converted from a tenement for Irish labourers. The landlord promised it would be 'just like Chelsea'. Their first child was due to be born at home because they were too late to register for a hospital under the National

Health Act. Although Sylvia was 'in spirit . . . all for home births with the father there', she had been warned by an American obstetrician against considering natural childbirth, the 'English method', and was sceptical and apprehensive. Sylvia became more cheerful as she began to 'get the routines under control' in the new flat, although the activity of living did not permit time for writing. For weeks there had been 'horrid raw grey sleety rain'; Sylvia developed another sinus infection.

At 5.45 on April 1, 1960, their first child, Frieda Rebecca, was born after an unexpectedly short labour. Sylvia found the experience 'amazing' and 'the intimacy, privacy, homeiness of it all seemed just what I needed'. After Sister Mardee, 'the little Indian' midwife had bathed the baby in Sylvia's largest Pyrex baking dish and left the house, Sylvia called her mother in the States, and by afternoon was eating spoonfuls of yoghurt and maple syrup while typing letters to friends on her Olivetti. In the next months she began to wonder 'If I shall ever write a good poem again', but her book of poems, now titled *The Colossus*, was accepted for fall publication by James Michie at William Heinemann Ltd.

The Hugheses borrowed a study from the W. S. Merwins. Sylvia used it in the morning and Ted in the afternoon. They shared household chores and baby care. Sylvia began making baby clothes although sewing had always been 'a deep seated hatred'. Again, she caught sinus-colds which affected her 'taste, sense of smell, vision and equilibrium', but she was 'becoming quite fond of this patchy district now and can't really imagine living anywhere else . . . except for a couple of auto collisions, housebreakings, deaths and babies, the jangle of rival ice-cream wagons and the regular noise of glass breaking outside, our square is peaceful and idyllic'.

By Frieda's first birthday Sylvia was 'over one third through a novel about a college girl building up for and going through a nervous breakdown'. She wrote:

I have been wanting to do this for ten years but had a terrible block about Writing A Novel. Then suddenly in beginning negotiations with a New York publisher for an American edition of my poems, the dykes broke and I stayed awake all night seized by fearsome excitement, saw how it should be done, started the next day & go every morning to my borrowed study as to an office & belt out more of it.

She had a fellowship on which to work, but the year was not easy. In rapid succession she had a miscarriage followed by an appendectomy, and then became pregnant again.

That summer the Hugheses bought a peaked thatched country house in Devon. As usual Sylvia threw herself into the new life with enthusiasm. It pleased her that the house, set in an orchard of seventy apple trees, facing a twelfth-century Anglican church across an acre of green field which in spring was filled with daffodils, was recorded in a medieval survey. She wrote, describing the thatch: 'How I love the millions of birds who live in it, even the blue tits who drink the cream off our milk.' She taught herself to ride a horse—bare-back—and began beekeeping, onion stringing, and potato digging. Worries about money became less acute and the work of making room after room habitable—the painting, carpentering, plumbing and electrification—occupied many days. In preparing the gardens in March for vegetables and roses, she thought she had suffered from stinging nettle bites, but the doctor diagnosed her problems as chilblains, which, she wrote, 'almost demoralized me, I thought I'd been vanquishing our 38° interior temperature with noble spirit, then to learn the cold had been secretly and nastily getting to me—well!'

The arrangement of days divided between child care, housework, and writing continued, but Sylvia began to feel she was doing little work and wrote, 'a couple of poems I like a year looks like a lot when they come out, but in fact are points of satisfaction separated by large vacancies.'

In addition there were other problems: Sylvia was determined to belong to the village, but with parental concern she wrote:

I think our little local church very lovely—it has 8 bellringers & some fine stained-glass windows, but I must say the Anglican religion seems terribly numb & cold & grim to me . . . All the awful emphasis on our weakness & sinfulness & being able to do nothing but through Christ . . . But I do want Frieda to have the experience of Sunday School, so I may keep up the unsatisfactory practice of going, although I disagree with almost everything.

Again, when she learned that it had long been local custom to come in spring to the manor house for daffodils, she collected and distributed them in the expected manner.

She is remembered in these years as vigorous, efficient, professional, and ambitious. Her social manner was poised and warm, and she was good at getting people to talk at awkward parties. She was described as physically big, and rawboned with high colouring; her hair hung in long braids or was coiled on her head. She was absorbed in local activities. There is no doubt that she loved England and planned to live there permanently, though she continued to consider herself an American.

On January 17th, 1962, Nicholas Farrar Hughes was born with his father and the local midwife in attendance. Sylvia described her new son as 'a true Hughes—craggy, dark, quiet, & smiley . . .' Subsequently, in a BBC broadcast, she said of her poem, 'Nick and the Candlestick':

A mother nurses her baby son by candlelight and finds in him a beauty which, while it may not ward off the world's ill, does redeem her share of it.

The following year was difficult. That summer she suffered repeated attacks of flu accompanied by high fevers. She was exhausted emotionally and physically. After a vacation in Ireland, another winter in Devon seemed impossible. She commuted bi-weekly to London where she was 'getting work with the BBC'. A few days before Christmas of 1962 she moved herself and her children to London:

. . . a small miracle happened—I'd been to Yeats' tower at Ballylea while in Ireland & thought it the most beautiful & peaceful place in the world; then, walking desolately around my beloved Primrose Hill in London and brooding on the hopelessness of *ever* finding a flat . . . I passed Yeats' house, with its blue plaque 'Yeats lived here' which I'd often passed & longed to live in. A sign board was up—flats to rent, I flew to the agent. By a miracle you can only know if you've ever tried to flat-hunt in London, I was first to apply . . . I am here on a 5 year lease & it is utter heaven . . . and it's Yeats' house, which right now means a lot to me.

She had begun to make plans with energetic assurance.

In the middle of January, 1963, *The Bell Jar* was published under the pseudonym, Victoria Lucas. Those close to Sylvia have said that she did not feel it was an adequate book, that she was agitated by the reviews. Perhaps it is to be regretted that Sylvia never knew that one of the professors she had esteemed at Smith College found her book 'vivid but excruciating' and said that her technique conveyed both a sense of immediacy and the projection of a schizophrenic condition which was 'amazingly successful'.

Sylvia's feelings about her first novel were only some of the problems with which she was wrestling at the time. She endured the coldest winter in London since the winter of 1813–14. The light and heat went off at unannounced intervals; pipes froze; there was no telephone; and, as always, a sinus infection developed.

Each morning before the children woke at eight, she worked on the *Ariel* poems. Here the sense of human experience as horrid and ungovernable, and of all relationships as puppetlike and meaningless, had come to dominate her imagination. Yet she wrote with intensity, convinced that what she was now writing could be said by no one else. Always there was a need to be practical, to find time for the deliberate expression of anguish. She wrote, 'I feel like a very efficient tool or weapon, used and in demand from moment to moment . . .' She hoped to find an *au pair* girl or mother's helper to replace the one she had fired, 'to help with the babes mornings so I can write . . . nights are no good, I'm so flat by then that all I can cope with is music & brandy & water.'

She had not given up the future. In the first week in February she began to anticipate, with plans of plays and dinners out, the 'spring tonic' of an April visit from friends in the States. She was eager for them to see 'my little Frieda and Nick . . . so beautiful and dear' and thought of return to the house in Devon, for 'around Mayday'.

Nevertheless, despite the care of a doctor and prescribed sedatives, she was unable to cope. She ended her life in the early morning of February 11, 1963.

THE BARFLY OUGHT TO SING

ANNE SEXTON

I can add, for Sylvia, only a small sketch and two poems—one poem written for her at the news of her death and the other, written a year later, written directly for both of us and for that place where we met . . . 'balanced there, suicides sometimes meet. . . .'

I knew her for a while in Boston. We did grow up in the same suburban town, Wellesley, Massachusetts, but she was about four years behind me and we never met. Even if we had, I wonder if we would have become close friends, back then—she was so bright, so precocious and determined to be special while I was only a pimply boy-crazy thing, flunking most subjects, thinking I was never special. We didn't meet, at any rate, until she was married to Ted Hughes and living in Boston. We met because we were poets. Met, not for protocol, but for truth. She heard, and George Starbuck heard, that I was auditing a class at Boston University given by Robert Lowell. They kind of followed me in, joined me there and so we orbited around the class silently. If we talked at all then we were fools. We knew too much about it to talk. Silence was wiser, when we could command it. We tried, each one in his own manner; sometimes letting our own poems come up, as for a butcher, as for a lover. Both went on. We kept as quiet as possible in view of the father.

Then, after the class, we would pile into the front seat of my old Ford and I would drive quickly through the traffic to, or near, The Ritz. I would always park illegally in a LOADING ONLY ZONE, telling them gaily, 'It's okay, because we are only going to get loaded!' Off we'd go, each on George's arm, into The Ritz to drink three or four or two martinis. George even has a line about this in his first book of poems, *Bone Thoughts*. He wrote, I *weave with two sweet ladies out of The Ritz*. Sylvia and I, such sleep mongers, such death mongers, were those two sweet ladies.

In the lounge-bar of The Ritz, not a typical bar at all, but very plush, deep dark red carpeting, red leather chairs around polite little tables and with waiters, white coated and awfully hushed where one knew upon stepping down the five velvet red steps that he was entering *something*, we entered. The waiters knew their job. They waited on the best of Boston, or at least, celebrities. We always hoped they'd make a mistake in our case and think us some strange Hollywood types. There had to be something to explain all our books, our snowboots, our clutter of poems, our oddness, our quick and fiery conversations—and always the weekly threesome hunched around their small but fashionable table.

Often, very often, Sylvia and I would talk at length about our first suicides; at length, in detail and in depth between the free potato chips. Suicide is, after all, the opposite of the poem. Sylvia and I often talked opposites. We talked death with burned-up intensity, both of us drawn to it like moths to an electric light bulb. Sucking on it! She told the story of her first suicide in sweet and loving detail and her description in *The Bell Jar* is just the same story. It is a wonder that we didn't depress George with our egocentricity. Instead, I think, we three were stimulated by it, even George, as if death made each of us a little more real at the moment. Thus we went on, in our fashion, ignoring Lowell and the poems left behind. Poems left behind were technique—lasting but, actually, over. We talked death and this was life for us, lasting in spite of us, or better, because of us, our intent eyes, our fingers clutching the glass, three pairs of eyes fixed on someone's—each one's gossip. I know that such fascination with death sounds strange (one does not argue that it isn't sick—one knows it *is*—there's no excuse), and that people cannot understand. They keep, every year, each year, asking me 'why, why?' So here is the Why-poem, for both of us, those sweet ladies at The Ritz. I do feel somehow that it's the same answer that Sylvia would have given. She's since said it for me in so many poems—so I try to say it for us in one of mine. . . .

WANTING TO DIE

Since you ask, most days I cannot remember.
I walk in my clothing, unmarked by that voyage.
Then the almost unnameable lust returns.

Even then I have nothing against life.
I know well the grass blades you mention,
the furniture you have placed under the sun.

But suicides have a special language.
Like carpenters they want to know *which tools*.
They never ask *why build*.

Twice I have so simply declared myself,
have possessed the enemy, eaten the enemy,
have taken on his craft, his magic.

In this way, heavy and thoughtful,
warmer than oil or water,
I have rested, drooling at the mouth-hole.

I did not think of my body at needle point.
Even the cornea and the leftover urine were gone.
Suicides have already betrayed the body.

Still-born, they don't always die,
but dazzled, they can't forget a drug so sweet
that even children would look on and smile.

To thrust all that life under your tongue!—
that all by itself becomes a passion.
Death's a sad bone; bruised, you'd say.

and yet she waits for me, year after year,
to so delicately undo an old wound,
to empty my breath from its bad prison.

Balance there, suicides sometimes meet,
raging at the fruit, a pumped up moon,
leaving the bread they mistook for a kiss.

leaving the page of the book carelessly open,
something unsaid, the phone off the hook
and the love, whatever it was, an infection.

And balanced there we did meet and never asking *why build*—
only asking *which tools*. This was our fascination. I neither could
nor would give you reasons why either of us wanted *to build*. It is
not my place to tell you Sylvia's why nor my desire to tell you
mine. But I do say, come picture us exactly at our fragmented
meetings, consumed at our passions and at our infections, as we
ate five free bowls of potato chips and consumed lots of martinis.

After this we would weave out of The Ritz to spend our last
pennies at The Waldorf Cafeteria—a dinner for 70 cents. George
was in no hurry. He was separating from his wife. Sylvia's Ted
was either able to wait or was busy enough with his own work
and I had to stay in the city (I live outside of it) for a 7 p.m.
appointment with my psychiatrist. A funny three.

I have heard since that Sylvia was determined from childhood
to be great, a great writer at the least of it. I tell you, at the time
I did not notice this in her. Something told me to bet on her but
I never asked it why. I was too determined to bet on myself to
actually notice where she was headed in her work. Lowell said, at
the time, that he liked her work and that he felt her poems got
right to the point. I didn't agree. I felt they really missed the
whole point. (These were early poems of hers—poems on the
way, on the working toward way.) I told Mr. Lowell that I felt
she dodged the point and did so perhaps because of her pre-
occupation with form. Form was important for Sylvia and each
really good poet has one of his own. No matter what he calls it—
free verse or what. Still, it belongs to you or it doesn't. Sylvia
hadn't then found a form that belonged to her. Those early
poems were all in a cage (and not even her own cage at that). I felt
she hadn't found a voice of her own, wasn't, in truth, free to be
herself. Yet, of course, I knew she was skilled—intense, skilled,
perceptive, strange, blonde, lovely, Sylvia.

From England to America we exchanged a few letters. I have them now, of course. She mentions my poems and perhaps I sent her new ones as I wrote—I'm not sure. The time of the LOADING ONLY ZONE was gone as now we sent aerograms back and forth, now and then. George was in Rome. He never wrote. He divorced and remarried over there. Sylvia wrote of one child, keeping bees, another child, my poems—happy, gossip-letters, and then, with silence between us, she died.

After her death, with the printing of her last poems, I read that she gave me credit on a BBC programme, credit as an influence upon her work. Certainly she never told me anything about it. But then, maybe she wouldn't have—nothing that ordinary, nothing that direct. She gave me and Robert Lowell (both in a rather casual lump, Sylvia!) credit for our breakthrough into the personal in poetry. I suppose we might have shown her something about daring—daring to tell it true. W. D. Snodgrass showed me in the first place. Perhaps he influenced Robert Lowell too—I can't speak for him. But let's get down to facts. I'm sure Sylvia's influences are hidden, as with most of us, and if one feels compelled to name an influence then let us begin with Theodore Roethke. I remember writing to Sylvia in England after *The Colossus* came out and saying something like . . . 'if you're not careful, Sylvia, you will out-Roethke Roethke', and she replied that I had guessed accurately and that he had been a strong influence on her work. Believe me, no one ever tells one's real influences—and certainly not on the radio or the TV or in interviews, if he can help it. As a matter of fact, I probably guessed wrong and she was lying to me. She ought to. I'd never tell anyone and she was smarter than I am about such hidden things. Poets will not only hide influences. They will bury them! And not that her lines reminded me of Roethke—but the openness to metaphor, the way they both have (and Sylvia even more so in her last work) of jumping straight into their own image and then believing it. No doubt of it—at the end, Sylvia burst from her cage and came riding straight out with the image-ridden-darer, Roethke. But maybe she buried her so-called influence deeper than that, deeper than any one of us would think to look, and if she did I say good luck to her. Her poems do their own work.

I don't need to sniff them for distant relatives of some sort. I'm against it. Maybe I did give her a sort of daring, but that's all she should have said. That's all that's similar about our work. Except for death—yes, we have that in common (and there must be enough other poets with that theme to fill an entire library). Never mind last diggings. They don't matter. What matters is her poems. These last poems stun me. They eat time. As for death——

SYLVIA'S DEATH

for Sylvia Plath

O Sylvia, Sylvia,
with a dead box of stones and spoons,

with two children, two meteors
wandering loose in the tiny playroom,

with your mouth into the sheet,
into the roofbeam, into the dumb prayer,

(O Sylvia, Sylvia,
where did you go
after you wrote me
from Devonshire
about raising potatoes
and keeping bees?)

what did you stand by,
just how did you lie down into?

Thief!—
how did you crawl into,

crawl down alone
into the death I wanted so badly and for so long,

the death we said we both outgrew,
the one we wore on our skinny breasts,

the one we talked of so often each time
we downed three extra dry martinis in Boston,

the death that talked of analysts and cures,
the death that talked like brides with plots,

the death we drank to,
the motives and then the quiet deed?

(In Boston
the dying
ride in cabs,
yes death again,
that ride home
with *our* boy.)

O Sylvia, I remember the sleepy drummer
who beat on our eyes with an old story,

how we wanted to let him come
like a sadist or a New York fairy

to do his job,
a necessity, a window in a wall or a crib,

and since that time he waited
under our heart, our cupboard,

and I see now that we store him up
year after year, old suicides

and I know, at the news of your death,
a terrible taste for it, like salt.

(And me,
me too.
And now, Sylvia,
you again,
with death again,
the ride home
with *our* boy.)

And I say only
with my arms stretched out into that stone place,

what is your death,
but an old belonging,

a mole that fell out
of one of your poems?

(O friend,
while the moon's bad,
and the king's gone
and the queen's at her wit's end,
the bar fly ought to sing!)

O tiny mother,
you too!
O funny duchess!
O blonde thing!

REMEMBERING SYLVIA

WENDY CAMPBELL

I first met Sylvia in 1956 when she was twenty-three. She had come as an American graduate, on a Fulbright, to read English at Cambridge. Dorothea Krook, who was a friend of mine, was giving a course of lectures on the English Moralists, and I was going to hear these at her invitation. (She wished me to see her point of view, and was adamant that I could only do so by hearing her lectures.) Sylvia was one of her most brilliant pupils, and in pursuit of Doris's point of view, it was arranged that I should be allowed to sit in on their supervisions. I liked Sylvia at once very much; she was so alive and warm and interested. She seemed to be entirely collected and concentrated and in focus: and she was charming to look at. Tall and slender and delicate wristed, she had pale honey hair, fine, thick and long, and beautiful dark brown eyes. And her skin was pale gold and waxy, the same even colour. I was immensely impressed by her essays, and her competent mastery of the authors she discussed. Although she was extremely intelligent she was entirely without the need to use her intelligence as a weapon. She did not feel the need to define herself in intellectual combat. In discussions at seminars she was very clever (as distinct from intelligent), without the least interest in cleverness as a mode. She had a sharp contempt for anything that verged on the precious or overheated. (There was at that time a contemporary novel being talked about which had been written by someone Sylvia knew. I had not liked its determined display of exquisite sensibilities, and when one day Sylvia asked me what I thought of it I told her with some hesitation. To my surprise and pleasure, she agreed with me, and we fell upon it together and sliced it up to our private satisfaction. This was really the beginning of our friendship.) There was nothing whatever of the preacher, the enthusiast or the persuader about Sylvia. Her point of reference was always firmly fixed within herself. She seemed to use her mind as a set of antennae with which she assessed her experience and felt it over. She wanted 'to know' for her own subjective purposes. Her intellectual traffic was largely with herself and related ultimately to her vision of the world and her experience.

She did not often talk to me about what she was writing but I remember her telling me one day about the girl who was the source of her poem, 'Spinster'. Sylvia felt that a drawing back in the face of any aspect of life was nothing less than horrible, a voluntary courting of deformity. It disgusted her, filled her with an angry contempt. And she saw in Newnham (and Girton) that the effect of academic pressure combined with academic ambition too often led to this kind of withdrawal; to an almost conscious sacrifice of the life of the feelings for the sake of undisturbed intellectualization. To her it was a hymn to winter.

I cannot recall exactly when she met Ted Hughes, but I can remember her arriving at one of her supervisions in an indignant rage because she had been turned out of her college when it was discovered that she had married him secretly. She thought the attitude of the college to her marriage was hysterical and absurd, as though the fact of being married had made her an initiate into something too dark and dangerous for the others to be near. It was a witness to what she protested against in 'Spinster'.

About this time I remember them both very clearly at a party I gave (standing by the fireplace, talking to some people, both of them smiling and smiling, almost incandescent with happiness). The Dean of Ted's college arrived and was standing in the doorway casting a delicately nauseated eye over the assembly when it came to rest on Ted. 'You do know some extraordinary people,' he murmured. I thought Ted so genuinely extraordinary that I laughed aloud and so did he, but the good dean spoke with feeling since Ted had apparently posed a certain problem for the college for a part of his time there. He lived with such vehemence, and such a perfect absence of self-consciousness, and such a total indifference to the modes of the Establishment that it was not always easy to preserve both Ted and the appearances which were thought to be necessary. At this party a friend of mine said as he was leaving, indicating Ted and Sylvia, 'Something going on between those two,' and I said, 'Well, yes, they've just been married.' And indeed something was undoubtedly going on. They seemed to have found solid ground in each other. Ted's gusto took more constructive forms and Sylvia had found a man on the same scale as herself. Her vividness demanded largeness, intensity, an extreme, and Ted was not only physically large, but he had a corresponding largeness of being. He was unfettered, he was unafraid: he didn't care, in a tidy bourgeois sense, he didn't care a damn for anyone or anything. They used to have dinner with me now and then and I found them enchanting company. I don't remember very much of what we talked about, but I have the clearest recollection of feeling that I was understood and received. I was recovering from the death of my husband and found people's kindness, and indeed everything to do with conventional sympathy almost unbearable. Ted and Sylvia had a spontaneous empathy with my state of mind which was very liberating to me. They gave me the incomparable restorative of understanding and there is very little else as valuable.

They moved into a flat in Eltisley Avenue, and though it was fairly small, they made it their own by lining one entire wall with their books and overcoming the landlady's effects with their own. Doris (Dorothea Krook) and I had dinner there and I was very impressed by Sylvia's telling us that she and Ted used to get up at about five o'clock in the morning so as to have time to do their own writing before the day properly began. She told us with relish how much she loved those early morning hours when the world was still a quiet private place before the noise of the day began. Ted told us how he felt the process of writing: I don't remember his precise words but he conveyed a clear picture of the process. He sank a shaft into the deepest part of himself and stood aside so to speak, and let the words, the matter, rise up. It was a marvellous image of the process of fishing the unconscious. It seemed to me that Sylvia had a sort of natural excellence at whatever she turned her hand to. If she wrote an essay it was effortlessly good, if she kept house it was done easily and well, and she even cooked superbly, with enthusiasm and discrimina-

184

tion and she enjoyed it almost as much as she enjoyed eating. But her very remarkable efficiency was also very natural to her, and was never accompanied by any sense of strain.

After Sylvia graduated they went to America, and taught and wrote and began to publish more poems. When they came back to England they lived in London for a while and I saw them once in their flat there. It was off Regent's Park, the top floor of a house which had been caught on the edge of collapse and nursed back to charm and usefulness by some enterprising person who was now spreading his restorations further. It was in 1960 when Sylvia had just had her first baby, Frieda. Their flat was painted white and excitingly filled with objects, and photographic blow-ups that made me long to stay and examine it minutely. But I had only time to rush in and out. Some months later they came to Cambridge for a day and a night, bringing Frieda and a friend of theirs who had been staying with them. I was interested to see the calm affectionate pleasure with which Sylvia dealt with Frieda. Once more the lack of fuss, the efficiency, the collected-ness. The friend however (of whom they were very fond) had begun to tax even Sylvia's reserves of resilience. He was an American sculptor who had been with them for six weeks and who was extremely neurotic about food. I had cooked a dish for Ted and Sylvia which I knew they particularly liked, but he declined to eat my concoction on the grounds that he only ate certain categories of food and this did not fall into any of them. Sylvia and I withdrew to the kitchen for a short hilarious interval while I wondered what to give him, and she said that he was so discriminating that he could frequently only bring himself to eat bread and butter. And that was what in fact on this occasion he eventually contented himself with. For all his charm, which was considerable, I congratulated Sylvia on not having strangled him, but although she laughed, she was irritable and on edge about him. This was the last time I saw them. They moved to Devon after that and seemed to be very busy and absorbed in their lives and their writing. When, two years later, I heard that Sylvia had killed herself I was simply unable to believe it. Suicide often seems to be a very reasonable means of leaving a disastrous life but it was very difficult to connect Sylvia with self-slaughter. Her attitude to life was, as I had seen it, so wholly and sensitively positive, that I had at first a ludicrous conviction that she must have been murdered. Then I read *The Bell Jar* and *Ariel*, and it became clearer to me how it had come about. Nevertheless for me, Sylvia's quality, her personal style of being, her vitality are summed up in an image of the Winged Victory as I have seen it flood-lit in the Louvre. She strides, her robes fly out, beautiful and huge. The disaster that befell Sylvia from within was a final version of the same disaster that is on a lesser scale recurrent for most of us. An eclipse of the light, temporary but recurring. She succumbed, in a dark phase of the moon, to the serpent that had followed her all her life.

Sylvia was serious and truthful and highly evolved—Forsterian terms; she was wholly remarkable for being wholly authentic. By which I mean that she was true to herself, or truly herself, something which is exceedingly rare. She was incapable of any sort of falsity or affectation or exaggeration. Her desire was to catch her life at its widest and richest stretch and live it with comprehension. But along with her remarkable abilities (in which she took no possessive pride since she took them for granted as the given), she had a streak of sharp contempt for anyone who appeared to refuse the full range of human experience. (She had no patience with compromises and smallness. To excel, she took for granted: that was merely the starting point: it was the thing itself that mattered to her.) She also had a bitter grief and resentment at the pain involved in being human, for herself and (by identification) for the rest of humanity. She could neither tolerate the pain herself, nor bear it for anyone else. It seems that an acceptance of the fact of pain is necessary for survival. The digestion of that excruciating fact is the price of survival. She explored everything that happened to her with precision and courage, and in time she would have arrived at that exciting point where tolerance fertilizes experience with compassion. If she had lived she would have paid that price.

NOTES ON THE CHRONOLOGICAL
ORDER OF SYLVIA PLATH'S POEMS

TED HUGHES

In a poet whose development was as phenomenal as hers, the chronological order of the poems is an important help to understanding them. Most readers will perceive pretty readily the single centre of power and light which her poems all share, but I think it will be a service if I point out just how little of her poetry is 'occasional', and how faithfully her separate poems build up into one long poem. She faced a task in herself, and her poetry is the record of her progress in the task. The poems are chapters in a mythology where the plot, seen as a whole and in retrospect, is strong and clear—even if the origins of it and the *dramatis personae*, are at bottom enigmatic. The world of her poetry is one of emblematic visionary events, mathematical symmetries, clairvoyance and metamorphoses. Her poetry escapes ordinary analysis in the way clairvoyance and mediumship do: her psychic gifts, at almost any time, were strong enough to make her frequently wish to be rid of them.

As will be shown by the sequence of her poems, and of her preoccupations right from the start, her initiation into this spiritual world was inevitable, and nothing very sudden. In her, as with perhaps few poets ever, the nature, the poetic genius and the active self, were the same. Maybe we don't need psychological explanations to understand what a difficult and peculiar destiny that means. She had none of the usual guards and remote controls to protect herself from her own reality. She lived right in it, especially during the last two years of her life. Perhaps that is one of the privileges, or prices, of being a woman and at the same time an initiate into the poetic order of events. Though the brains, the strength, the abundance and vivacity of spirits, the artistic virtuosity, the thousand incidental gifts that can turn it into such poetry as hers are another matter.

Before her first book, *The Colossus*, she had written great quantities of verse, all of it characteristic and unique, with a dense crop of inspired phrases that a poet of any age would have been glad to have secured. But she never saved lines or phrases. She wrote her early poems very slowly, Thesaurus open on her knee, in her large, strange handwriting, like a mosaic, where every letter stands separate within the work, a hieroglyph to itself. If she didn't like a poem, she scrapped it entire. She rescued nothing of it. Every poem grew complete from its own root, in that laborious inching way, as if she were working out a mathematical problem, chewing her lips, putting a thick dark ring of ink around each word that stirred for her on the page of the Thesaurus.

THE FAUN was one of the earliest poems she saved. This dates from spring, 1956, while she was an undergraduate at Cambridge, in England.

STRUMPET SONG: dates from about the same time.

SPINSTER: dates from this time. The opposition of a prickly, fastidious defence and an imminent volcano is, one way or another, an element in all her early poems. A variant on the theme is the dreary meaninglessness and exhaustion of those times when for some reason or another the volcano is inactive or under a flood.

ALL THE DEAD DEARS: belongs here.

WATERCOLOR OF GRANTCHESTER MEADOWS: belongs here.

DEPARTURE: is a memory of the summer of 1956, which we spent renting a house in Benidorm, a Spanish fishing village, not much spoiled at that time.

HARDCASTLE CRAGS: is a deep narrow valley in the Pennines in West Yorks, and makes the southern boundary of the moorland made famous by Emily Brontë in *Wuthering*

Heights. The village she describes, which is on a hilltop overlooking this valley, is very ancient.

SOW: commemorates a great sow that lived near this village.

Between these and the next poems we moved to the United States, where she took up a teaching post on the English faculty at Smith College.

MUSSEL HUNTER AT ROCK HARBOUR: she wrote this in the summer, on Cape Cod, before she started teaching. This was one of her first poems in syllabics, which were her first step, technically, in her self-exploration. She was a lucky fisherman.

The next group of poems belongs to the time she was teaching. They all share a likeness—and there were others of the same family, as good and as chilling. THE THIN PEOPLE, LORELEI, FULL FATHOM FIVE, FROG AUTUMN, THE DISQUIETING MUSES, SNAKECHARMER, THE GHOST'S LEAVETAKING, SCULPTOR, NIGHT SHIFT, are the ones she saved.

In THE DISQUIETING MUSES, as in SNAKECHARMER, THE GHOST'S LEAVETAKING and several poems not collected, she shows clearly how native she was to the world of the Primitive Painters. Her vision, particularly in its aspect—strong at this time—of the deathly paradise, belongs with theirs perhaps more readily than with anything in poetry, but these poems are, ultimately, about her world, not theirs, and it is not a world of merely visual effects. SNAKECHARMER, after a picture by Rousseau, is what she did not know, a specific vision revealed to yogis at a certain advanced stage, to take just one instance.

SCULPTOR: Leonard Baskin's work struck her very hard, as well it might, since some of the gods he was carving at the time were also part of her pantheon—namely, the huge bald angels, the mutilated dead men, the person with the owl growing out of his shoulder.

LORELEI and FULL FATHOM FIVE: she was prompted to these by reading one of Cousteau's accounts of his diving and underwater explorations. At this distance of time, one can see that in these poems for the first time she accepts the invitation of her inner world. These poems coincided with a decision, made with great difficulty and against great tactical opposition from individuals she regarded as her benefactors, to leave teaching and throw herself on writing for a few years.

Between these last and the next group of poems is a gap of some months. From late summer 1958 to mid-1959, we lived in Boston. It was a difficult time for her: a lifetime's training, and fierce and highly successful effort to prepare herself to teach in a University, with many other deep compulsions to the same end, were not surrendered so easily. From this year there was not much poetry, but it was a decisive time.

THE EYE-MOTE dates from this period. The mention of Oedipus, and the Greek Tragedians' figures elsewhere, may seem literary, but if one can take her dream life as evidence, those personalities were deeply involved in her affairs. Her openness to the ambiguous populations of 'the living ether' took its toll. Her reactions to hurts in other people and animals, and even tiny desecrations of plant-life were extremely violent. The chemical poisoning of nature, the pile-up of atomic waste, were horrors that persecuted her like an illness—as her latest poems record. Auschwitz and the rest were merely the open wounds, in her idea of the great civilized crime of intelligence that like the half-imbecile, omnipotent, spoiled brat Nero has turned on its mother.

THE MAN IN BLACK belongs here.

THE HERMIT AT OUTERMOST HOUSE is a fore-runner of the style that she possessed completely only after her first book was completed. It has the comic goblin, the tricksterish spirit, the crackling verbal energy, that was the nymph-form—a lot of Caliban in it—of *Ariel*.

THE BEEKEEPER'S DAUGHTER is one of a group of poems that she wrote at this time about her father. Besides being a general biologist and botanist, he was a specialist in bees, and wrote a book called *Bumblebees and Their Ways*. This poem, one of her chilliest, recounts a key event in her *Vita Nuova*.

POINT SHIRLEY was a deliberate exercise in Robert Lowell's early style. The setting is the bit of coast off Boston Harbour where she spent her first years.

AFTERMATH, TWO VIEWS OF A CADAVER ROOM, and SUICIDE OFF EGG ROCK come clear of the domination of heavy iambic lines, have the casual fluency of her syllabic poems, yet a greater naturalness of tone and a warmer fullness of phrasing than anything she had done before. Also, they steer in quite masterfully towards some point in her life that had been painful. For the first time, she tried deliberately to locate just what it was that hurt.

In the Autumn of 1959, after touring around the States, we were invited to Yaddo. The weeks spent at Yaddo—with only three or four other residents—completed the poems in *The Colossus*. It was, in several ways, the culmination of the first part of her life. For three months, while seeing the States, she had not touched verse. Her first child would be born six months later. We had decided to live in Europe, and were to go there straight from Yaddo. It was an end and a new beginning. She took childbearing in a deeply symbolic way. Maybe it is truer to say that she accepted the symbolic consequences of an event. In those weeks, she changed at great speed and with steady effort.

BLUE MOLES records two dead moles we found in the grounds at Yaddo.

FLUTE NOTES FROM A REEDY POND: like most of the pieces she wrote at this time, it is an elegy for an old order, the promise of a new. The sudden enrichment of the texture of her verse, and the nimble shifting of focus, were something new and surprised her. At this time she was concentratedly trying to break down the tyranny, the fixed focus and public persona which descriptive or discoursive poems take as a norm. We devised exercises of meditation and invocation.

THE WINTER SHIP belongs here.

MUSHROOMS: this developed from an invocation.

THE BURNT-OUT SPA: records an old spa near Yaddo.

THE MANOR GARDEN: This is about the last of the old order, and the new birth is requisitioning all nature to its delivery. The new style is just under the surface. YOU'RE, in *Ariel*, is another poem, written some months later, with a similar combination of elements, which shows how close natural kin she was, at this point in her development, with Emily Dickinson.

THE STONES was the last poem she wrote at Yaddo, and the last in America. The immediate source of it was a series of poems she began as a deliberate exercise in experimental improvisation on set themes. She had never in her life improvised. The powers that compelled her to write so slowly had always been stronger than she was. But quite suddenly she found herself free to let herself drop, rather than inch over bridges of concepts.

She was reading Paul Radin's collection of African folktales with great excitement. In these, she found the underworld of her worst nightmares throwing up intensely beautiful adventures, where the most unsuspected voices thrived under the pressures of a reality that made most accepted fiction seem artificial and spurious. At the same time she was reading—closely and sympathetically for the first time—Roethke's poems. The result was a series of pieces, each a monologue of some character in an underground, primitive drama. STONES was the last of them, and the only one not obviously influenced by Roethke. It is full of specific details of her experience in a mental hospital, and is clearly enough the first eruption of the voice that produced *Ariel*. It is the poem where the self, shattered in 1953, suddenly finds itself whole. The series was called POEM FOR A BIRTHDAY.

That was the end of the first phase of her development. When she consolidated her hold on the second phase, two years later, she dismissed everything prior to THE STONES as Juvenilia, produced in the days before she became herself. In England, she wrote one more poem, YOU'RE, which I have already mentioned, before her first child was born, at home, without anaesthetic, with great ease and speed, at exactly sunrise, on the first day of April, the day she regularly marked as the first day of Spring.

Once she had arrived so surely at her own centre of gravity, everything that happened to her or that she undertook, enriching and enlarging herself, also enriched and enlarged her poetry. With the birth of her first child she received herself, and was able to turn to her advantage all the forces of a highly-disciplined, highly intellectual style of education which had, up to this point, worked mainly against her, but without which she could hardly have gone so coolly into the regions she now entered. The birth of her second child, in January of 1962, completed the preparation.

The two years between 1960 and 1962 had produced some beautiful poems, but only three that she selected for *Ariel*. She had heard what her real voice sounded like, and now had new standard for herself. The poem called TULIPS, was the first sign of what was on its way. She wrote this poem without her usual studies over the Thesaurus, and at top speed, as one might write an urgent letter. From then on, all her poems were written in this way.

TULIPS belongs to March 1961, and records some tulips she had in the hospital where she was recovering from an appendectomy. Another poem, written at the same time and in almost identical form, published in *The London Magazine*, but not collected, the weaker twin of this one, was the monologue of a body completely, impatiently, enclosed in a plaster cast—which was the actual condition of a patient in a bed near her.

MORNING SONG, a poem about her daughter Frieda, dates from this time, and from later in the year comes LITTLE FUGUE. Her interest in music was average. As a young girl she had played the viola, and could play on the piano any number of popular hits from the early 1950s. But suddenly now she became absorbed by the late quartet music of Beethoven, particularly the Grosse Fugue.

The first poem of the final phase was ELM. This particular tree, enormous, stands over our yard in England. The poems dates from April 1962.

THE MOON AND THE YEW TREE came soon after. Opposite the front of our house stands a church. Early one morning, in the dark, I saw the full moon setting on to a large yew that grows in the churchyard, and I suggested she make a poem of it. By midday, she had written it. It depressed me greatly. It's my suspicion that no poem can be a poem that is not a statement from the powers in control of our life, the ultimate suffering and decision in us. It seems to me that this is poetry's only real distinction from the literary forms that we call 'not poetry'. And I had no doubt that this was a poem, and perhaps a great poem. She insisted that it was an exercise on the theme.

THE RIVAL is a poem left over from a series specifically about that woman in the moon, the disquieting muse.

BERCK-PLAGE: In June, 1961, we had visited Berck-Plage, a long beach and resort on the coast of France north of Rouen. Some sort of hospital or convalescent home for the disabled fronts the beach. It was one of her nightmares stepped into the real world. A year later—almost to the day—our next door neighbour, an old man, died after a short grim illness during which time his wife repeatedly needed our help. In this poem that visit to the beach and the death and funeral of our neighbour are combined. It belongs to July 1962.

The next group of poems, including everything in *Ariel* up to the end of the Bee sequence, arrived in October and November of 1962. There were a few others not collected. She occasionally wrote two or three in the same day. The Bee poems came first.

NICK AND THE CANDLESTICK: Nicholas is the name of the little boy, her second child.

THE NIGHT DANCES: This records Nicholas' dancing in his cot. He devised an eerie set of joyful, slow prancing movements which must be called a dance, and which he used to go through when he woke up at night.

ARIEL was the name of the horse on which she went riding weekly. Long before, while she was a student at Cambridge (England), she went riding with an American friend out towards Grantchester. Her horse bolted, the stirrups fell off, and she came all the way home to the stables, about two miles, at full gallop, hanging around the horse's neck.

The final group of poems dates from mid-January 1963.

THE MUNICH MANNEQUINS and TOTEM were composed over the same two days.

PARALYTIC soon after.

BALLOONS, CONTUSION, KINDNESS, EDGE and WORDS belong to the last week of her life.

Surveyed as a whole, with attention to the order of composition, I think the unity of her opus is clear. Once the unity shows itself, the logic and inevitability of the language, which controls and contains such conflagrations and collisions within itself, becomes more obviously what it is—direct, and even plain, speech.

PART IV

WARNINGS FROM THE GRAVE

STEPHEN SPENDER

Poetry is a balancing of unconscious and conscious forces in the mind of the poet, the source of the poetry being the unconscious, the control being provided by the conscious. If the poet thinks about his poetic ego, he visualizes, I suppose, a point at which consciousness and unconsciousness meet. The unconscious forces are below the threshold at which he becomes aware of himself as having an identity; but his 'name' also is below the threshold where it requires attributes of character, performer, reputation, family, and all those things. That is why labels attached by chairmen, editors and award givers to poets are so irrelevant. Today, it is true, they have become the apparatus whereby the poet keeps himself afloat in life for the purpose of writing his poetry. But that as much importance is attached to labels is part of the general disgrace attached to the life of the imagination in our time.

If you consider the quality suggested by the name 'Keats' in a poem by that poet, it has little to do with his biography, his critical reputation, his place in the anthologies. It has, rather, two aspects. First, 'Keats' is a suffusing quality of sensibility in a poem of Keats, a climate, or like the colour of a sunset, a glow affecting all objects seen in that light. Secondly, though, there is something more personal than this, something like the feel of a pulse on the wrist, the throb of blood in the rhythm of:

> Forlorn! The very word is like a bell
> To toll thee back from thee to my sole self!

Today, true poets must feel, I think, a growing distrust of their own 'names' which are to an ever-increasing extent sold to the reading public, or listening audience, on grounds totally irrelevant to poetry (the poet's achievements, academic status, or unacademic misdemeanours, etc.). The result is that poets find themselves forced to escape from their public persona, either into their unconscious pre-named-and-labelled activity, or into an intellectualism which rises superior to the givers of labels. Sometimes, as with Robert Lowell, these two opposites seem combined: an extreme intellectuality is fused with an ability to plunge into the subconscious depths. Reading Berryman, Jarrell, Lowell, Roethke, and now this posthumous collection of Sylvia Plath, one is forced to take note that with some of the best recent poets, even though one does not immediately connect them with Rimbaud, a programme of the poet 'cultivating his hysteria' seems to have become very serious indeed.

Sylvia Plath's poems in this volume (which were written immediately after the birth of a child, and shortly before she committed suicide) come out of a consciousness which is unique, immensely forceful, but which is below the threshold of what I have here described as the second kind of poetic naming, in which you can put your finger on a line and say 'this is Sylvia Plath'. Their power, their decisiveness, the positiveness and starkness of their outline, are decided not by an identifiable poetic personality expressing herself, but by the poet, a woman finding herself in a situation, out of which she produces these disconcerting, terrifying poems. The guarantees of the authenticity of the situation are insanity (or near-insanity) and death. All the way through we feel that the last thing the poet cares about is her book, her name, whether she will get a critical accolade, a Book Award, a Pulitzer, a Guggenheim, or whatever. She is writing out of a pure need of expression, certified, as I say, by death. The miracle is an effect of controlled uncontrolledness. As one reads on, one begins to seek the dark places which provide the structure of the control, the landmarks among which the poetry is moving. There is the German and Austrian background (Sylvia Plath was born in Boston in 1932 of German and Austrian parents), feelings about her German father (which correspond rather to those of Theodore Roethke about his), concentration camps, her daughter, and her son, her husband (the English poet, Ted Hughes), the Devonshire landscape, villagers, the sea. Probably at some later stage, critics will chart this autobiographic territory. One will be grateful when they do this, but one can be grateful also that they have not done so already. Part of the impressiveness of these poems is the feeling they give the reader of finding his way darkly through a dark and ominous landscape.

The landscape is an entirely interior, mental one in which external objects have become converted into symbols of hysterical vision:

> This is my property,
> Two times a day
> I pace it, sniffing
> The barbarous holly with its viridian
> Scallops, pure iron,
>
> And the wall of old corpses.
> I love them.
> I love them like history.
> The apples are golden,
> Imagine it—
>
> My seventy trees
> Holding their gold-ruddy balls
> In a thick grey death-soup,
> Their million
> Gold leaves metal and breathless.
>
> 'Letter in November'

One can enjoy the 'description' in this, the autumn-golden apples in the grey-soup mist. All the same, this nature is not in the least alleviating, it is not outside the poet, it is not the great furniture of the continuity of the seasonal earth, on which the distraught mind can rest. Or if there are some externals in these poems (they do give one a strong panicky feeling of kitchens, utensils, babies, gardens) they exist in an atmosphere where the external is in immediate process of becoming the internal, opposites identical with one another.

The same fusion of opposites applies to the feelings expressed. Sylvia Plath's imagination does not, like D. H. Lawrence's, merely oscillate between feelings of love and of hatred. With her the two attitudes seem completely fused. How else can one take lines like these?

> Darling, all night
> I have been flickering, off, on, off, on.
> The sheets grow heavy as a lecher's kiss.
>
> Three days. Three nights.
> Lemon water, chicken
> Water, water make me retch.
>
> I am too pure for you or anyone.
> Your body
> Hurts me as the world hurts God.
>
> 'Fever 103°'

Considered simply as art, these poems have line to line power and rhythm which, though repetitive, is too dynamic to be monotonous. Beyond this, they don't have 'form'. From poem to poem they have little principle of beginning or ending, but seem fragments, not so much of one long poem, as of an outpouring which could not stop with the lapsing of the poet's hysteria. In this respect they have to be considered emotional-mystical poetry, like the poems of St. John of the Cross, in which the length of the poem is decided by the duration of the poet's vision, which is far more serious to the poet than formal considerations.

They are like nothing more than poems of prophecy, written by some priestess cultivating her hysteria, come out of Nazi and war-torn Europe, gone to America, and then situated on the rocky Cornish Atlantic coast. One does not think of Clytemnestra as a *hysteric*; one thinks of her as hysterical for very good reasons, against which she *warns*. Sylvia Plath would have agreed with Wilfred Owen that 'all a poet can do today is to warn'. But being a woman, her warning is more shrill, penetrating, visionary than Owen's. Owen's came out of the particular circumstances of the trenches, and there is nothing to make us think that if he had not been on the Western Front—the mud and blood into which his nose was rubbed—he would not have warned anyone

202

about anything at all. He would have been a nice chap and a quiet poet. With Sylvia Plath, her femininity is that her hysteria comes completely out of herself, and yet seems about all of us. And she has turned our horrors and our achievements into the same witches' brew. In the following lines one feels that a space-man promenading in space is not too distant a relation from a man in a concentration camp, and that everything is a symptom of the same holocaust:

> The same fire
>
> Melting the tallow heretics,
> Ousting the Jews.
> Their thick palls float
>
> Over the cicatrix of Poland, burnt-out
> Germany.
> They do not die.
>
> Grey birds obsess my heart,
> Mouth-ash, ash of eye.
> They settle. On the high
>
> Precipice
> That emptied one man into space
> The ovens glowed like heavens incandescent.
>
> It is a heart,
> This holocaust I walk in,
> O golden child the world will kill and eat.
>
> 'Mary's Song'

As with all visionary poetry, one can sup here on horror even with enjoyment.

ON SYLVIA PLATH

A. E. DYSON

I first saw the name Sylvia Plath on a poem called 'Snake'. It was submitted with thousands of others for a competition run by the *Critical Quarterly* for poets who had not yet published a volume. All three judges (Philip Larkin, C. B. Cox and myself) were immensely struck by it. Of course it won the prize; and then we met Sylvia Plath, and discovered that she was the American wife of Ted Hughes. The year after, she edited for us a poetry supplement called *American Poetry Now*, which first introduced a number of the best younger American poets to a wide British audience. It was in this year that her first volume was published, *The Colossus* (Heinemann).

This was an exciting event; it is not often that one feels with complete assurance the arrival of a major poet. Though certain of the poems fail by the highest standards, all are interesting, and some soon became, for me at least, among that small class of work which comes back to haunt—in lines, phrases, whole stanzas. Where did one hear that, one wonders? It could hardly be better put.

One immediately felt a highly distinctive new voice, and sensibility—something cool, refreshing, healing, like the personality of the poet herself; but something darker, too, at the heart. The title poem is significantly named; a sense of the huge and continuing dominated her sensibility. But the grandeur of nature oppressed, as well as fascinated her: apprehensions of lurking menace, more likely to test endurance than joy, are seldom absent. In 'Hardcastle Crags', the young woman who walks at night through a bleak landscape is offered nothing, unless it be the satisfaction of pitting flesh and blood against the iron of the universe itself:

All the night gave her, in return
For the paltry gift of her bulk and the beat
Of her heart was the humped indifferent iron
Of its hills, and is pastures bordered by black stone set
On black stone.

In battling with the encroachments of rock, wind, the sea which
is 'brutal endlessly', a temporary, almost humdrum heroism may
be earned, as poems like 'Point Shirley' and 'The Hermit at
Outermost House' suggest; but nature outlasts man, and wins
again in the end:

A labour of love and that labour lost.
Steadily the sea
Eats at Point Shirley.

When Sylvia Plath encountered a landscape that had been
tamed and reduced by man, she responded as to a type of trifling.
Walking in Grantchester Meadows, since Rupert Brooke the very
touchstone of English nostalgia, she notes that 'Nothing is big
or far'. The birds are 'thumb-size', the cygnets 'tame', the Granta
'bland', the water rats 'droll'. Even the students, lost in a 'moony
indolence of love', are unmenaced, and therefore somewhat un-
real. 'It is a country on a nursery plate', a pretty place, but Sylvia
Plath was more at home when she sensed behind nature its naked
inhospitality to man.

Wind and sea were only the more natural of the forces she
detected waiting to batter or supplant the human race, or patiently
take over when it was gone. In 'Ouija', there is an eerie evocation
of 'those unborn, those undone' as they crowd into the seance
room, drawn to the living by envy:

Imagine their deep hunger, deep as the dark
For the blood-heat that would ruddle or reclaim.

In 'The Thin People', the threat comes from devitalized
humanity, from those who in Blake's words 'restrain Desire . . .
because theirs is weak enough to be restrained', who having resisted energy, put the 'Giants who formed the world into its
sensual existence' in chains. Sylvia Plath sees the thin folk as a

menace, as Blake does, but she fears too 'their talent to persevere/ In thinness, to come, later, / Into our bad dreams'. In 'Mushrooms', the quality of menace is even more chillingly detected, in the sinister, almost cancerous proliferation of fungus. This macabrely ironic vision of a form of life infinitely lower than man, simply waiting in endless patience to 'Inherit the earth', has the vividness of science fiction at its best, without being in the least sensational. (The associations which the word 'mushroom' have for us since Hiroshima may enhance the effectiveness, which is not, however, dependent upon them.) In 'Sculptor', by a further surprising stroke, the forms the sculptor is about to create are felt as bodiless realities waiting to use him for incarnation, after which they will both dwarf and outlast him:

> His chisel bequeathes
> Them life livelier than ours.

The theme sounds again in 'Frog Autumn', and in the longer 'Mussel Hunter at Rock Harbour'. Perhaps the most remarkable variant, however, is in 'All the Dead Dears', a poem which starts, as a note informs us, from the Archaeological Museum in Cambridge, where there is 'a stone coffin of the fourth century A.D. containing the skeletons of a woman, a mouse and a shrew. The ankle-bone of the woman has been slightly gnawn'. From the stark statement:

> These three, unmasked now, bear
> Dry witness
> To the gross eating game

the poet goes on to sense, in the long dead, a host waiting to revisit the living in memories, and later claim them to itself:

> How they grip us through thick and thin,
> These barnacle dead!
> This lady here's no kin
> Of mine, yet kin she is: she'll suck
> Blood and whistle my marrow clean
> To prove it . . .

And then this inexorable community is still more strikingly explored, in a manner reminding us again of 'Ouija' and 'Mushrooms', whilst reaching even nearer, perhaps, to the heart of the thematic menace:

> All the long gone darlings: they
> Get back, though, soon,
> Soon: be it by wakes, weddings,
> Childbirths or a family barbecue:
> Any touch, taste, tang's
> Fit for those outlaws to ride home on,
>
> And to sanctuary: usurping the armchair
> Between tick
> And tack of the clock, until we go,
> Each skulled-and-crossboned Gulliver
> Riddled with ghosts, to lie
> Deadlocked with them, taking root as cradles rock.

The affinity which Sylvia Plath felt with the dead and the alien was not unlike a form of pity; a conviction of kinship with everything that lives or has lived, however inaccessible or sinister. Her feeling for animals is similar in kind, not only in 'Frog Autumn' and 'Mussel Hunter at Rock Harbour', but in one of the most moving of her earlier poems, 'Blue Moles'.

One further theme running through *The Colossus* was her occasional sense of being teased by glimpses of better worlds, also lurking just beyond the surface of things, but now in the realm of acknowledged fantasy. Siren voices from under water, at Lorelei,

> sing
> Of a world more full and clear
>
> Than can be . . .

The 'lost otherworld' of dreams presents itself like 'hieroglyphics / Of some godly utterance', yet the sleeper 'merely by waking up' comes to know its lack of substance. In the fine poem 'Black Rook in Rainy Weather', Sylvia Plath reflects, half philosophically, half ironically on the nature of her own poetic gift.

She does not expect 'miracle', but nonetheless, 'a certain minor light' might still at times shine out, transfiguring the everyday world in a manner

> to seize my sense, haul
> My eyelids up, and grant
>
> A brief respite from fear
> Of total neutrality.

Continuing the logic of this she moves, consciously and delicately tentative, to a limited claim for poetry itself:

> With luck,
> Trekking stubborn through this season
> Of fatigue, I shall
> Patch together a content
>
> Of sorts. Miracles occur,
> If you care to call those spasmodic
> Tricks of radiance miracles.

And indeed, of these early poems some such claim can be made, except that it seems too modest; certainly the craftsmanship is expert, and one senses that it is through craftsmanship that she has arrived at the distinctive voice, the 'content / Of sorts'. It was only in the last two years of her life that another kind of miracle occurred; the dark undercurrent of her experience became a new and fierce possession, and a terrible beauty was born. Between *The Colossus* and the very late poems, there was a period when her earlier mode took on a new, almost ethereal quality in poems such as 'I am Vertical', where a longing for death more explicit than anything expressed earlier is transmuted, however, by an altogether refreshing and spring-like quality of style. And then, something further happened; it seems as though having mastered form, she transcended it, and the central drama of her troubled consciousness was wholly released. In 'Daddy', violence erupts through the poem's powerful rhythm, which seems generated, however, by the actual experience of the poem, and imbued with organic life. The rhythm is hinted at in the first stanza, temporarily lost in the second, recovered powerfully but still fitfully in the next six; and then from stanza nine onwards it takes over completely, as though generated by the creative ferment itself. And in two of the other unforgettable poems of this period—'Lady Lazarus' and 'A Birthday Present'—something altogether exalted and ecstatic controls the verse. In literary terms, one is aware of the influence of Robert Lowell, and of Sylvia Plath's close friend of genius, Anne Sexton; but the label 'confessional' poetry, which has already been used to link them, seems more inadequate, even, than labels usually do. Certainly much of the greatest poetry since the Romantics (since Shakespeare, indeed) has dealt with the deranged mind; with the paradox of wisdom and folly, of true vision wholly alienated from the rational mind. In Sylvia Plath, it is as though the poet finds in personal experience a depth of derangement, but then, in the magnificent sanity of creation, transmutes this into a myth for her age. As Professor Alun Jones put it in a fine article:[1]

> T. S. Eliot's assertion that 'The more perfect the artist, the more completely separate in him will be the man who suffers and the mind which creates' indicates the dualism that is operating in these poems, for in so far as the *persona* represents the 'man who suffers', the artist creates the poem within which the suffering is contained and given meaning. If the man is patient and passive under suffering, the creative mind is certainly both agent and active. The creative mind—which is largely released and refined in suffering—knows freedom and achieves Grace, through the act of creation itself. The poet exercises his traditional power in using the beneficent passion of poetry to expel the malignant forces of private suffering.

This puts its finger on one aspect of these amazing poems: our sense that, unlike much Beat poetry, they are not the expression only, but the transmutation, of suffering; that they are in the highest degree creative art, and that in art, there is healing of a kind.

Yet what healing, one is forced to wonder?—few poems are

[1] A. R. Jones, 'Necessity and Freedom: The Poetry of Robert Lowell, Sylvia Plath, and Anne Sexton'. (*Critical Quarterly*, Vol. VII, No. I, 1965.)

more searing in their impact, or more unanswerable. Perhaps it is in the use of Nazi imagery that their challenge is intensified; if this suffering is the private hell of paranoia, it is an image, too, of the world that we know. It is this bifocal vision which reminds one, irresistibly, of Kafka, and disturbs with the same kind of power. One cannot forget that Anne Sexton quotes as *her* epigraph phrases from a letter Kafka wrote to Oskar Pollak:

. . . the books we need are the kind that act upon us like a misfortune, that make us suffer like the death of someone we love more than ourselves, that make us feel as though we were on the verge of suicide, or lost in a forest remote from all human habitation—a book should serve as the axe for the frozen sea within us.

In Sylvia Plath's last poems, as in the work of Robert Lowell and Anne Sexton, we are reminded that the Modern Movement, as Kafka himself exemplified it, is not dead, but still with us; that its mutations are if anything more terrifying than those we have learned to accept in Yeats, Eliot and Joyce; that an art which *does* confront our present nuclear world fully and totally must be an art on the brink of the abyss; that perhaps the creative mind exploring its innermost anguish is the only mirror art can hold up to us today.

The paradoxes of Sylvia Plath's last poems are inexhaustible. In 'Lady Lazarus' she faces with bitter irony our modern response to the miraculous, but in a poem where the miracle of dignity, at least, is achieved. At moments, it seems almost as if the writer's unhealed suffering is required for the poem's aesthetic success. Yet no reader of the poem can respond to suffering like the crowd depicted *in* the poem. There remains this tincture of salvation in art.

DYING IS AN ART

GEORGE STEINER

I have not read *The Bell Jar,* a novel that Sylvia Plath published under the name of Victoria Lucas. The rest of her work consists of two volumes of poems: *The Colossus,* first published in England in 1960, and *Ariel,* published in London in the spring of 1965, two years after her death, together with a number of poems first printed in *Encounter.* Some of these have not been included in the posthumous collection.

It is fair to say that no group of poems since Dylan Thomas's *Deaths and Entrances* has had as vivid and disturbing an impact on English critics and readers as has *Ariel.* Sylvia Plath's last poems have already passed into legend as both representative of our present tone of emotional life and unique in their implacable, harsh brilliance. Those among the young who read new poetry will know 'Daddy', 'Lady Lazarus', and 'Death & Co.' almost by heart, and reference to Sylvia Plath is constant where poetry and the conditions of its present existence are discussed.

The spell does not lie wholly in the poems themselves. The suicide of Sylvia Plath at the age of thirty-one in 1963, and the personality of this young woman who had come from Massachusetts to study and live in England (where she married Ted Hughes, himself a gifted poet), are vital parts of it. To those who knew her and to the greatly enlarged circle who were electrified by her last poems and sudden death, she had come to signify the specific honesties and risks of the poet's condition. Her personal style, and the price in private harrowing she so obviously paid to achieve the intensity and candour of her principal poems, have taken on their own dramatic authority.

All this makes it difficult to judge the poems. I mean that the vehemence and intimacy of the verse is such as to constitute a very powerful rhetoric of sincerity. The poems play on our nerves with their own proud nakedness, making claims so immediate and sharply urged that the reader flinches, embarrassed by the routine discretions and evasions of his own sensibility. Yet if these poems are to take life among us, if they are to be more than exhibits in the history of modern psychological stress, they must be read with all the intelligence and scruple we can muster. They are too honest, they have cost too much, to be yielded to myth.

One of the most striking poems in *The Colossus*, 'All the Dead Dears', tells of a skeleton in the Cambridge museum of classical antiquities:

> How they grip us through thin and thick,
> These barnacle dead!
> This lady here's no kin
> Of mine, yet kin she is; she'll suck
> Blood and whistle my marrow clean
> To prove it. As I think now of her head,
>
> From the mercury-backed glass
> Mother, grandmother, great grandmother
> Reach hag hands to haul me in,
> And an image looms under the fishpond surface
> Where the daft father went down
> With orange duck-feet winnowing his hair—

On a small scale, the lines illustrate a good deal of Sylvia Plath's tactics and syntax of feeling. The short lines are paced with delicate, seemingly offhand control. The half-rhymes, cross-rhymes, and alliterations give tautness to what might otherwise appear an arbitrary measure. The allusion to *The Duchess of Malfi* ('When I look into the fish-pond in my garden, / Methinks I see a thing armed with a rake') is nicely judged. The motifs touched on are those which organize much of Sylvia Plath's poetry: the generation of women knit by blood and death, the dead reaching out to haul the living into their shadowy vortex, the personage of the father somehow sinister and ineffectual, the poet literally bled and whistled clean by the cruel, intricate quality of felt life.

'Watercolour of Grantchester Meadows' is explicitly conventional in setting and tone. But at the close, this version of pastoral deflects abruptly into darkness and muted hysteria:

> Droll, vegetarian, the water rat
> Saws down a reed and swims from his limber grove,
> While the students stroll or sit,
> Hands laced, in a moony indolence of love—
> Black-gowned, but unaware
> How in such mild air
> The owl shall stoop from his turret, the rat cry out.

The black gowns, which are merely the ordinary garb of the Cambridge undergraduate, are so placed as to alert the reader to mourning; the vegetarian cries out under the sudden beak of the carnivore. One recognizes the props: the moon, the reed-fringed water, the owl and turret. They are a part of that Gothic strain which is so constant beneath the surface of English lyric poetry, and which has been reinforced in modern verse by its consonance with the mortalities and erotic conceits of the Metaphysicals and Jacobeans.

This penchant for the Gothic effect seems to me to weaken much of Sylvia Plath's earlier verse, and it extends into her mature work. She used Gothicism in a particular way, making the formal terrors an equivalent to genuine and complex shocks of feeling, but the modish element is undeniable. Her resources were, however, more diverse. Possessed of a rare intensity and particularity of nervous response—the 'disquieting muses' had stood at the left side of her crib 'with heads like darning-eggs'—Sylvia Plath tested different symbolic means, different modes of concretion, with which to articulate what rang so queer and clear inside her. It is almost silly to argue 'influences' when dealing with a young poet of this honesty and originality. But one can locate the impulses that helped her find her own voice. Wallace Stevens for one:

> Death whitens in the egg and out of it.
> I can see no colour for this whiteness.
> White: it is a complexion of the mind.
>   'Moonrise'

213

Or Emily Dickinson, whose authority gives a poem like 'Spinster' its spiky charm:

> And round her house she set
> Such a barricade of barb and check. . . .

The tactile, neutral precision of D. H. Lawrence's observations of animal and vegetable is recognizable in 'Medallion' and 'Blue Moles'. These poets, together with Andrew Marvell and the Jacobean dramatists, seem to have meant a lot. But the final poem in *The Colossus*, a seven-part garland 'For a Birthday', is unmistakable. In at least three sections, 'Dark House', 'Maenad', and 'The Stones', Sylvia Plath writes in a way that is entirely hers. Had one been shown only the last six lines, one would have known—or should have—that a formidable compulsion was implicit and that a new, mature style had been achieved:

> Love is the bone and sinew of my curse.
> The vase, reconstructed, houses
> The elusive rose.
>
> Ten fingers shape a bowl for shadows.
> My mendings itch. There is nothing to do.
> I shall be good as new.

Undoubtedly, the success of this poem arises from the fact that Sylvia Plath had mastered her essential theme, the situation and emotive counters around which she was henceforth to build much of her verse: the infirm or rent body, and the imperfect, painful resurrection of the psyche, pulled back, unwilling, to the hypocrisies of health. It is a theme already present in *The Colossus* ('Two Views of a Cadaver Room'). It dominates, to an obsessive degree, much of *Ariel*. As 'Lady Lazarus' proclaims:

> Dying
> Is an art, like everything else.
> I do it exceptionally well.
>
> I do it so it feels like hell.
> I do it so it feels real.
> I guess you could say I've a call.

214

It requires no biographical impertinence to realize that Sylvia Plath's life was harried by bouts of physical pain, that she sometimes looked on the accumulated exactions of her own nerve and body as 'a trash / To annihilate each decade'. She was haunted by the piecemeal, strung-together mechanics of the flesh, by what could be so easily broken and then mended with such searing ingenuity. The hospital ward was her exemplary ground:

> My patent leather overnight case like a black pillbox,
> My husband and child smiling out of the family photo;
> Their smiles catch onto my skin, little smiling hooks.
>
> 'Tulips'

This brokenness, so sharply feminine and contemporary, is, I think, her principal realization. It is by the graphic expression she gave to it that she will be judged and remembered. Sylvia Plath carries forward, in an intensely womanly and aggravated note, from Robert Lowell's *Life Studies*, a book that obviously had a great impact on her. This new frankness of women about the specific hurts and tangles of their nervous-physiological make-up is as vital to the poetry of Sylvia Plath as it is to the tracts of Simone de Beauvoir or to the novels of Edna O'Brien and Brigid Brophy. Women speak out as never before:

> The womb
> Rattles its pod, the moon
> Discharges itself from the tree with nowhere to go.
>
> 'Childless Woman'

> They have swabbed me clear of my loving associations.
> Scared and bare on the green plastic-pillowed trolley. . . .
>
> 'Tulips'

It is difficult to think of a precedent to the fearful close of 'Medusa' (the whole poem is extraordinary):

> I shall take no bite of your body,
> Bottle in which I live,

Ghastly Vatican.
I am sick to death of hot salt.
Green as eunuchs, your wishes
Hiss at my sin.
Off, off, eely tentacle!

There is nothing between us.

The ambiguity and dual flash of insight in this final line are of a richness and obviousness that only a very great poem can carry off.

The progress registered between the early and the mature poems is one of concretion. The general Gothic means with which Sylvia Plath was so fluently equipped become singular to herself and therefore fiercely honest. What had been style passes into need. It is the need of a superbly intelligent, highly literate young woman to cry out about her especial being, about the tyrannies of blood and gland, of nervous spasm and sweating skin, the rankness of sex and childbirth in which a woman is still compelled to be wholly of her organic condition. Where Emily Dickinson could—indeed was obliged to—shut the door on the riot and humiliations of the flesh, thus achieving her particular dry lightness, Sylvia Plath 'fully assumed her own condition'. This alone would assure her of a place in modern literature. But she took one step further, assuming a burden that was not naturally or necessarily hers.

Born in Boston in 1932 of German and Austrian parents, Sylvia Plath had no personal, immediate contact with the world of the concentration camps. I may be mistaken, but so far as I know there was nothing Jewish in her background. But her last, greatest poems culminate in an act of identification, of total communion with those tortured and massacred. The poet sees herself on

An engine, an engine
Chuffing me off like a Jew.
A Jew to Dachau, Auschwitz, Belsen.
I began to talk like a Jew.
I think I may well be a Jew.

216

The snows of the Tyrol, the clear beer of Vienna
Are not very pure or true.
With my gypsy ancestress and my weird luck
And my Tarot pack and my Tarot pack
I may be a bit of a Jew.
                              'Daddy'

Distance is no help; nor the fact that one is 'guilty of nothing'. The
dead men cry out of the yew hedges. The poet becomes the loud
cry of their choked silence:

                    Herr God, Herr Lucifer
                    Beware
                    Beware.
                    Out of the ash
                    I rise with my red hair
                    And I eat men like air.
                              'Lady Lazarus'

Here the almost surrealistic wildness of the gesture is kept in place
by the insistent obviousness of the language and beat; a kind of
Hieronymus Bosch nursery rhyme.
   Sylvia Plath is only one of a number of young contemporary
poets, novelists, and playwrights, themselves in no way implicated
in the actual holocaust, who have done most to counter the
general inclination to forget the death camps. Perhaps it is only
those who had no part in the events who *can* focus on them ration-
ally and imaginatively; to those who experienced the thing, it has
lost the hard edges of possibility, it has stepped outside the real.
   Committing the whole of her poetic and formal authority to
the metaphor, to the mask of language, Sylvia Plath *became* a
woman being transported to Auschwitz on the death trains. The
notorious shards of massacre seemed to enter into her own being:

                    A cake of soap,
                    A wedding ring,
                    A gold filling.
                              'Lady Lazarus'

In 'Daddy' she wrote one of the very few poems I know of in any language to come near the last horror. It achieves the classic act of generalization, translating a private, obviously intolerable hurt into a code of plain statement, of instantaneously public images which concern us all. It is the 'Guernica' of modern poetry. And it is both histrionic and, in some ways, 'arty', as is Picasso's outcry.

Are these final poems entirely legitimate? In what sense does anyone, himself uninvolved and long after the event, commit a subtle larceny when he invokes the echoes and trappings of Auschwitz and appropriates an enormity of ready emotion to his own private design? Was there latent in Sylvia Plath's sensibility, as in that of many of us who remember only by fiat of imagination, a fearful envy, a dim resentment at not having been there, of having missed the rendezvous with hell? In 'Lady Lazarus' and 'Daddy' the realization seems to me so complete, the sheer rawness and control so great, that only irresistible need could have brought it off. These poems take tremendous risks, extending Sylvia Plath's essentially austere manner to the very limit. They are a bitter triumph, proof of the capacity of poetry to give to reality the greater permanence of the imagined. She could not return from them.

Already there are poets writing like Sylvia Plath. Certain of her angular mannerisms, her elisions and monotonies of deepening rhyme, can be caught and will undoubtedly have their fashion. But minor poets even of a great intensity— and that is what she was—tend to prove bad models.[1] Sylvia Plath's tricks of voice can be imitated. Not her desperate integrity.

[1] Ed.—Mr. Steiner is borne out here, as most any editor of a literary review will testify. Her death occasioned literally hundreds of poems, and her imitators by now are legion— and almost always unexceptional.

PART V

THE BELL JAR
An American Girlhood

MARY ELLMANN

A poet's novel, a casebook almost in stanzas, each episode brief, brittle, encapsulated. The past consists of 'Atoms that cripple', minute totalities of pain which spill out separately. They lack the essential sprawl and waste of the novel. The progress from one to another is poetic too, less in time than in image. Whatever scene is settled upon, is drawn up to its sharpest point, until it hurts. And yet, the disparate scenes gather congruity. They lean forward, crowding closer together in the momentum of madness; then slowly and less successfully they move back upward, against expectation, to a second sanity.

The method is nervous, a formalized jerkiness rather like Dorothy Richardson's, but without her gasps and flutters. This instability is plain, awkward, laughable. The girl's words make fun of her own ingenuous disorder. *The Bell Jar* is perhaps closest to a poem like 'Cut', that series of macabre conceits on the theme of one decapitated thumb. Here it is one cracked mind. The further range within the poems, of the 'cry', is withheld from the novel. Its cries are only mouthed, like grins. The poem 'Two Views of a Cadaver Room' notices that 'In their jars the snail-nosed babies moon and glow.' But here 'the baby in the last bottle' seems to be 'smiling a little piggy smile', and in the newspaper Eisenhower's face, 'bald and blank as the face of a foetus in a bottle', *beams* up. The same narrow and reiterative memories pervade both the poems and the novel. The same segment of Atlantic shore emerges in both: the prison, the rock, the public hotdog grills, the garbage hem of the water. The difference: each object in the novel is a photograph taken at a

Ed.—*The Bell Jar* was never available from an American publisher.

fun-house, nut-house angle, a displaced vision in the poems.

The comparative outwardness of *The Bell Jar* makes clear what the poems transcend: how much can be wrung out of very little. The novel exposes Sylvia Plath's first milieu, the poverty of suggestion by which her talent was nonetheless roused. The American Girl is the topic. Her growing up suburban, with saddle shoes and 'fifteen years of straight A's', her eastern women's college, her scholarships and weekends at Yale; her summer month, at the end of her third year, on a New York f(ashion)-f(iction) magazine, playing editor. The novel opens with twelve little editors, soaking up the calculated largesse of their sponsors—free lessons in millinery, free lunches, free sunglasses cases. Pretty, brainy, ambitious virgins riding four abreast in taxicabs: the ideal coming-of-age in America. And then the breakdown—the only implement required to separate 'Esther Greenwood' from her banality, to pull her like a letter from hell out of her innocuous envelope. Her friend Doreen, an all-white creature, lies down to sleep in her own brown vomit. In disarray, her bright hair admits an original darkness, crawling out of its roots. The crabmeat at the *Ladies' Day* lunch fills the girls' flat tummies with ptomaine. The $40 shantung sheath is ripped off in the dark by one Marco-the-woman-hater: 'Your dress is black and the dirt is black as well.' The cheap smart lie is gone, and there is nothing left but the self, which seems to have been always waiting, like the dullest of truths, to reclaim attention.

Still, the collapse hangs on to the terms of the previous competence, it keeps a kind of faith. To date the American Girl who caves into Crazy Girl, there is Buddy Willard the American Boy, the white-toothed medical student, who caves into Death Boy. A careerist (in disease) like the girl, a winner like her too. Buddy Willard wins the prize for the medical student who persuades the most relatives to allow autopsies of their dead, also the sanatorium scholarship for the medical student who catches TB. But it is his literary criticism which the girl remembers best:

'Do you know what a poem is, Esther?'
'No, what?' I said.
'A piece of dust.'

That, and his body:

> The only thing I could think of was turkey neck and turkey gizzards and I felt very depressed.

'They had four men laid out, black as burnt turkey.' The referents are all like that, as domestic as they are grotesque. The same things are recalled insidiously as were lived naïvely.

Madness only alters their perspective: objects come in too close or recede too far. Buddy Willard's face looms over the girl's 'like a distracted planet', sailors on the Boston Common look as big as pigeons. And the proper boundaries between things fall down. The animal invades the human—comically (pregnant Dodo Conway's head balances like a sparrow's egg on the duck's egg of her body) or hideously:

> I felt the darkness, but nothing else, and my head rose, feeling it, like the head of a worm.

The inanimate becomes mischievous, unreliable: printed letters wriggle about and written letters persist in hanging down like strings. What should flow is rigid. Days are 'bright, white boxes' with sleep 'like a black shade' between them. Each shade snaps up for the girl, exposing her to unmitigated glare.[1] Worst, the mechanical invades the living. The features of a suicide's face revert, as in pop art, to the dots of the newspaper surface. Faces are 'empty as plates', nineteen years are nineteen telephone poles, 'threaded together by wires'. The first sentence of the novel raises the issue of electricity in the body:

> It was a clear, sultry summer, the summer they electrocuted the Rosenbergs. . . . It had nothing to do with me, but I couldn't help wondering what it would be like, being burned alive all along your nerves.

It has something to do with her later, with her shock treatment:

> Then something bent down and took hold of me and shook me like the end of the world. Whee-ee-ee-ee, it shrilled, through an air crackling with blue light, and with each flash a

---

[1] The nights snapped out of sight like a lizard's eyelid:
A world of bald white days in a shadeless socket.
                                                    'The Hanging Man'

great jolt drubbed me till I thought my bones would break and the sap fly out of me like a split plant.[2]

I wondered what terrible thing it was that I had done.

Yet the young girl is still young, easily cowed and uncomprehending: this is certainly punishment, but what is crime? ('I'm stupid about executions,' she said at the start.) The present voice has none of the later decision:

> A vulturous boredom pinned me in this tree.
> If he were I, he would do what I did.
>
> 'The Hanging Man'

Invasions of the flesh take place in cages. It is always because the person is caught, that she must witness or undergo them—as the dead woman entombed with a mouse and a shrew must be gnawed by them, until the animals die too. Every step into madness brings another dark pit into view. In New York, 'the fusty peanut-smelling mouth' of the subway matches the mouth ('the blind cave behind her face') of the girl who says of the Rosenbergs, 'I'm so glad they're going to die.' (The remark splits in two, like the novel, between the girlish and the deadly.) A Mrs. Tomolillo, in childbirth, moves down a 'long, blind, doorless and windowless corridor of pain'. A bus door shuts 'silently, on gloved hinges' behind the girl's back. Her body is another cage:

> I would simply have to ambush it with whatever sense I had left, or it would trap me in its stupid cage for fifty years without any sense at all.

The best of all her suicide attempts is made in a crawl space, a dirt hole dug out beyond the basement of the house. Her body is dragged out of there, still alive, but the mind is in another cage of its own: the bell jar, the fluted glass form which descends around the mad person, separating the air she breathes from the air of the sane.[3]

---

[2] By the roots of my hair some god got hold of me.
I sizzled in his blue volts like a desert prophet.
('The Hanging Man')

[3] In her autobiographical sketch, 'Ocean 1212-W', Sylvia Plath described her childhood as still another glass enclosure, now one from which the adult is shut out:
Whereon those nine first years of my life sealed themselves off like a ship in a bottle.

Release in the novel, as in the poems, takes the form of precipitate movement. But while the two share a hatred of stasis, the novel is not capable of that terrible resurgence of 'Ariel':

> The dew that flies
> Suicidal, at one with the drive
> Into the red
>
> Eye, the cauldron of morning.

The novel retains its girlish ambiance: the *things* of girls, their penchant for losing and falling, not rising. From a hotel roof, Esther Greenwood throws her wardrobe, beginning with a strapless slip, out into the sky, to fall down into the city 'like a loved one's ashes'. Buddy Willard takes her ski-ing, and she comes down the slope alone:

> People and trees receded on either hand like the dark sides of a tunnel as I hurtled on to the still, bright point[4] at the end of it, the pebble at the bottom of the well, the white sweet baby cradled in its mother's belly.

Death, for the mad virgin, is a conception—as, recovering, she determines to be seduced. She arranges the encounter like an appointment with a gynaecologist—the man need only be a stranger and intelligent—and almost loses her life again. She bleeds uncontrollably, her shoes fill up like cups under a faucet. It is apparent that if such events constitute reality, madness is as plausible as sanity. Esther Greenwood survives the haemorrhage, but another patient, a Lesbian, hangs herself because of it.

The novel scarcely indicates what there is to be sane *for*, beyond escaping the fustiness of insanity. And yet the relief of the bell jar's lifting even temporarily, of the girl's breathing fresh air again, suggests something more. It is still girlish (perhaps still American), it keeps the simplicity of her denied preferences. The obverse of desperation in the novel, as in the poems, is startlingly wholesome. The girl in New York never knew what drink to

---

[4] Is there no still place
Turning and turning in the middle air,
Untouched and untouchable.
                            ('Getting There')

order in a bar. What she liked best was to eat avocadoes and take hot baths. After her ptomaine poisoning, she drank bouillon: 'I felt purged and holy and ready for a new life.' And after an insulin reaction, she was given milk:

> . . . I fanned the hot milk on my tongue as it went down, tasting it luxuriously the way a baby tastes its mother.

Babies gleam in and out of the novel, sometimes forms of horror, more often of desire. The girl stands under her bell jar 'blank and stopped as a dead baby'. But when death looked like the 'white sweet baby' in the womb, she plunged down to reach it. All cleanliness and clarity are associated with the living child ('What is so pure/As the cry of a child'. . . . 'The clear vowels rise like balloons' . . . . 'Your mouth opens clean as a cat's') and with the mundane family:

> It would be nice, living by the sea with piles of little kids and pigs and chickens, wearing what my grandmother called wash dresses, and sitting about in some kitchen with bright linoleum and fat arms, drinking pots of coffee.

Perhaps, within sanity, there might be such simple horizontal bonds. ('I am vertical.') Mutual satisfactions seem to be available to others:

> I looked at the baby in the lap of the woman opposite. I had no idea how old it was, I never did, with babies—for all I knew it could talk a blue streak and had twenty teeth behind its pursed pink lips. It held its little wobbly head up on its shoulders—it didn't seem to have a neck—and observed me with a wise Platonic expression.

The extremes of the novel are those of the poems, suicide and childbirth, erasing a line or writing a new one. Before madness, the person is crude, self-made and self-sufficient. After it, she is taken up by two élite societies—the dead inviting her to die, the unborn requesting to be born. Between these rival importunities she draws, for a time, her breath.

ON *THREE WOMEN*[1]

DOUGLAS CLEVERDON

Three Women is the first and only poetic work that Sylvia Plath wrote specifically for broadcasting. Early in 1962 I had produced for the BBC Third Programme a radio feature in dramatic form by her husband Ted Hughes, entitled *The Wound*,[2] with music by Alexander Goehr. One admirable function of the BBC Features Department (now defunct: to which I belonged) was to encourage poets to create works for the medium of radio, which, by its concentration on the spoken word, offer opportunities for dramatic or poetic evocation that none of the other mass media can rival. So it was natural that when the broadcast of *The Wound* was occupying our minds, the idea should emerge of a radio piece by Sylvia Plath also.

Already, during the previous eighteen months, she had broadcast some of her poems in *The Poet's Voice, New Poetry,* and *The Living Poet.* In an interview that she later recorded[3] for the Harvard Poetry Room, she mentions that the poems in her first book, *The Colossus*, were not written to be read aloud; but of her more recent poems, she says, 'I have found myself having to read them aloud to myself . . . I've got to say them, I speak them to myself, and I think that this in my own writing development is quite a new thing with me, and whatever lucidity they may have comes from the fact that I say them to myself, I say them aloud.'

One may speculate how far the experience of broadcasting poetry may have encouraged this development in Sylvia Plath— as, perhaps, in poets generally. It coincided, as the critic A. Alvarez

---

[1] This introduction to *Three Women* was first printed in the limited edition published by Turret Books in 1968.

[2] Printed in *Wodwo*, by Ted Hughes (Faber and Faber, 1967).

[3] Subsequently issued by the British Council in the L.P. series, *The Poet Speaks* (Argo Record Co.), and published in *The Poet Speaks*, edited by Peter Orr (Routledge Ltd.).

has pointed out, with the sudden liberation 'into her real self' that followed the birth of her daughter Frieda in 1960, and with the creative outburst after her son Nicholas was born in January, 1962. These poems, she said, came directly from her own 'very serious, very personal emotional experiences'; but she maintained that a poet should be able to control and manipulate even the most terrifying experiences, like madness or being tortured, with an informed and intelligent mind. It is this disciplined quality that characterizes the superb poems in her second and posthumous volume, *Ariel*.

Apart from 'Morning Song', none of these published poems is concerned with the experience of child-bearing. Considering the vast range of poems on death and mortality, it is surprising that such a fundamental experience as birth has so little literature of its own—until, of course, one remembers how few great poets have themselves been mothers. My wife recalls the enthusiasm with which Sylvia Plath talked about the birth of her two children —the first in a London flat in a somewhat seedy square near Primrose Hill, with a sweet and gentle Indian girl as midwife; the second in a Devonshire village, where the local midwife was also one of the bee-keepers whose rituals are celebrated in 'The Bee Meeting'. 'What I admire most,' she said, 'is the person who masters an area of practical experience, and can teach me something. I mean, my local midwife has taught me how to keep bees. Well, she can't understand anything I write. And I find myself liking her more than most poets.'

Throughout the last twelve months of her life—she died in February 1963—Sylvia Plath was writing with extraordinary speed and intensity. Towards the end, it is said, she was sometimes writing two or three poems a day. In the introduction to some poems that she sent me for broadcasting, she wrote, 'These new poems of mine have one thing in common. They were all written at about four in the morning—that still blue, almost eternal hour before cockcrow, before the baby's cry, before the glassy music of the milkman setting his bottles.'

It was early in May, 1962, that she sent me the script of *Three Women*. It was immediately accepted by the Third Programme; the production was recorded on August 2, and broadcast on

September 13. Technically, it is an admirably straightforward piece of radio writing, a simple but dramatically effective sequence of monologues by three women: before, during and after childbirth or miscarriage. (Unfortunately, two of the three readers engaged for the production were, at almost the last moment, unable to take part, and had to be replaced at short notice; consequently the voices of the three women were not differentiated as clearly as they should have been.)

As with many of Sylvia Plath's finest poems, *Three Women* is rooted in comparatively recent personal experience. The setting, admittedly, is a maternity ward; but this recalls not only her own emotions as a hospital patient but also the fascination that she felt, when she was young, in accompanying doctors around the wards and seeing babies born. Against the whiteness of the hospital, the white sheets, the white cold wing of the great swan, the white clouds rearing, a world of snow, there is projected 'a garden of black and red agonies'. The Wife, 'center of an atrocity', gives birth to 'this blue, furious boy', the Girl to 'my red, terrible girl'; beneath the moon that 'drags the blood-black sea around, month by month', the Secretary is bled white as wax. The evocation of vivid colour is matched in intensity by the startling directness of the imagery; and the emotional experience is shaped by poetic discipline into the most austere and monosyllabic forms. In radio, nothing can equal a poet's visualizing imagination, dramatically expressed in clear and speakable language.

ON 'DADDY'

A. R. JONES

The accepted procedure in psychology is to study the diseased personality not merely for its intrinsic interest, but more importantly for the light such a study will throw on the workings of the normal adjusted personality. The assumption is that the psychotic personality presents an extension, a caricature almost, of the normal mind; the life of the psychotic is different only in degree from that of what is accepted vaguely as normality. Literature has always interested itself in perverse states of mind and from the time of Browning's monologues and Edgar Allan Poe's stories this interest has grown stronger. Yeats, in the Crazy Jane poems, for instance, and Dylan Thomas in poems such as 'Love in the Asylum' both use the deranged mind as a means by which they explore that area of human experience on the fringes of consciousness to arrive at a different, perhaps more profound view of the human predicament. The poet is, after all, traditionally mad—'the lover, the lunatic and the poet' sharing their derangement—and the assumption is that the poet's madness, like that of Lear, enables him to attain a vision of truth beyond the horizon of ordinary mental states. This 'fine frenzy' of the poet which once associated him with inspiration and even divinity, in the twentieth century has linked him with the psychotic personality. An extension of the argument is the one used in connection with *The Waste Land*—that only a poetic structure which is itself fragmented can truthfully reflect a world in which all values are themselves in fragments: only a maladjusted, psychotic personality can faithfully interpret the maladjusted, psychotic personality of the age in which we live. The truth about ourselves and about the *Zeitgeist* is not available to those who cling to the traditional, outmoded concepts of order or normality. Clearly from this point of view, the Johnsonian ideal of passing one's life in the common forms is a dangerous and smug illusion, or, at the very least, the common forms are those of the mentally sick. The last poems of Sylvia Plath draw their compulsive intensity not so much from their element of naked confession but from this assumption that in a deranged world, a deranged response is the only possible reaction of the sensitive mind. This is seen in her poem 'Daddy':

You do not do, you do not do
Any more, black shoe
In which I have lived like a foot
For thirty years, poor and white,
Barely daring to breathe or Achoo.

Daddy, I have had to kill you.
You died before I had time—
Marble-heavy, a bag full of God,
Ghastly statue with one grey toe
Big as a Frisco seal

And a head in the freakish Atlantic
Where it pours bean green over blue
In the waters off beautiful Nauset.
I used to pray to recover you.
Ach, du.

In the German tongue, in the Polish town
Scraped flat by the roller
Of wars, wars, wars.
But the name of the town is common.
My Polack friend

Says there are a dozen or two.
So I never could tell where you
Put your foot, your root,
I never could talk to you.
The tongue stuck in my jaw.

It stuck in a barb wire snare.
Ich, ich, ich, ich,
I could hardly speak.
I thought every German was you.
And the language obscene

An engine, an engine
Chuffing me off like a Jew.
A Jew to Dachau, Auschwitz, Belsen.
I began to talk like a Jew.
I think I may well be a Jew.

The snows of the Tyrol, the clear beer of Vienna
Are not very pure or true.
With my gypsy ancestress and my weird luck
And my Tarot pack and my Tarot pack
I may be a bit of a Jew.

I have always been scared of *you*,
With your Luftwaffe, your gobbledygoo.
And your neat moustache,
And your Aryan eye, bright blue.
Panzer-man, panzer-man, O You—

Not God but a swastika
So black no sky could squeak through.
Every woman adores a Fascist,
The boot in the face, the brute
Brute heart of a brute like you.

You stand at the blackboard, daddy,
In the picture I have of you,
A cleft in your chin instead of your foot
But no less a devil for that, no not
Any less the black man who

Bit my pretty red heart in two.
I was ten when they buried you.
At twenty I tried to die
And get back, back, back to you.
I thought even the bones would do.

But they pulled me out of the sack,
And they stuck me together with glue.
And then I knew what to do.
I made a model of you,
A man in black with a Meinkampf look

And a love of the rack and the screw.
And I said I do, I do.
So, daddy, I'm finally through.
The black telephone's off at the root,
The voices just can't worm through.

If I've killed one man, I've killed two—
The vampire who said he was you
And drank my blood for a year—
Seven years, if you want to know.
Daddy, you can lie back now.

There's a stake in your fat black heart
And the villagers never liked you.
They are dancing and stamping on you.
They always *knew* it was you.
Daddy, daddy, you bastard, I'm through.

The rhythm of a poem such as 'Daddy' has its basis in nursery
rhyme, and in this respect may be compared with the rhythms
used by the witches in *Macbeth* or, more recently, by T. S. Eliot in
Sweeney Agonistes—a dramatic fragment surprisingly close to
Sylvia Plath's poem in feeling and theme. The rhythmic patterns
are extremely simple, almost incantatory, repeated and giving a
very steady return. The first line, for example, 'You do not do,
you do not do', with its echoes of the witches winding up their
sinister spell, 'I'll do, I'll do, and I'll do' or T. S. Eliot's repetition
of 'How do you do. How do you do' denies the affirmation of
the marriage service which is later introduced into the poem,
'And I said I do, I do', and suggests a charm against some brooding but largely undefined curse. As in nursery rhyme, the force,
almost compulsive, of the rhythmical pattern of the poem gives a

sense of certainty, psychologically a sense of security, to a world of otherwise remarkably haphazard and threatening events. The dilemma of the old woman who lived in the shoe, of Dr. Foster, or of Miss Muffet terrified by the spider, is largely contained and appears acceptable and almost reassuring in the comforts of an incantatory rhythmical pattern, for order is imposed, often, indeed, superimposed, on an otherwise fortuitous and even terrifying reality. Also the subject of the nursery rhyme tends to accept his situation with something like a matter-of-fact stoicism; often he seems to co-operate with the events that beset him.

The effectiveness of 'Daddy' can largely be accounted for by Sylvia Plath's success in associating the world of the poem with this structure of the nursery rhyme world, a world of carefully contained terror in which rhythm and tone are precariously weighed against content to produce a hardly achieved balance of tensions.

Sylvia Plath's *persona* exemplifies, she has said, the Electra complex and is involved in the classical psychological dilemma of hatred for her mother, with whom she identifies herself, and love for her German father whom she rejects as tyrannous, brutal and life-denying. The animus that sustains her is both directed towards the father and driven in on herself as if, in the wish to prove her love for those who persecute her, she must outdo them in persecuting herself. The area of experience on which the poem depends for its images is rawly personal, even esoteric, and yet she manages to elevate private facts into public myth, and the sheer intensity of her vision lends it a kind of objectivity. The detachment she achieves in this sudden, terrifying insight into a private world of suffering and humiliation far from dragging the reader into a vortex of suffering and humiliation curiously releases him into a sense of objectivity and freedom from such emotions. The central insight is that of the *persona*, her awareness of her own schizophrenia, of herself as a victim, a centre of pain and persecution; but there is also awareness of a love/hate relation with those responsible for persecuting her. It is this insight into her schizophrenic situation that gives the poem its terrifying but balanced polarity; the two forces, persecutor and victim, are brought together because the *persona* cannot completely renounce the brutality which is embodied in the father/lover image without also renouncing the love she feels for the father/lover figure. The love/hate she feels is the very centre of her emotional life without which she can have neither emotion nor life. In this sense she can be said to co-operate with those that persecute her and, indeed, to connive at her own suffering. As in nursery rhyme, the heroine loves her familiar terrors.

The main area of conflict in the poem is not that covered by the relation of persecutors and persecuted but is within the psyche of the persecuted herself. It is between the *persona* as suffering *victim* and the *persona* as detached, discriminating will. In this poem the diseased psyche takes the place of sensibility and the problem is to establish the relations between subconscious psyche and conscious will. Torn between love and violence, the *persona* moves towards self-knowledge, the awareness that she loves the violence or, at least, towards the recognition that the principles of love and violence are so intimately associated one with the other that the love can only express itself in terms of the violence. By accepting the need for love, she exposes herself to the pain and humiliation of a brutal persecution. The traditional associations of love with tenderness, respect, beauty, and so on, have been utterly destroyed; love is now associated with brutality, contempt and sadistic ugliness. Love does not bring happiness but only torture, 'the rack and the screw'. Moreover, far from admiring the traditional qualities of a lover, the poem insists that:

> Every woman adores a Fascist,
> The boot in the face, the brute
> Brute heart of a brute like you.

Furthermore, brutality is not only a necessary part of love but is also a central and inevitable principle of life. In the last stanza of the poem the community itself joins the heroine in a savage, primitive ritual of brutality—

> And the villagers never liked you.
> They are dancing and stamping on you.

The poem avoids self-pity by hardening its tone into one of self-contempt. The *persona* is divided and judges itself. The only escape from such self-knowledge is in death which the poem acknowledges not only as a release but also as a refining and purifying force, a way of cleansing. It is not annihilation of the personality but the freeing of it from the humiliating persecution of love and violence.

The poem is a terrifyingly intimate portrait, but it achieves something much more than the expression of a personal and despairing grief. The poem is committed to the view that this ethos of love/brutality is the dominant historical ethos of the last thirty years. The tortured mind of the heroine reflects the tortured mind of our age. The heroine carefully associates herself and her suffering with historical events. For instance, she identifies herself with the Jews and the atrocities of 'Dachau, Auschwitz, Belsen' and her persecutors with Fascism and the cult of violence. The poem is more than a personal statement for by extending itself through historical images it defines the age as schizophrenic, torn between brutality and a love which in the end can only manifest itself, today, in images of violence. This love, tormented and perverse, is essentially life-denying: the only escape is into the purifying freedom of death. This is the hideous paradox, that the only release from a world that denies the values of love and life is in the world of death. The nursery rhyme structure of the poem lends this paradox the force of matter-of-fact reasonableness and an air of almost reasonable inevitability. In this we are persuaded almost to co-operate with the destructive principle—indeed, to love the principle as life itself.

APPENDIX OF POEMS AND
PROSE BY SYLVIA PLATH

The purpose of this section is to provide the reader with material which, in all likelihood, he has not seen, but also to indicate the variety and thematic development of Sylvia Plath's work. — Ed.

Dialogue en Route

'If only something would happen!'
sighed Eve, the elevator-girl ace,
to Adam the arrogant matador
as they shot past the forty-ninth floor
in a rocketing vertical clockcase,
fast as a fallible falcon.

'I wish millionaire uncles and aunts
would umbrella like liberal toadstoods
in a shower of Chanel. Dior gowns,
filet mignon and walloping wines,
a pack of philanthropical fools
to indulge my extravagant wants.'

Erect in his folderol cloak,
sham Adam the matador cried:
'O may G-men all die of the choler,
and my every chimerical dollar
breed innumerable bills, bona fide:
a hot hyperbolical joke.'

Said Eva: 'I wish venomous nematodes
were bewitched to assiduous lovers,
each one an inveterate gallant
with Valentino's crack technical talent
for recreation down under the covers:
erotic and elegant episodes.'

Added Adam, that simian swell,
with his modish opposable thumb:
'O for ubiquitous free aphrodisiacs,
and for pumpkins to purr into Cadillacs
and voluptuous Venus to come
waltzing up to me out of her cockle-shell.'

Breaking through gravity's garrison,
Eve, the elevator-girl ace,
and Adam the arrogant matador
shot past the ninety-fourth floor
to corral the conundrum of space
at its cryptic celestial origin.

They both watched the barometer sink
as the world swivelled round in its orbit
and thousands were born and dropped dead,
when, from the inane overhead,
(too quick for the pair to absorb it)
came a gargantuan galactic wink.

SYLVIA PLATH (about 1951–2)*

*Unpublished poems are asterisked.—Ed.

Miss Drake Proceeds to Supper

No novice
In those elaborate rituals
Which allay the malice
Of knotted table and crooked chair,
The new woman in the ward
Wears purple, steps carefully
Among her secret combinations of egg-shells
And breakable humming-birds,
Inching sallow as a mouse
Between the cabbage-roses
Which are slowly opening their furred petals
To devour and drag her down
Into the carpet's design.

Eye cocked askew,
She can see in the nick of time
How perilous needles grain the floorboards
And outwit their brambled plan.
Now through an air
Adazzle with bright shards
Of broken glass
She edges with wary breath,
Fending off jag and tooth,
Until, turning sideways,
She lifts one webbed foot after the other
Into the still, sultry weather
Of the patients' dining-room.

SYLVIA PLATH (1956)*

On the Plethora of Dryads

Hearing a white saint rave
About a quintessential beauty
Visible only to the paragon heart,
I tried my sight on an apple-tree
That for eccentric knob and wart
Had all my love.

Without meat or drink I sat
Starving my fantasy down
To discover that metaphysical Tree which hid
From my worldling look its brilliant vein
Far deeper in gross wood
Than axe could cut.

But before I might blind sense
To see with the spotless soul,
Each particular quirk so ravished me
Every pock and stain bulked more beautiful
Than flesh of any body
Flowed by love's prints

Battle however I would
To break through that patchwork
Of leaves' bicker and whisk in babel tongues,
Streak and mottle in tawn bark,
No visionary lightnings
Pierced my dense lid.

Instead, a wanton fit
Dragged each dazzled sense apart
Surfeiting eye, ear, taste, touch, smell,
Now, snared by this miraculous art,
I ride earth's burning carrousel
Day in, day out,

And such grit corrupts my eyes
I must watch sluttish dryads twitch
Their multifarious silks in the holy grove
Until no chaste tree but suffers blotch
Under flux of those seductive
Reds, greens, blues.

SYLVIA PLATH (1956)*

Epitaph for Fire and Flower

You might as well string up
This wave's green peak on wire
To prevent fall, or anchor the fluent air
In quartz, as crack your skull to keep
These two most perishable lovers from the touch
That will kindle angels' envy, scorch and drop
Their fond hearts charred as any match.

Seek no stony camera-eye to fix
The passing dazzle of each face
In black and white, or put on ice
Mouth's instant flare for future looks;
Stars shoot their petals, and suns run to seed,
However you may sweat to hold such darling wrecks
Hived like honey in your head.

Now in the crux of their vows, hang your ear
Still as a shell: hear what an age of glass
These lovers prophesy to lock embrace
Secure in museum diamond for the stare
Of astounded generations; they wrestle
To conquer cinder's kingdom in the stroke of an hour
And hoard faith safe in a fossil.

But though they'd rivet sinews in rock
And have every weathercock kiss hang fire
As if to outflame a phoenix, the moment's spur
Drives nimble blood too quick
For a wish to tether; they ride nightlong
In their heartbeats' blazing wake until red cock
Plucks bare that comet's flowering.

Dawn snuffs out star's spent wick
Even as love's dear fools cry evergreen,
And languor of wax congeals the vein
No matter how fiercely lit; staunch contracts break
And recoil in the altering light: the radiant limb
Blows ash in each lover's eye; the ardent look
Blackens flesh to bone and devours them.

SYLVIA PLATH (1956)

Battle-Scene from the Comic Operatic Fantasy
The Seafarer

It beguiles—
This little Odyssey
In pink and lavender
Over a surface of gently-
Graded turquoise tiles
That represent a sea
With chequered waves and gaily
Bear up the seafarer,
Gaily, gaily,
In his pink plume and armor.

A lantern-frail
Gondola of paper
Ferries the fishpond Sinbad
Who poses his pastel spear
Toward three pink-purple
Monsters which uprear
Off the ocean-floor
With fanged and dreadful head.
Beware, beware
The whale, the shark, the squid.

But fins and scales
Of each scrolled sea-beast
Troll no slime, no weed.
They are polished for the joust,
They gleam like easter eggshells,
Rose and amethyst.
Ahab, fulfil your boast:
Bring home each storied head.
One thrust, one thrust,
One thrust: and they are sped.

So fables go.
And so all children sing
Their bathtub battles deep,
Hazardous and long,
But oh, sage grownups know
Sea-dragon for sofa, fang
For pasteboard, and siren-song
For fever in a sleep,
Laughing, laughing
Of greybeards wakes us up.

SYLVIA PLATH (1957)

Words for a Nursery

Rosebud, knot of worms,
Heir of the first five
Shapers, I open:
Five moony crescents
For eyes to light me
Toward what I can grasp,
Milk-spout, big finger
So many ladders
Giving a leg up
To these limber hooks.

I learn, good circus
Dog that I am, how
To move, serve, steer food,
Index the arrow,
Thumbhead, blunt helper.
My master's fetcher,
Whipper of itches,
No pocket dozer,
I shut on the key
Of this blue-green toy.

Five-antlered, branching
Touchy antenna,
I nose out the lay
Of thistle and silk,
Cold pole and hot plate.
Old historian,
My page this desert
Crossed by three causeways,
Leathery, treeless,
With five whorled landspits.

Brown-backed, white-bellied
As a flatfish, I
Swim the Sea of Do,
The left my lackey,
My backward image.
Penbearer, scrubnurse,
The captain's batman,
By heart here I hold
Coin, button, trigger
And his love's body.

Ill-served he'll be when
Age manhandles me
(A crab to nap on
Chair arm and tables,
Five wickless candles
To wag at the dark)
And worse-served when death
Makes off with this rose,
Five worms in a box
To feed the thin crows.

SYLVIA PLATH (1957)

249

Mushrooms

Overnight, very
Whitely, discreetly,
Very quietly

Our toe, our noses
Take hold on the loam,
Acquire the air.

Nobody sees us,
Stops us, betrays us;
The small grains make room.

Soft fists insist on
Heaving the needles,
The leafy bedding,

Even the paving.
Our hammers, our rams,
Earless and eyeless,

Perfectly voiceless,
Widen the crannies,
Shoulder through holes. We

Diet on water,
On crumbs of shadow,
Bland-mannered, asking

Little or nothing.
So many of us!
So many of us!

We are shelves, we are
Tables, we are meek,
We are edible,

Nudgers and shovers
In spite of ourselves
Our kind multiplies:

We shall by morning
Inherit the earth.
Our foot's in the door.
SYLVIA PLATH (1959)

In Plaster

I shall never get out of this! There are two of me now:
This new absolutely white person and the old yellow one,
And the white person is certainly the superior one.
She doesn't need food, she is one of the real saints.
At the beginning I hated her, she had no personality—
She lay in bed with me like a dead body
And I was scared, because she was shaped just the way I was

Only much whiter and unbreakable and with no complaints.
I couldn't sleep for a week, she was so cold.
I blamed her for everything, but she didn't answer.
I couldn't understand her stupid behaviour!
When I hit her she held still, like a true pacifist.
Then I realized what she wanted was for me to love her:
She began to warm up, and I saw her advantages.

Without me, she wouldn't exist, so of course she was grateful.
I gave her a soul, I bloomed out of her as a rose
Blooms out of a vase of not very valuable porcelain,
And it was I who attracted everybody's attention,
Not her whiteness and beauty, as I had at first supposed.
I patronized her a little, and she lapped it up—
You could tell almost at once she had a slave mentality.

I didn't mind her waiting on me, and she adored it.
In the morning she woke me early, reflecting the sun
From her amazingly white torso, and I couldn't help but notice
Her tidiness and her calmness and her patience:
She humoured my weakness like the best of nurses,
Holding my bones in place so they would mend properly.
In time our relationship grew more intense.

She stopped fitting me closely and seemed offish.
I felt her criticizing me in spite of herself,
As if my habits offended her in some way.
She let in the drafts and became more and more absent-minded.
And my skin itched and flacked away in soft pieces
Simply because she looked after me so badly.
Then I saw what the trouble was: she thought she was immortal.

She wanted to leave me, she thought she was superior,
And I'd been keeping her in the dark, and she was resentful—
Wasting her days waiting her days waiting on a half-corpse!
And secretly she began to hope I'd die.
Then she could cover my mouth and eyes, cover me entirely,
And wear my painted face the way a mummy-case
Wears the face of a Pharaoh, though it's made of mud and water.

I wasn't in any position to get rid of her.
She'd supported me for so long I was quite limp—
I had even forgotten how to walk or sit,
So I was careful not to upset her in any way
Or brag ahead of time how I'd avenge myself.
Living with her was like living with my own coffin:
Yet I still depended on her, though I did it regretfully.

I used to think we might make a go of it together—
After all, it was a kind of marriage, being so close.
Now I see it must be one or the other of us.
She may be a saint, and I may be ugly and hairy,
But she'll soon find out that that doesn't matter a bit.
I'm collecting my strength; one day I shall manage without her,
And she'll perish with emptiness then, and begin to miss me.

SYLVIA PLATH (1961)

An Appearance

The smile of iceboxes annihilates me.
Such blue currents in the veins of my loved one!
I hear her great heart purr.

From her lips ampersands and percent signs
Exit like kisses.
It is Monday in her mind: morals

Launder and present themselves.
What am I to make of these contradictions?
I wear white cuffs, I bow.

Is this love then, this red material
Issuing from the steel needle that flies so blindingly?
It will make little dresses and coats,

It will cover a dynasty.
How her body opens and shuts—
A Swiss watch, jewelled in the hinges!

O heart, such disorganization!
The stars are flashing like terrible numerals.
ABC, her eyelids say.

SYLVIA PLATH (1962)

Lesbos

Viciousness in the kitchen!
The potatoes hiss.
It is all Hollywood, windowless,
The fluorescent light wincing off and on like a terrible migraine.
Coy paper strips for doors . . .
Stage curtains, a widow's frizz!
And I, love, am a pathological liar,
And my child—look at her, face down on the floor!
Little unstrung puppet, kicking to disappear!
Why she is a schizophrenic,
Her face red and white, a panic.
You have stuck her kittens outside your window
In a sort of cement well
Where they crap and puke and cry and she can't hear.
You say you can't stand her.
The bastard's a girl!
You who have blown your tubes like a bad radio
Clear of voices and history, the staticky
Noise of the new.
You say I should drown the kittens. Their smell!
You say I should drown my girl.
She'll cut her throat at ten if she's mad at two.
The baby smiles, fat snail,
From the polished lozenges of orange linoleum.
You could eat him. He's a boy.
You say your husband is just no good for you,
His Jew-mama guards his sweet sex like a pearl.
You have one baby, I have two.
I should sit on a rock off Cornwall and comb my hair.
I should wear tiger pants, I should have an affair.
We should meet in another life, we should meet in the air,
Me and you.

Meanwhile there's a stink of fat and baby crap.
I'm doped and thick from my last sleeping pill.
The smog of cooking, the smog of hell

Floats our heads, two venomous opposites,
Our bones, our hair.
I call you Orphan, orphan. You are ill.
The sun gives you ulcers, the wind gives you t.b.

Once you were beautiful.
In New York, Hollywood, the men said; 'Through?
Gee, baby, you are rare'.
You acted, acted, acted for the thrill.
Your impotent husband slumps out for a coffee.
I try to keep him in,
An old pole for the lightning,
The acid baths, the skyfulls off of you.
He lumps it down the plastic cobbled hill,
Flogged trolley. The spars are blue.
The blue sparks spill,
Splitting like quartz into a million bits.
O jewel! O valuable!
That night the moon
Dragged its blood bag, sick
animal
Up over the harbor lights.
And then grew normal,
Hard and apart and white.
The scale-sheen on the sand scared me to death.
We kept picking up handfuls, loving it,
Working it like dough, a mulatto body,
The silk grits.
A dog picked up your doggy husband. They went on.

Now I am silent, hate
Up to my neck,
Thick, thick!
I do not speak.
I am packing the hard potatoes like good clothes,
I am packing the babies,
I am packing the sick cats.
O vase of acid!

It is love you are full of. You know who you hate.
He is hugging his ball and chain down by the gate
That opens to the sea
Where it drives in, white and black,
Then spews it back.
Every day you fill him with soul-stuff, like a pitcher.

You are so exhausted!
Your voice my ear-ring,
Flapping and sucking, blood-loving bat.
That is that! That is that!
You peer from the door,
Sad hag. 'Every woman's a whore.
I can't communicate'.

I see your cute décor
Close on you like the fist of a baby
Or an anemone, that sea
Sweetheart, that kleptomaniac.
I am still raw.
I say I may be back.
You know what lies are for!

Even in your Zen heaven we shan't meet.

Sylvia Plath (1962)

Purdah

Jade—
Stone of the side,
The agonized

Side of green Adam, I
Smile, cross-legged,
Enigmatical,

Shifting my clarities.
So valuable!
How the sun polishes this shoulder!

And should
The moon, my
Indefatigable cousin

Rise, with her cancerous pallors,
Dragging trees—
Little bushy *polyps*,

Little nets,
My visibilities hide.
I gleam like a mirror.

At this facet the bridegroom arrives
Lord of the mirrors!
It is himself he guides

In among these silk
Screens, these rustling *appurtenances*.
I breathe, and the mouth

Veil stirs its curtain
My eye
Veil is

A *concatenation* of rainbows.
I am his.
Even in his

Absence, I
Revolve in my
Sheath of impossibles,

Priceless and quiet
Among these parakeets, *macaws*!
O chatterers

Attendants of the eyelash!
I shall unloose
On feather, like the peacock.

Attendants of the lip!
I shall unloose
One note

Shattering
The chandelier
Of air that all day flies

Its crystals
A million ignorants.
Attendants!

Attendants!
And at his next step
I shall unloose

I shall unloose—
From the small jeweled
Doll he guards like a heart—

The lioness,
The shriek in the bath,
The cloak of holes.

SYLVIA PLATH (1962)

Mystic

The air is a mill of hooks—
Questions without answer,
Glittering and drunk as flies
Whose kisses sting unbearably
In the fetid wombs of black air under pines in summer.

I remember
The dead smell of sun on wood cabins,
The stiffness of sails, the long salt winding sheets.
Once one has seen God, what is the remedy?
Once one has been seized up

Without a part left over—
Not a toe, not a finger—and used,
Used utterly, in the sun's conflagrations, the stains
That lengthen from ancient cathedrals,
What is the remedy?

The pill of the Communion tablet,
The walking beside still water? Memory?
Or picking up the bright pieces
Of Christ in the faces of rodents,
The tame flower-nibblers, the ones

Whose hopes are so low they are comfortable—
The humpback in her small, washed cottage
Under the spokes of the clematis?
Is there no great love, only tenderness?
Does the sea
Remember the walker upon it?
Meaning leaks from the molecules.
The chimneys of the city breathe, the window sweats,
The children leap in their cots.
The sun blooms, it is a geranium.

The heart has not stopped.

SYLVIA PLATH (1963)

Excerpt from the radio play: 'Three Women'

WIFE: Who is he, this blue, furious boy,
Shiny and strange, as if he had hurtled from a star?
He is looking so angrily!
He flew into the room, a shriek at his heel.
The blue color pales. He is human after all.
A red lotus opens in its bowl of blood;
They are stitching me up with silk, as if I were a material.

What did my fingers do before they held him?
What did my heart do, with its love?
I have never seen a thing so clear.
His lids are like the lilac-flower
And soft as a moth, his breath.
I shall not let go.
There is no guile or warp in him. May he keep so.

SECY: There is the moon in the high window. It is over.
How winter fills my soul! And that chalk light
Laying its scales on the windows, the windows of empty
offices,
Empty schoolrooms, empty churches. O so much
emptiness!
There is this cessation. This terrible cessation of everything.
These bodies mounded around me now, these polar
sleepers—
What blue, moony ray ices their dreams?
I feel it enter me, cold, alien, like an instrument.
And that mad, hard face at the end of it, that O-mouth
Open in its gape of perpetual grieving.
It is she that drags the blood-black sea around,
Month after month, with its voices of failure.
I am helpless as the sea at the end of her string.
I am restless. Restless and useless. I, too, create corpses.

I shall move north. I shall move into a long blackness.
I see myself as a shadow, neither man nor woman,
Neither a woman, happy to be like a man, nor a man
Blunt and flat enough to feel no lack.
                    I feel a lack.
I hold my fingers up, ten white pickets.
See, the darkness is leaking from the cracks.
I cannot contain it. I cannot contain my life.

I shall be a heroine of the peripheral.
I shall not be accused by isolate buttons,
Holes in the heels of socks, the white mute faces
Of unanswered letters, coffined in a letter case.
I shall not be accused, I shall not be accused.
The clock shall not find me wanting, nor these stars
That rivet in place abyss after abyss.

GIRL: I see her in my sleep, my red, terrible girl.
She is crying through the glass that separates us.
She is crying, and she is furious.
Her cries are hooks that catch and grate like cats.
It is by these hooks she climbs to my notice.
She is crying at the dark, or at the stars
That at such a distance from us shine and whirl.

I think her little head is carved in wood,
A red, hard wood, eyes shut and mouth wide open.
And from the open mouth issue sharp cries
Scratching at my sleep like arrows,
Scratching at my sleep, and entering my side.
My daughter has no teeth. Her mouth is wide.
It utters such dark sounds it cannot be good.

WIFE: What is it that flings these innocent souls at us?
Look, they are so exhausted, they are all flat out
In their canvas-sided cots, names tied to their wrists,
The little silver trophies they've come so far for.

There are some with thick black hair, there are some bald.
Their skin tints are pink or sallow, brown or red;
They are beginning to remember their differences.

I think they are made of water; they have no expression.
Their features are sleeping, like light on quiet water.
They are the real monks and nuns in their identical
                    garments.
I see them showering like stars onto the world—
On India, Africa, America, these miraculous ones,
These pure, small images. They smell of milk.
Their footsoles are untouched. They are walkers of air.

Can nothingness be so prodigal?
Here is my son.
His wife eye is that general, flat blue.
He is turning to me like a little, blind, bright plant.
One cry. It is the hook I hang on.
And I am a river of milk.
I am a warm hill.

SECY: I am not ugly. I am even beautiful.
The mirror gives back a woman without deformity.
The nurses give back my clothes, and an identity.
It is usual, they say, for such a thing to happen.
It is usual in my life, and the lives of others.
I am one in five, something like that. I am not hopeless.
I am beautiful as a statistic. Here is my lipstick.

I draw on the old mouth.
The red mouth I put by with my identity
A day ago, two days, three days ago. It was a Friday.
I do not, even need a holiday; I can go to work today.
I can love my husband, who will understand.
Who will love me through the blur of my deformity
As if I had lost an eye, a leg, a tongue.

And so I stand, a little sightless. So I walk
Away on wheels, instead of legs, they serve as well.
And learn to speak with fingers, not a tongue.
The body is resourceful.
The body of a starfish can grow back its arms
And newts are prodigal in legs. And may I be
As prodigal in what lacks me.

GIRL: She is a small island, asleep and peaceful,
And I am a white ship hooting: Goodbye, goodbye.
The day is blazing. It is very mournful.
The flowers in this room are red and tropical.
They have lived behind glass all their lives, they have been
                    cared for tenderly.
Now they face a winter of white sheets, white faces.
There is very little to go into my suitcase.

There are the clothes of a fat woman I do not know.
There is my comb and brush. There is an emptiness.
I am so vulnerable suddenly.
I am a wound walking out of hospital.
I am a wound that they are letting go.
I leave my health behind. I leave someone
Who would adhere to me: I undo her fingers like bandages:
                    I go.

SECY: I am myself again. There are no loose ends.
I am bled white as wax, I have no attachments.
I am flat and virginal, which means nothing has happened,
Nothing that cannot be erased, ripped up and scrapped,
                    begun again.
These little black twigs do not think to bud,
Nor do these dry, dry gutters dream of rain.
This woman who meets me in windows—she is neat,

So neat she is transparent, like a spirit.
How shyly she superimposes her neat self
On the inferno of African oranges, the heel-hung pigs.
She is deferring to reality.
It is I, It is I—
Tasting the bitterness between my teeth,
The incalculable malice of the everyday.

OCEAN 1212-W

Sylvia Plath

My childhood landscape was not land but the end of the land—the cold, salt, running hills of the Atlantic. I sometimes think my vision of the sea is the clearest thing I own. I pick it up, exile that I am, like the purple 'lucky stones' I used to collect with a white ring all the way round, or the shell of a blue mussel with its rainbowy angel's fingernail interior; and in one wash of memory the colours deepen and gleam, the early world draws breath.

Breath, that is the first thing. Something is breathing. My own breath? The breath of my mother? No, something else, something larger, farther, more serious, more weary. So behind shut lids I float awhile;—I'm a small sea captain, tasting the day's weather—battering rams at the seawall, a spray of grapeshot on my mother's brave geraniums, or the lulling shoosh-shoosh of a full, mirrory pool; the pool turns the quartz grits at its rim idly and kindly, a lady brooding at jewellery. There might be a hiss of rain on the pane, there might be wind sighing and trying the creaks of the house like keys. I was not deceived by these. The motherly pulse of the sea made a mock of such counterfeits. Like a deep woman, it hid a good deal; it had many faces, many delicate, terrible veils. It spoke of miracles and distances; if it could court, it could also kill. When I was learning to creep, my mother set me down on the beach to see what I thought of it. I crawled straight for the coming wave and was just through the wall of green when she caught my heels.

I often wonder what would have happened if I had managed to pierce that looking-glass. Would my infant gills have taken over, the salt in my blood? For a time I believed not in God nor Santa Claus, but in mermaids. They seemed as logical and possible to me as the brittle twig of a seahorse in the Zoo aquarium or the skates lugged up on the lines of cursing Sunday fishermen—skates the shape of old pillow-slips with the full, coy lips of women.

And I recall my mother, a sea-girl herself, reading to me and my brother—who came later—from Matthew Arnold's 'Forsaken Merman':

Sand-strewn caverns, cool and deep,
Where the winds are all asleep;
Where the spent lights quiver and gleam;
Where the salt weed sways in the steam–
Where the sea-beasts ranged all round
Feed in the ooze of their pasture-ground;
Where the sea-snakes coil and twine
Dry their mail and bask in the brine;
Where great whales come sailing by,
Sail and sail with unshut eye,
Round the world forever and aye.

I saw the gooseflesh on my skin. I did not know what made it. I was not cold. Had a ghost passed over? No, it was the poetry. A spark flew off Arnold and shook me, like a chill. I wanted to cry; I felt very odd. I had fallen into a new way of being happy.

Now and then, when I grow nostalgic about my ocean childhood—the wauling of gulls and the smell of salt, somebody solicitous will bundle me into a car and drive me to the nearest briny horizon. After all, in England, no place is what? more than 70 miles from the sea. 'There,' I'll be told, 'there it is.' As if the sea were a great oyster on a plate that could be served up, tasting just the same, at any restaurant the world over. I get out of the car, I stretch my legs, I sniff. The sea. But that is not it, that is not it at all.

The geography is all wrong in the first place. Where is the grey thumb of the water tower to the left and the sickle-shaped sand-bar (really a stone bar) under it, and the Deer Island prison at the tip of the point to the far right? The road I knew curved into the waves with the ocean on one side, the bay on the other; and my grandmother's house, half-way out, faced east, full of red sun and sea lights.

To this day I remember her phone number: OCEAN 1212-W. I would repeat it to the operator, from my home on the quieter bayside, an incantation, a fine rhyme, half expecting the black earpiece to give me back, like a conch, the susurrous of the sea out there as well as my grandmother's Hello.

The breath of the sea, then. And then its lights. Was it some huge, radiant animal? Even with my eyes shut I could feel the glimmers off its bright mirrors spider over my lids. I lay in a watery cradle, and sea gleams found the chinks in the dark green window blind, playing and dancing, or resting and trembling a little. At naptime I clinked my fingernail on the hollow brass bedstead for the music of it and once, in a fit of discovery and surprise, found the join in the new rose paper and with the same curious nail bared a great bald space of wall. I got scolded for this, spanked, too, and then my grandfather extracted me from the domestic furies for a long beachcoming stroll over mountains of rattling and cranking purple stones.

My mother was born and brought up in the same sea sea-bitten house; she remembered days of wrecks where the townspeople poked among the waves' leavings as at an open market—tea-kettles, bolts of soaked cloth, the lone, lugubrious shoe. But never, that she could remember, a drowned sailor. They went straight to Davy Jones. Still, what mightn't the sea bequeath? I kept hoping. Brown and green glass nuggets were common, blue and red ones rare: the lanterns of shattered ships? Or the sea-beaten hearts of beer and whisky bottles. There was no telling.

I think the sea swallowed dozens of tea sets—tossed in abandon off liners, or consigned to the tide by jilted brides. I collected a shiver of china bits, with borders of larkspur and birds or braids of daisies. No two patterns ever matched.

Then one day the textures of the beach burned themselves on the lens of my eye forever. Hot April. I warmed my bottom on the mica-bright stone of my grandmother's steps, staring at the stucco wall, with its magpie design of egg-stones, fan shells, coloured glass. My mother was in hospital. She had been gone three weeks. I sulked. I would do nothing. Her desertion punched a smouldering hole in my sky. How could she, so loving and faithful, so easily leave me? My grandmother hummed and thumped out her bread dough with suppressed excitement. Viennese, Victorian, she pursed her lips, she would tell me nothing. Finally she melted a little. I would have a surprise when mother came back. It would be something nice. It would be—a baby.

A baby.

I hated babies. I who for two and a half years had been the

268

centre of a tender universe felt the axis wrench and a polar chill immobilize my bones. I would be a bystander, a museum mammoth. Babies!

Even my grandfather, on the glassed-in verandah, couldn't woo me from my huge gloom. I refused to hide his pipe in the rubber plant and make it a pipe tree. He stalked off in his sneakers, wounded too, but whistling. I waited till his shape rounded Water Tower Hill and dwindled in the direction of the sea promenade; its ice-cream and hotdog stalls were boarded up still, in spite of the mild pre-season weather. His lyrical whistle beckoned me to adventure and forgetting. But I didn't want to forget. Hugging my grudge, ugly and prickly, a sad sea urchin, I trudged off on my own, in the opposite direction toward the forbidding prison. As from a star I saw, coldly and soberly, the *separateness* of everything. I felt the wall of my skin: I am I. That stone is a stone. My beautiful fusion with the things of this world was over.

The tide ebbed, sucked back into itself. There I was, a reject, with the dried black seaweed whose hard beads I liked to pop, hollowed orange and grapefruit halves and a garbage of shells. All at once, old and lonely, I eyed these—razor clams, fairy boats, weedy mussels, the oyster's pocked grey lace (there was never a pearl) and tiny white 'ice-cream cones'. You could always tell where the best shells were—at the rim of the last wave, marked by a mascara of tar. I picked up, frigidly, a stiff pink starfish. It lay at the heart of my palm. a joke dummy of my own hand. Sometimes I nursed starfish alive in jam jars of seawater and watched them grow back lost arms. On this day, this awful birthday of otherness, my rival, somebody else, I flung the starfish against a stone. Let it perish. It had no wit.

I stubbed my toe on the round, blind stones. They paid no notice. They didn't care. I supposed they were happy. The sea waltzed off into nothing, into the sky—the dividing line on this calm day almost invisible. I knew, from school, the sea cupped the bulge of the world like a blue coat, but my knowledge somehow never connected with what I *saw*—water drawn half-way up the air, a flat, glassy blind; the snail trails of steamers along the rim. For all I could tell, they circled that line forever. What lay behind it? 'Spain', said owl-eyed Harry Bean, my friend. But the parochial map of my mind couldn't take it in. Spain. Mantillas and gold castles and bulls. Mermaids on rocks, chests of jewels, the fantastical. A piece of which the sea, ceaselessly eating and churning, might any minute beach at my feet. As a sign.

A sign of what?

A sign of election and specialness. A sign I was not forever to be cast out. And I *did* see a sign. Out of a pulp of kelp, still shining, with a wet, fresh smell, reached a small, brown hand. What would it be? What did I *want* it to be? A mermaid, a Spanish infanta?

What it was, was a monkey.

Not a real monkey, but a monkey of wood. Heavy with the water it had swallowed and scarred with tar, it crouched on its pedestal, remote and holy, long-muzzled and oddly foreign. I brushed it and dried it and admired its delicately carved hair. It looked like no monkey I had ever seen eating peanuts and moony-foolish. It had the noble pose of a simian Thinker. I realize now that the totem I so lovingly undid from its caul of kelp (and have since, alas, mislaid with the other baggage of childhood) was a Sacred Baboon.

So the sea, perceiving my need, had conferred a blessing. My baby brother took his place in the house that day, but so did my marvellous and (who knew?) even priceless baboon.

Did my childhood seascape, then, lend me my love of change and wildness? Mountains terrify me—they just sit about, they are so *proud*. The stillness of hills stifles me like fat pillows. When I was not walking alongside the sea I was on it, or in it. My young uncle, athletic and handy, rigged us a beach swing. When the tide was right you could kick to the peak of the arc, let go, and drop into the water.

Nobody taught me to swim. It simply happened. I stood in a ring of playmates in the quiet bay, up to my armpits, rocked by ripples. One spoilt little boy had a rubber tyre in which he sat and kicked, although he could not swim. My mother would never let my brother or me borrow water wings or tyres or swimming pillows for fear they would float us over our depth and rubbish us to an early death. 'Learn to swim first,' was her stern motto. The little boy climbed off his tyre, bobbed and clung, and wouldn't share it. 'It's mine,' he reasonably said. Suddenly a cat's paw scuffed the water dark, he let go and the pink, lifesaver-shaped tyre skimmed out of his grip. Loss widened his eyes; he began to cry. 'I'll get it,' I said, my bravado masking a fiery desire for a ride. I jumped with a sideflap of hands; my feet ceased to touch. I was in that forbidden country— 'over my head'. I should, according to mother, have sunk like a stone, but I didn't. My chin was up, hands and feet milling the cold green. I caught the scudding tyre and swam in. I was swimming. I could swim.

The airport across the bay unloosed a blimp. It went up like a silver bubble, a salute.

That summer my uncle and his petite fiancée built a boat. My brother and I carried shiny nails. We woke to the tamp-tamp of the hammer. The honey-colour of the new wood, the white shavings (turned into finger rings) and the sweet dust of the saw were creating an idol, something beautiful—a real sailboat. From the sea my uncle brought back mackerel. Greeny-blue-black brocades unfaded, they came to table. And we did live off the sea. With a cod's head and tail my grandmother could produce a chowder that set, when chilled, in its own triumphal jelly. We made suppers of buttery steamed clams and laid lines of lobster pots. But I never could watch my grandmother drop the dark green lobsters with their waving, wood-jammed claws into the boiling pot from which they would be, in a minute, drawn—red, dead and edible. I felt the awful scald of the water too keenly on my skin.

The sea was our main entertainment. When company came, we set them before it on rugs, with thermoses and sandwiches and coloured umbrellas, as if the water—blue, green, grey, navy or silver as it might be, were enough to watch. The grown-ups in those days, still wore the puritanical black bathing suits, that make our family snapshot albums so archaic.

My final memory of the sea is of violence—a still, unhealthily yellow day in 1939, the sea molten, steely-slick, heaving at its leash like a broody animal, evil violets in its eye. Anxious telephone calls crossed from my grandmother, on the exposed ocean-side, to my mother, on the bay. My brother and I, kneehigh still, imbibed the talk of tidal waves, high ground, boarded windows and floating boats like a miracle elixir. The hurricane was due at nightfall. In those days, hurricanes did not bud in Florida and bloom over Cape Cod each autumn as they now do—bang, bang, bang, frequent as firecrackers on the Fourth and whimsically named after women. This was a monstrous specialty, a leviathan. Our world might be eaten, blown to bits. We wanted to be in on it.

The sulphurous afternoon went black unnaturally early, as if what was to come could not be star-lit, torch-lit, looked at. The rain set in, one huge Noah douche. Then the wind. The world had become a drum. Beaten, it shrieked and shook. Pale and elate in our beds, my brother and I sipped our nightly hot drink. We would, of course, not sleep. We crept to a blind and hefted it a notch. On a mirror of rivery black our faces wavered like moths, trying to pry their way in. Nothing could be seen. The only sound was a howl, jazzed up by the bangs, slams, groans and splinterings of objects tossed like crockery in a giant's quarrel. The house rocked on its root. It rocked and rocked and rocked its two small watchers to sleep.

The wreckage the next day was all one could wish—overthrown trees and telephone poles, shoddy summer cottages bobbing out by the lighthouse and a litter of the ribs of little ships. My grandmother's house had lasted, valiant—though the waves broke right over the road and into the bay. My grandfather's seawall had saved it, neighbours said. Sand buried her furnace in golden whorls; salt stained the upholstered sofa and a dead shark filled what had been the geranium bed, but my grandmother had her broom out, it would soon be right.

And this is how it stiffens, my vision of that seaside childhood. My father died, we moved inland. Whereon those nine first years of my life sealed themselves off like a ship in a bottle—beautiful, inaccessible, obsolete, a fine, white flying myth.

Thalidomide

Seven pages of poem from first handwritten draft to final typed version. (Originals on quarto typewriting paper.)

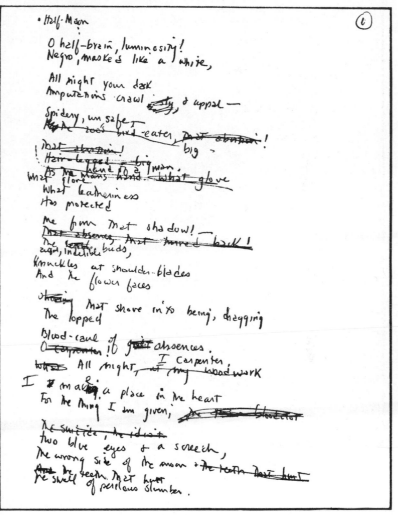

Half-Moon

O' half-brain, luminosity!
Negro, masked like a white,

All night your chink
Amputation's crawl & appal —

Spidery, unsafe.
What glove

What leatheriness
Has protected

Me from that shadow! —
The awful, indelible buds,

Knuckles at shoulder-blades,
And the flower faces

That shoere into being, dragging
The lopped

Blood-caul of absences.
All night I carpenter

A space for the thing I am given —
two blue eyes & a screech,

He mounts backside
The smell of perilous slumber

He smiles at perfection's, a slumber
Perilous to him as an eyelid. Of accident & indifference
A slumber   You turn & turn.

Perilous, thin as an eyelid. Dark fruit!
An eyelid a pane of ice.
O unholy light,

Child's eyelid,.   of accident & indifference.
A leaf of ice!
White spit   Nothingness! Black ice!

Half-Man

The dark points revolve & fell.

~~It is a~~ sin

It is sin that cries
through the cracked glass

O moon-smoke,

unholy light!
The glass ~~warps~~ & cracks across

the image
Flees & aborts like dropped mercury

Half-Moon

November 4
1962.
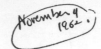

O half-brain, luminosity!
Negro, masked like a white,

All night your dark
Amputations crawl and appal---

Spidery, unsafe.
What glove

What leatheriness
Has protected

Me from that shadow!---
The awful, indelible _ubs,

Knuckles at shoulder-blades,
And the flower faces

That shove into being, dragging
The lopped

Blood-caul of absences.
All night I carpenter

A space for the thing I was given---
Two blue eyes and a screech,

~~A slumbers~~ Sleep
~~perilous, Fearful as an eyelid~~   Imperilled sleep,
                                      Fearful as an eyelid.
~~All night~~   Sleep, perilous   Sleep, thin as an eyelid.
~~White spit~~   O white spit
Of ~~accident and indifference!~~

~~Not black . . .~~
The dark fruits revolve and fall.
~~O . . . smoke,~~

~~Unholy light!~~
The glass cracks across,

The image
Flees and aborts like dropped mercury.

Mirr

(Half Moon)

O half-brain, luminosity!
Negro, masked like a white,'

~~All night~~ Your dark
Amputations crawl and appal---

Spidery, unsafe.
What glove

What leatheriness
Has protected

Me from that shadow!---
The indelible buds,

Knuckles at shoulder-blades,
~~And the~~ Flower faces ~~that~~

~~That~~ Shove into being, dragging
The lopped

Blood-caul of absences.
All night I carpenter

A space for the thing I am given---
~~Two blue eyes and a screech,~~ Alove

~~Sleep, thin as an eyelid.~~ Of two blue eyes & a screech
Of White spit

Of indifference!
The dark fruits revolve and fall.

The glass cracks across,
The image

Flees and aborts like dropped mercury.

Sylvia Plath
Court Green
North Tawton
Devonshire, England

Thalidomide

O Half Moon——

Half-brain, luminosity
Negro, masked like a white,

Your dark
Amputations crawl and appal———

Spidery, unsafe.
What glove

What leatheriness
Has protected

Me from that shadow———
The indelible buds,

Knuckles at shoulder-blades, the
Faces that

Shove into being, dragging
The lopped

Blood-caul of absences.
All night I carpenter

A space for the thing I am given,
A love

Of two wet eyes and a screech.
White spit

Of indifference
The dark fruits revolve and fall.

The glass cracks across,
The image

Flees and aborts like dropped mercury.

Sylvia Plath
Court Green
North Tawton
Devonshire, England

Thalidomide

O half moon——

Half-brain, luminosity———
Negro, masked like a white,

Your dark
Amputations crawl and appal———

Spidery, unsafe.
What glove

What leatheriness
Has protected

Me from that shadow———
The indelible buds,

Knuckles at shoulder-blades, the
Faces that

Shove into being, dragging
The lopped

Blood-caul of absences.
All night I carpenter

A space for the thing I am given,
A love

Of two wet eyes and a screech.
White spit

Of indifference!
The dark fruits revolve and fall.

The glass cracks across,
The image

Flees and aborts like dropped mercury.

Pen Drawings by Sylvia Plath

Wuthering Heights

Benidorm

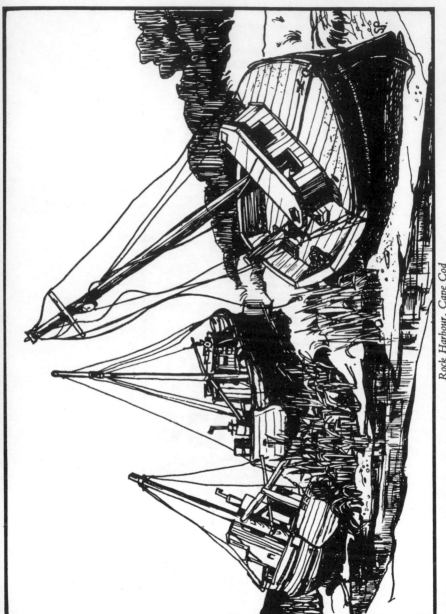

Rock Harbour, Cape Cod

An Informal Check List of Criticism

MARY KINZIE

Critical essays on Sylvia Plath's work are arranged here chronologically, in conjunction with some comments of my own. Not all of the reviews are annotated, as my primary interest has been to trace the development of the so-called 'cult' through the reviews, noting the effect that her death has had on the tenor and substance of the critical comment. I have not commented on essays in this volume, nor on those which did not, in my opinion, raise any substantive questions.

Reader's Guides and Indices have not proven sufficient for compiling a bibliography of critical material, partly because the material is recent, and partly because it is piecemeal, scattered in American and British journals. Therefore, I am certain to have missed some articles, but hope that the authors involved will not be offended and will communicate with the editor, so that appropriate mention can be made in any subsequent editions.

There are, all too clearly, two 'periods' of Plath criticism; the first is divided from the second by her death on February 11, 1963. Until that time, the reviews of *The Colossus* and *The Bell Jar* had been brief, reserved, entirely conventional. It is interesting to speculate whether 'the meanings' which M. L. Rosenthal subsequently found 'to call out from nearly every poem' would even have been divined, had people not been motivated by her death to go back and re-read.

Moraes, Dom
Review of *The Colossus* (London, 1960), *Time and Tide*, vol. 41,
no. 46 (November 19, 1960), 1413. 400 words.
Objections and praise are consistent. *The Colossus* is 'probably
too long'; Miss Plath is too tricky with 'wordage'; but it is 'one
of the best first books for a long time'; Plath has 'learnt her craft'.

Bergonzi, Bernard
'The Ransom Note', *The Manchester Guardian*, no. 35,583
(November 25, 1960), 9. Review of *The Colossus* (London,
1960). 240 words.
Plath's 'Spinster' is cited for its debt to John Crowe Ransom,
whom he calls 'a profitable master'. Bergonzi remarks on the
poet's 'fastidious vocabulary and a delicate feeling for the
placing of the individual word'.

Dickinson, Peter
Review of *The Colossus* (London, 1960), *Punch*, vol. 239,
no. 6,273 (December 7, 1960), 829. 70 words.
'American too, but different . . . the forceful symbolism of a
good surrealist painting. Miss Plath's outlook is gloomy but
she is exhilarating to read.'

Alvarez, A.
Review of *The Colossus* (London, 1960), *The Observer Weekend
Review*, no. 8,842 (December 18, 1960). 250 words.
'Sylvia Plath's *The Colossus* needs none of the usual throat-
clearing qualifications, to wit: "impressive, considering, of
course, it is a *first* volume by a *young* (excuse me), *American
poetess*". Miss Plath neither asks excuses for her work nor offers
them. She steers clear of feminine charm, deliciousness, gen-
tility, supersensitivity and the act of being a poetess. She simply
writes good poetry. And she does so with a seriousness that
demands only that she be judged equally seriously . . . There is
an admirable no-nonsense air about this; the language is bare
but vivid and precise, with a concentration that implies a good
deal of disturbance with proportionately little fuss. I think Miss

Plath can allow herself this undemonstrativeness because most of her poems rest secure in a mass of experience that is never quite brought out into daylight . . . It is this sense of threat, as though she were continually menaced by something she could see only out of the corners of her eyes, that gives her work its distinction.'

Blackburn, Thomas
Review of *The Colossus* (London, 1960), *The New Statesman*, vol. 60, no. 1,554 (December 24, 1960), 1016. 130 words.
The 'baffling obliqueness' of the work in general and the particular 'unruliness' of the imagery are 'worthy faults'.

Wain, John
Review of *The Colossus* (London, 1960), *The Spectator*, vol. 206, no. 6916 (January 13, 1961), 50. 180 words.
Miss Plath 'has fun with poetry', and, despite obvious models in Roethke and Stevens, she has been 'surprisingly' successful 'in finding an individual manner'.

Fuller, Roy
Review of *The Colossus* (London, 1960), *The London Magazine*, vol. 8, no. 3 (March, 1961), 69–70. 400 words.
'The strongest impression these poems leave is of cleverness, a quality,' says Mr. Fuller, 'that I for one admire inordinately . . .' But he notes that the poet's voice is still 'ventriloquial'; 'too many poems have no other point than their own skill. For all the strangeness and power, the book exudes taste—taste in the tradition that puts a good poet in an academic sinecure.' His hopes for her next book are appropriately premonitory; 'If Miss Plath can let things slip a bit without gushing, her next book may remove all one's doubts.'

Times Literary Supplement
Review of *The Colossus* (London, 1960), no. 3103 (August 18, 1961), 550. 120 words.
'Miss Plath tends to be elusive and private in a way, as if what the poems were "about" in a prose sense were very much her own business.'

Myers, E. Lucas
Review of *The Colossus* (New York, 1962), *The Sewanee Review*, vol. 70, no. 2 (Spring, 1962), 216–17. 400 words.
Myers wants Plath to 'shorten the emotional distance' in her second volume of poetry. *Departure* is reprinted entire.

Hurd, Pearl Strachan
Review of *The Colossus* (New York, 1962), *The Christian Science Monitor*, vol. 54, no. 225 (August 20, 1962), 9c. 70 words.

King, Nicholas
Review of *The Colossus* (New York, 1962), *The New York Herald Tribune Book Review*, vol. 122, no. 42 (August 26, 1962), 4. 60 words.

Simon, John
Review of *The Colossus* (New York, 1962), *The Hudson Review*, vol. 15, no. 3 (Autumn, 1962), 464. 170 words.
A just and decent commentary. The faults of Plath's first volume: (*a*) 'blowing up' of 'the tiniest personal experience into an event of vast, universal, and, preferably, mythic importance'; (*b*) 'intoxication with the rare word which she displays with *nouveau riche* ostentation; and obsessive fiddling with certain forms. . . . But with time—the deepening of perception and strengthening . . . of control—these temporary improprieties can become the proper pursuits of poetry: holding nature's immensities in the poem's pocket mirror; redeeming the language'; and letting the 'voices of form lead on to a meeting point in, and with infinity'.

Dickey, William
Review of *The Colossus* (New York, 1962), *The Kenyon Review*, vol. 24, no. 4 (Autumn, 1962), 760–64. 600 words.
A wholly unsuccessful attempt to compare the poetry of Plath, John Hollander and Barbara Guest. Comments such as 'each passage establishes a consistent, personal tone of voice, which contributes to the individuality and unity of the poem', pass for criticism.

Howard, Richard
Review of *The Colossus* (New York, 1962), *Poetry*, vol. 101,
no. 6 (March, 1963) 412–13. 500 words.
'Miss Plath's burden is, throughout, the disaster inscribed
within the surface of life and landscape.' Mr. Howard notes
'a new departure' in the final poem, 'The Stones'. A thoughtful,
short review.

Owen, Guy
Review of *The Colossus* (New York, 1962), *Books Abroad*,
vol. 37, no. 3 (Spring, 1963), 209. 250 words.

Jerome, Judson
Review of *The Colossus* (New York, 1962), *The Antioch Review*,
vol. 23, no. 1 (Spring, 1963), 110–11. 130 words.
A pleasant, funny, but not very informative review. Mr. Jerome
says he 'likes her animals—especially goats and pigs'. 'Playing
along even in the eeriest and most grotesque of the poems is a
bubble of unabashed humor; she likes life—oh rare response!'

The Bell Jar

Most reviews of *The Bell Jar* are illiterate. Without the 'light' of
Ariel, the dropping of the Victoria Lucas pseudonym on its second
publication in 1967, and the suicide, which gave a biographical
dimension to literary discussion, *The Bell Jar* created only minor
interest. Reviews of it usually appeared alongside those of *The
Thin Red Line*, by James Jones (which made a tremendous splash
in England and is generally accorded twice the time given the
Lucas novel); *The Gift*, by Emyr Humphreys; *One Day in the Life
of Ivan Denisovich*, by Alexander Solzhenitsyn; *The Carpetbaggers*,
by Harold Robbins; and *Pigeon Feathers*, by John Updike.
    Most of these reviews appeared in the latter part of January and
some in February of 1963. Simon Raven's appeared four days after
her death. Not until Alvarez's article in *The Review* (or, more
accurately, until the broadcast of which the article is a transcript),
did most critics know that Lucas and Plath were one and the
same writer.

Taubman, Robert
Review of *The Bell Jar*, by Victoria Lucas (London, 1963), *The New Statesman*, vol. 65, no. 1663 (January 25, 1963), 128. 230 words.
'Inner-direction' is the descriptive thread which leads Mr. Taubman from *The Bell Jar* into *The Carpetbaggers*. But he does see the former as 'the first feminine novel in a Salinger mood'.

Times Literary Supplement
Review of *The Bell Jar*, by Victoria Lucas (London, 1963), no. 3178 (January 25, 1963), 53. 300 words.
Esther Greenwood's relationships are 'zany fiascos', but her spokesman, Miss Lucas, 'can certainly write'. 'If she can learn to shape,' says the reviewer, 'as well as she imagines, she may write an extremely good book.'

Lerner, Laurence
Review of *The Bell Jar,* by Victoria Lucas (London, 1963), *The Listener*, vol. 69, no. 1766 (January 31, 1963), 215. 320 words.
Mr. Lerner takes pains to show that Esther Greenwood's mental illness does not denigrate the truth of her observations. 'There are criticisms of America,' he says, 'that the neurotic can make as well as anyone, perhaps better, and Miss Lucas makes them brilliantly.'

Butler, Rupert
Review of *The Bell Jar*, by Victoria Lucas (London, 1963), *Time and Tide*, vol 44, no. 5 (January 31 through February 4, 1963), 34. 160 words. The theme of mental illness is 'tricky'.

Raven, Simon
Review of *The Bell Jar*, by Victoria Lucas (London, 1963), *The Spectator*, vol 210, no. 7025 (February 15, 1963), 203. 50 words.
Mr. Raven advises his English readers to 'stick to home produce' in the field of 'unpleasant, competent, and funny female novelists'.

II

After her death, Sylvia Plath was increasingly treated as a commodity, packaged in *Ariel* and sealed off by her birth and death dates. She did not become a 'confessional poet' until she committed suicide. I do not mean that the more conscientious criticis, like Spender or Rosenthal, lacked only the space for an obituary in order to launch Plath in the 'confessional' school; they needed, in addition, the 'evidence' (a word which appears fairly often) of some forty-three poems, read singly or in small groups as they were published in British magazines and newspapers, before her death. But by the time *Ariel* was published entire in 1965, lesser critics realized that they had better decide who Sylvia Plath was as there was no more to come from her quarter. So it was that Sylvia Plath became 'confessional', and her poetry 'suicidal'; two overly used terms which rapidly passed from the moment when their discovery was still part of an organic, elemental insight, to the secure realm of journalistic repetition.

And 'repetitive' is the best way to characterize the ensuing criticism of her work. Whether they are pedantic, musing, miffed, or so obviously confused that they can't find cover, most reviewers become 'adjectival' to a fault. The following terms appear with an alarming, juggernaut regularity whether in praise or blame:

Anguished, arch, afflicted, boiling, biting, bitter, crippling, confessional, coy, crumbling, demonic, disturbed, dangerous, dark, delirious, enigmatic, fierce, feverish, frightening, ghastly, horrible, horrifying, hysterical, hair-raising, incredible, intolerable, insufferable, intense, murderous, nightmarish, negative, nay-saying, obsessed, outraged, ominous, ruthless, sick, self-pitying, self-indulgent, self-referring, solipsistic, shocking, scalding, suicidal, terrifying, terrible, throbbing, twisted, tragic, violent.

This desperate vocabulary probably derives from the shock that such talent could endure a despair sufficient to annihilate itself, as well as the suspicion that her 'evidence' is incontrovertible. A genuine reverence and awe before the poet's articulated pain runs through most of these reviews; they sense her importance, but they cannot verbalize it.

In the more venomous reviews, where the authors find it boring or unworthy to sit the book out, they betray, more than anything else, a kind of heinous envy. Jealous, not of the experiencing of internal hardship, but of the awesomeness which attends it in the period since her death, some critics get remarkably short-tempered.

There is another curiosity, and that is the frequency of the claim that Sylvia Plath's poetry is inseparable from her life, or that she erased the boundaries between art and experience. In its most extreme form, the feeling is that her aesthetic, after all, is nothing more than the chronicle of a nervous breakdown. When it is assumed that the pages of *Ariel* are populated by the coincidentally successful phrases of a 'disturbed consciousness'—and when those 'accidents' are lauded by one critic after another—some reviewers may have felt justified in setting their lives against hers and judging her, not by her poems, but against the measure of their own decorum.

Another group seems perturbed because this now-famous poetess does not speak from their humanist tradition. As one reviewer lamented, the poems don't perch sedately on the page; they do not represent the 'leavings of a great heart . . . preoccupied elsewhere' (Brinnin re: Dickinson); E. R. Taylor regrets that the 'confessional' poem 'deprives the reader of one chief pleasure of poetry, the feeling of having come upon a silence, a privacy, upon intellect existing unselfconsciously somewhere out of reach of camera'. These critics are not so much angry with Plath as they are genuinely regretful at the passing of an older order.

Whether *Ariel* is 'evidence' for the dangers of the 'confessional' school, or of a 'highly cultivated sensibility', or of the 'cultivation of hysteria', or simply of writing good poetry when you're badly disturbed, the volume has become an artifact of sensibility in which the craft of the poetry is frequently lost amidst speculation about how one ought to confront life.

The Interim

Alvarez, A.
'A Poet's Epitaph', *The Observer*, no. 8955 (February 17, 1963), 23. 80 words.
Sylvia Plath had died the Monday before, on February 11, 1963. Alvarez's closing tribute is: 'The loss to literature is inestimable.' 'Edge', 'The Fearful', 'Kindness' and 'Contusion', were reprinted here.

Starbuck, George
Eulogy, *The Spectator*, vol. 210, no. 7026 (February 22, 1963), 220. 90 words.
'So soon after her early death I do not find it appropriate to try to say anything in the form of a judgment of her work. But I and many others read and enjoyed her poems, and perhaps that is the best epitaph a poet could wish.'

Hamilton, Ian
Review of *The Colossus* (London, 1960) and several later poems, *The London Magazine*, vol. 3, no. 4 (July, 1963), 54–56. 1,500 words.
A rather indifferent review, except for a quote from Paul Valéry concerning the 'confident realist, the confronter of things as they are': 'the universe cannot for one instance [*sic*] endure to be only what it is . . . the mistakes, the appearances, the play of the dioprics of the mind deepen and quicken the world's miserable mass . . . the idea introduces into what is, the leaven of what is not.' Hamilton feels that Plath's illusions—and he uses 'Sow' for his example—are signs of a misspent playfulness; 'the "real" is known to the poet from the beginning, and the spirit in which it is withheld from the reader is the spirit of fun-and-games; the strategy can easily come to seem a way of using up powers of invention for which no more serious function can, meantime, be found.'

Hughes, Ted
Note introducing ten poems by Sylvia Plath, *Encounter*, vol. 21, no. 4 (October, 1963), 45.

Alvarez, A.
'Sylvia Plath', *The Review*, no. 9 (October, 1963), 20–26. 2,600 words. From 'The All-Round Image', a talk prepared for the BBC Third Programme. This is a review of *The Colossus* (London, 1960), and a group of last poems, 'Poppies in October', 'Ariel', 'Daddy', 'Lady Lazarus' and 'Fever 103°'. Expanded, and given a prefix and suffix, this article appears as 'Sylvia Plath' in *Tri-Quarterly* no. 7 (Fall, 1966), 65–74. 3,000 words.

Read, Herbert
Remarks on 'Ocean 1212-W' in the introduction to *Writers on Themselves* (London, 1964), iii–iv. The book is a collection of BBC interviews in which Sylvia Plath's piece, as well as a piece by Ted Hughes called 'The Rock' appeared.

Jones, A. R. and C. B. Cox
'After the Tranquillized Fifties', *Critical Quarterly*, vol. 6, Summer, 1964, pp. 107–12.

Jones, A. R.
'Necessity and Freedom: The Poetry of Robert Lowell, Sylvia Plath, and Anne Sexton', *Critical Quarterly*, vol. 7, no. 1 (January, 1965), 13–30. 6,000 words.
This is a very intelligent and graceful essay, but it perhaps implies more about the differences between British and American criticism than what the three poets hold in common. 'American poetry is moving towards an acceptance of the dramatic monologue as the predominant poetic mode.' He quotes Yeats's objection to Wilfred Owen, 'passive suffering is not a theme for poetry', and then goes on to define the mode of these poets: 'The creative mind—which is largely released and refined in

suffering—knows freedom and achieves Grace, through the act of creation itself.' In speaking of *Ariel*, Mr. Jones says, 'The *persona* of many of these poems is willful and even perverse in its responses, at most maintaining a precarious balance of terrors, victim of the nightmare world that lies below the threshold of consciousness but that relates, only too readily, to the daylight world of the mind. Though recognisably a world of sensibility, nothing could be farther from the "only connect" world of beautiful personal relationships; here the sensibility is fractured and dissociated, a world in which "the deaf and dumb Signal the blind", and the blind are images of monstrous fascination. . . .' He ends this discussion by saying, 'There is no doubt that in *Ariel* Sylvia Plath submits herself entirely to this destructive element, or equally that her creative mind realized in poems of burning intensity what her suffering self experienced as tormenting desolation. Yet, strangely, these poems are affirmative in that tentative way, perhaps, of Stein's questionings' [In Lord Jim] which is a good description of his own attitude towards the poems, but perhaps not of the poems themselves.

Ariel

Furbank, P. N.
Review of *Ariel* (London, 1965), *The Listener and BBC Television Review*, vol. 73, no. 1876 (March 11, 1965), 379. 240 words.
For the Union Dead, by Robert Lowell, was published by Faber and Faber Ltd., in 1965 and was considered alongside *Ariel* in many reviews. Here, Lowell's verse is 'healthy' in comparison with Sylvia Plath's. Not only is Plath's verse 'sick', but her 'victories' are 'Pyrrhic', her 'gaiety' is 'helpless', and she exhibits 'an hysterical bravado in the face of insuperable calamity'. Although Furbank is fairly prodigal with terms such as 'life-hatred', as well as in his adherence to what becomes, in time, the working vocabulary of Plath reviewers (i.e., 'desperation', 'horror', 'anguish' and 'hysteria'), he mentions the similarity

between some of Plath's poetry and 'black cinema'. Very few critics, A. E. Dyson and perhaps Anne Sexton are exceptions, have touched upon the peculiar kind of Gothic tone which is very closely related to the Expressionism of the twenties and thirties, particularly in the German cinema. 'The *persona* of the last poems', says Furbank, 'is still recognizably the limbless fairy-tale homunculus "All-mouth" (from 'Poem for a Birthday') muttering and mythologizing to itself. The poems are an attempt to give words to what psychiatrists call the "not-me".'

Furbank calls the attempt successful 'up to a point' but doesn't define that point.

Alvarez, A.

'Poetry in Extremis', *The Observer*, no. 9063 (March 14, 1965), 26. 1,200 words. Review of *Ariel* (London, 1965).

The 'myth has to do with her extraordinary outburst of creative energy in the months before her death, culminating in the last few weeks. . . .' It is a curious fact that in this and following reviews, whenever the critic admits to the growth of a 'cult' or a 'myth' of Sylvia Plath, he then dedicates most of his resources and space to defining what her 'objective achievement' is *not*, rather than what it is: 'the verse has an originality that keeps it apart from any poetic fads. It is too concentrated and detached and ironic for "confessional" verse, with all that implies of self-indulgent cashing-in on misfortunes. . . .'

Rosenthal, M. L.

'Poets of the Dangerous Way', *The Spectator*, vol. 214, no. 7134, (March 19, 1965), 367. Review of *Ariel* (London, 1965). 540 words.

The myth grows. Rosenthal intimates that there is something inexplicable behind the arrival of these poems, perhaps the 'almost demonically intense commitment to the confessional mode'; the poet no longer 'solders her consciousness of responsibility for evil events to the tinier moments of her daily life'— as Rosenthal elsewhere defines the 'confessional' mode—Sylvia Plath is quickly becoming a laboratory culture, a sick yet admirable mind exposing its sensibilities while infected by them.

By saying that 'we shall never be able to sort out clearly the unresolved, unbearably exposed suggestibility and agitation of these poems from the purely aesthetic energy that shaped the best of them', Rosenthal is admitting that there's no longer any use to discuss that 'purely aesthetic energy' at all; it has been subsumed under the vague 'suggestibility and agitation', that is to say, under the demon of the poet herself. In his final paragraph, Rosenthal asks 'whether the cultivation of sensibility is after all worth the candle. The answer,' he says, 'is yes, for reasons that I hope we all know—yet it seems important to raise the question anyway.' Such a statement is particularly revealing, especially after Rosenthal's mention of black magic and incantation in Plath's poems, since his rhetorical question does not exorcize the doubt that maybe *nothing* is 'worth the candle'. This is not to denigrate his honesty, but it is easy to miss the point. For example: 'Mr. Rosenthal believes it is [worth the candle],' says a man named John Tripp in a letter in *The Spectator* on April 9, 'and he is right. Better a world inhabited by the supersensitive than one trampled over by philistine herds.' Mr. Tripp goes on to say that Miss Plath 'looked around her and saw the mess and she cracked'. Then he quotes James Thurber on F. Scott Fitzgerald: 'A sense of humor might have saved him.'

Press, John
Review of *Ariel* (London, 1965), *Punch*, vol. 248, no. 6499 (March 31, 1965), 486. 200 words.
'Her self-knowledge and her love of life could not save her, but at least she was able to write these terrifying poems and to achieve the momentary calmness of her self-epitaph: "Dying/is an art . . ."'

Hope, Francis
Review of *Ariel* (London, 1965), *The New Statesman*, vol. 69, no. 1781 (April 30, 1965), 687–88. 500 words.
Although 'Suffer and Observe', as this review of five poetry

volumes is called, follows closely on the heels of one on Norman Mailer's *The American Dream*, it is not a bad short review. But Mr. Hope spends most of his time defining the critic's headaches when confronted with '. . . just the sort of poems that force the poet's life and death onto the reader, that refuse to lie down on the page where decency and good taste want them to stay'. The 'neutral qualities' of imagery, syntax, and general poetics are given a nod, just so we know they're still operative.

Ross, Alan
Review of *Ariel* (London, 1965), *The London Magazine*, vol. 5, no. 2 (May, 1965), 99–101. 720 words.
Mr. Ross provides an interesting definition of Sylvia Plath's discipline when he says: 'What, in fact, to the writer were these poems? In a sense they seem familiar, alternative and more buoyant expressions of flesh that had already foregone its pleasures, even its mobility.'

Skelton, Robin
Review of *Ariel* (London, 1965), *The Massachusetts Review*, vol. 6, no. 6 (Autumn, 1965), 834–35. 340 words.
The violence in *Ariel* is that 'of the disturbed mind rather than that of society'.

Steiner, George
'Dying is an Art', *The Reporter*, vol. 33, no. 6 (October 7, 1965), 51–54. Review of *Ariel* (London, 1965). 3,000 words.
Reprinted with deletions in *Smith Alumni Review* (Winter, 1966), 85–87; and printed in full in *Language and Silence*, by George Steiner, Faber & Faber Ltd (London, 1967, pp. 324–331) and Atheneum (New York, 1967, 295–302).

Lowell, Robert
Introduction to *Ariel*, Harper & Row (New York, 1966), pre-published in the *New York Review of Books*, vol. 6, no. 8 (March 12, 1966). 1,000 words.
Mr. Lowell shares equal billing on the cover with Plath, though he is at pains to point out in the introduction that 'she was never a student of mine, but for a couple of months seven years ago, she

used to drop in on my poetry seminar at Boston University. . . . She showed us the poems that later, more or less unchanged, went into *The Colossus*. . . . Somehow none of it sank very deep into my awareness. I sensed her abashment and distinction, and never guessed her later appalling and triumphant fulfillment.' He finds her 'one of those super-real hypnotic, great classical heroines', and that 'her art's immortality is life's disintegration'. It is hardly Mr. Lowell's fault, however, that so many critics have chosen to interpret her poetry through his modest commentary, and ultimately confront his work at her expense.

Lask, Thomas
'A kind of Heroism', *The New York Times*, vol. 115, no. 39 (June 8, 1966), 49m, 582. Review of *Ariel* (New York, 1966). 400 words.

Time
Review of *Ariel*, vol 87, no. 23 (June 10, 1966), 118–20. 1,000 words. *Time*'s descriptions (Sylvia Plath was 'a pretty little poppet', a 'compulsive' everything, from talker to student to writer, finally a 'literary dragon who . . . breathed a burning river of bale across the literary landscape') are as demeaning, in their pop-snotty way, as the jargon of the belletrists, and make the path of any writer seem hasty, predictable, and banal. However, 'Daddy' is reprinted entire (118).

Spender, Stephen
'Warnings from the Grave', *The New Republic*, vol. 154, no. 25 (June 18, 1966), 23, 25–26. Review of *Ariel* (New York, 1966). 1,550 words.

Feldman, Irving
'The Religion of One', *Book Week* (June 19, 1966), 3. Review of *Ariel* (New York, 1966). 1,600 words.
Sylvia Plath is 'our infirm prophet'. Many critics have agreed with Mr. Feldman on this point, but few have attempted to define her aesthetic contribution in terms of aesthetics, i.e., a philosophical understanding. When Mr. Feldman tries, however, he falls into his own trap; he defines aesthetics in terms of

Plath's 'madness', and her religiosity in terms of super-psycho-logized nonsense: 'Aesthetically,' he says, 'the madness within which these poems locate themselves is the ultimate term of the objectivity and narrowness of the lyric poem, which tends to view the world as an aspect of the self. Religiously, this mad-ness dissolves the neutral objectifications of the universe and uncovers its bare power and will, for "universe" (and "God") is a concept of the will and as such is always implicit with will.' He does not, at any rate, tell us what is meant by 'will'; the will has obviously very little to do with choice or intellection, and one possessed of 'the ravenously dissolving power' attri-butable to Sylvia Plath can create only 'disembodied' poetry. Her words, he says, are 'the motions of the disembodied will—arbitrary, capricious, arch, hysterical—on its own in the void, unsupported by any pressure of circumstances'. Further on, he says that this 'disembodiment takes the form of a sort of pure style, of words released from their weight of meaning, or moral concern'.

Newsweek
'Russian Roulette', vol. 67, no. 25 (June 20, 1966), 109a–110. Review of *Ariel* (New York, 1966). 550 words.
It is interesting that *Newsweek* draws a parallel between Plath and Keats, since A. Alvarez mentions the death of Keats' brother as an impetus for Keats' intense creative activity. Spender, too, in the promising first paragraphs of 'Warnings from the Grave', when he began to explain the poet's sense of voice and the 'naming' process, held Keats up to the light. Here, however, 'pain and exacerbation were for Sylvia Plath what voluptuousness was for Keats'.

Friedberg, Martha
'With Feeling and Color', *Books Today* (June 26, 1966), 6. Review of *Ariel* (New York, 1966). 600 words.
This reviewer bent over backwards to find 'three happy poems' and she thinks that at least Miss Plath 'knew that her writing life flourished to the end'.

Baro, Gene
    Review of *Ariel* (New York, 1966), *New York Times Book Review* (June 26, 1966), 10–11. 550 words.
    Mr. Baro agrees with Feldman that 'Miss Plath didn't often pursue logical development, but relied upon an electric leap of insight among images to bring a poem off', but he calls her materials 'associative' instead of demonic.

The Christian Science Monitor
    Review of *Ariel* (New York, 1966), vol. 85, no. 182 (June 30, 1966), 11. One of the first hints of a counter-reaction: reviewers are beginning to be 'miffed' by the 'habit of breakdown'.

Davison, Peter
    'Inhabited by a Cry: The Last Poetry of Sylvia Plath', *Atlantic* (August, 1966), 76–77.
    A review which accepts the cult interpretation completely. On *The Colossus*: '. . . it seems to have no absolute necessity for being: they read like advanced exercises. She wrote a lot of prose as well, including a novel, but the two that I have read seem to me not much out of the ordinary . . . Sylvia Plath's talent, though intensely cultivated, did not bloom into genius until the last months of her life . . . The poems in *Ariel* are poems of defeat except in one sense: that they exist at all.'

Smith, William Jay
    Review of *Ariel* (New York, 1966), *Harper's*, vol. 233, no. 1394 (August, 1966), 92. 330 words.
    Substantially a quote from Robert Lowell's introduction.

Jaffe, Dan
    Review of *Ariel* (New York, 1966), *The Saturday Review*, vol. 49, no. 42 (October 15, 1966), 29. 550 words.
    '*Ariel*', says Mr. Jaffe, 'asks us to feel emotions based on a delirium we do not share. It is best viewed as a case study. . . .

Most of us have visited the regions of horror too often to savor the book masochistically.' Mr. Jaffe not only dislikes 'delirium', he also dislikes 'subjects' which 'become opportunities for the personality to impose itself', and he seems particularly to dislike Plath's suicide because it 'crowns the confessional school with a symbolic act'.

Claire, William F.
'That Rare, Random Descent: The Poetry and Pathos of Sylvia Plath', *The Antioch Review*, vol. 26, no. 4 (Winter, 1966–67), 552–60. 2,200 words.
A general review with the public biographical data and the usual confused and compassionate sentiments.

Kenner, Hugh
'On Ariel', *Triumph* (September, 1966), 33–34. 1,200 words.
Mr. Kenner rejects the notion that Sylvia Plath's poems are 'unmediated shrieks from the heart of the fire,' noting the rhetorical discipline evident in the 'control, sometimes *look* of control, . . . as cunning in its power over our nerves as the stream of repulsions. It in fact enacts its own inability to govern. Naked negation spilling down the sides of improvised vessels, that is the formal drama of poem after poem.'
Although 'naked negation' may unfairly serve Kenner in much the same way that 'unmediated shriek' has served his unnamed respondents/critics—since neither phrase attempts to explain in other than circular terms those words shrieked or negating— the image ('spilling down . . . improvised vessels') nevertheless marks Mr. Kenner's resolve to discuss Plath as poet.
Yet the tumbrils inevitably roll: and the moulding indices of Sylvia Plath's progress retain a nearly uniform, external character: 'The book's nausea is insidious because the denizens of the IBM-Playtex-Cadillac world has been coached, as much by his mentors as by his psyche, to accept as sincerity nothing less than repudiation.'

Klein, Elinor
'A Friend Recalls Sylvia Plath', *Glamour* (November, 1966), 168–84. An incredibly tasteless reminiscence. 'Already a legend is springing up, and it is a dark one. But along with the tragic aspects of her life and death, there was a happy side to her nature and years when she found great joy in living. They are recalled here, though her letters and remembered shared experiences by a close college-and-after friend.' Sample: 'Sylvia won a Fulbright to Cambridge University in England, and after graduation in 1955, she was determined to spend her summer pursuing both her muse and a tan.'

Virginia Quarterly Review
Review of *Ariel* (New York, 1966), vol. 42, no. 4, 140. 170 words.
'These last poems . . . are as intense and as frightening as any verse published in recent years. . . . Unlike much of the current "confessional poetry", however, these poems are self-defeating without being self-indulgent.'

Taylor, Eleanor Ross
'Sylvia Plath's Last Poems', *Poetry*, vol. 89, no. 4 (January, 1967), 260–62. Review of *Ariel* (New York, 1966). 950 words.
The reviewer sympathizes with the 'woman's special experience', calls Plath's poems 'self-consciously womanly', but she does not state why such a quality should be admirable, or poetic, or brought in their half-coherent state to bear upon Plath's works.

Brinnin, John Malcolm
Review of *Ariel* (New York, 1966), *The Partisan Review*, vol. 34, no. 1 (Winter, 1967), 156–57. 300 words.
Brinnin compares Plath with Emily Dickinson, making the distinction that 'anguish in Emily Dickinson is a consequence; it partakes of a classical notion of anguish; the great heart victimized by its own humanity. In Sylvia Plath, by contrast, anguish is not a consequence but the whole relentless subject itself.' Brinnin therefore prefers to take Plath in 'small . . . medicinal doses'.

Howes, Barbara
'A Note on *Ariel*', *The Massachusetts Review*, vol. 8, no. 1 (Winter, 1967), 225–26. 500 words.
This is a peculiarly vitriolic review and belongs in the counter-reactionary group with Jaffe's and, to a lesser degree, Taylor's, Hope's, Feldman's and Brinnin's. The collective verdict is 'solipsism'. Howes laments here the difficulty of 'separating her (Plath's) work from her psychology', since 'disorder, suffering, even madness are not, in themselves, necessarily interesting.'

Newman, Charles
'Candor is the Only Wile: The Art of Sylvia Plath', *Tri-Quarterly*, no. 7, (Fall, 1966), 39–64. 8,000 words.

Alvarez, A.
'Sylvia Plath', *Tri-Quarterly*, no. 7 (Fall, 1966), 65–74.

Dyson, A. E.
'On Sylvia Plath', *Tri-Quarterly*, no. 7 (Fall, 1966), 75–80.

Hughes, Ted
'The Chronological Order of Sylvia Plath's Poems', *Tri-Quarterly*, no. 7 (Fall, 1966), 81–88.

Sexton, Anne
'The Barfly Ought to Sing', *Tri-Quarterly*, no. 7 (Fall, 1966), 89–93.

Ames, Lois
'Notes Towards a Biography', *Tri-Quarterly*, no. 7 (Fall, 1966), 95–107.

Davis, Douglas M.
Review of *Ariel* (New York, 1966), *The National Observer*, vol. 6, no. 6 (February 6, 1967), 31. 180 words.
Here again, 'the personal tragedy somehow reinforces poetry'.

Rosenthal, M. L.
'Other Confessional Poets', *The New Poets: American and British Poetry Since World War II*, Oxford University Press (New York, 1967), 79–89. An expansion of Rosenthal's 'Metamorphosis of a Book' (on *Colossus*) and 'Poets of the Dangerous Way' (On *Ariel*).

The Colossus and *The Bell Jar* revisited

Wall, Stephen
Review of *The Bell Jar,* by Sylvia Plath (London, 1966), *The Observer*, no. 91,040 (September 11, 1966), 27. 50 words.
'Sylvia Plath's attention had the quality of ruthlessness, and here—even more perhaps than in her last poems—imagery and rhetoric is disciplined by an unwinking intelligence.' This is an unusual comment for two reasons: first of all, because 'ruthlessness' was a term which no other reviewer used; secondly, words similar to 'unwinking' have been used by the pound in reviews of *Ariel*, but more to delimit Plath's psyche than her mind.

Taubman, Robert
Review of *The Bell Jar*, by Sylvia Plath (London, 1966), *The New Statesman*, vol. 72, no. 1853 (September 16, 1966), 402. 130 words.

Times Literary Supplement
Review of *The Colossus* (London, 1967), no. 3394 (March 16, 1967), 220. 80 words.
The Colossus now seems 'in the light of *Ariel*, a good deal darker and more interestingly obsessive than it did seven years ago'.

The Observer
Review of *The Colossus* (London, 1967), no. 9167 (March 26, 1967), 23. 50 words.

Press, John
Review of *The Colossus* (London, 1967), *Punch*, vol. 252, no. 6604 (April 5, 1967), 508. 130 words.
'Reading it (*Colossus*) four years after her death we may detect in it traces of the mental pain and of the obsessions which later overwhelmed her—the intuitive understanding of a suicide in "Suicide Off Egg Rock", the preoccupation with inhuman purity in "Moonrise", the queerness . . . the attraction for death.'

Symons, Julian
Review of *The Colossus* (London, 1967), *The New Statesman*, vol. 73, no. 1882 (April 7, 1967), 479. 80 words.
The Colossus 'contains only hints of the raw genius shown in *Ariel*. . . .'

Rosenthal, M. L.
'Metamorphosis of a Book', *The Spectator*, vol. 218, no. 7243 (April 21, 1967), 456–57. 800 words.
'I feel rebuked not to have sensed all these meanings in the first place, for now they seem to call out from nearly every poem.'

BIBLIOGRAPHY

MARY KINZIE
DANIEL LYNN CONRAD
SUZANNE D. KURMAN

I. BOOKS

Ariel, London, Faber and Faber Ltd., 1965.
New York, Harper and Row Inc., 1966.

The Bell Jar, by Victoria Lucas, London, William Heinemann Ltd., 1963.

The Bell Jar, by Sylvia Plath, London, Faber and Faber Ltd., 1966.

The Colossus and Other Poems, London, William Heinemann Ltd., 1960 (hereafter *The Colossus*), New York, Alfred A. Knopf, Inc., 1962.
London, Faber and Faber Ltd., 1967.

Uncollected Poems, London, Turret Press, 1965.[1]

II. SHORT FICTION

'The Day Mr. Prescott Died', *Granta*, vol. 60, no. 1166 (October 20, 1956), 20–23.

'The Wishing Box', *Granta*, vol. 61, no. 1169 (January 26, 1957), 3–5. *Atlantic*, vol. 214, no. 4 (October, 1964), 86–89.

'The Daughters of Blossom Street', *London Magazine*, no. 7 (May, 1960), 34–48.

'The Fifteen-Dollar Eagle', *The Sewanee Review*, no. 68 (Fall, 1960), 603–18.

'The Fifty-ninth Bear', *London Magazine*, no. 8 (February, 1961), 11–20.

---

[1] The poems included in this edition of 150 copies are: 'Blackberrying', 'Private Ground', 'An Appearance', 'Finisterre', 'Insomniac', 'I Am Vertical', 'Candles', 'Parliament Hill Fields'. Bound into the booklet, as the centre-spread, is the manuscript (in facsimile) one page of an early draft of the poem 'Thalidomide'. The poem, 'Insomniac' won the Guinness Poetry Award at the Cheltenham Festival for 1961, and was first printed in the festival programme for that year.

'Johnny Panic and the Bible of Dreams', *Atlantic*, vol. 222, no. 3 (September, 1968), 54–60.

III. NON-FICTION

'Context', *London Magazine*, no. 1 (February, 1962), 45–46.

'Ocean 1212-W', *The Listener and BBC Television Review* (hereafter: *The Listener*), no. 70 (August 29, 1963), 312–13. *Writers on Themselves*, ed. Herbert Read, London, Cox and Wyman Ltd., 1964.

'Poets on Campus', *Mademoiselle*, vol. 37, no. 10 (August, 1953), 290–91.

IV. DRAMA

Three Women, a Monologue for Three Voices, produced by Douglas Cleverdon for the BBC Third Programme, first transmitted Sunday, August 19, 1962, 9.40–10.10 p.m. Cast: The Wife: Penelope Lee; The Secretary: Jill Balcon; The Girl: Janette Richer.[2]

V. POETRY

Page numbers for *The Colossus and Other Poems* are from the 1967 Faber reissue of the original 1960 Heinemann edition which contains the following nine poems excluded from the 1962 Knopf edition: 'Metaphors', 'Black Rook in Rainy Weather', 'Maudlin', 'Ouija', 'Two Sisters of Persephone', and four of the poems included in the section 'Poems for a Birthday': 'Who', 'Dark House', 'Maenad', and 'The Beast'. Page numbers for the poems as they appear in the 1962 Knopf edition are in parentheses.

Page numbers for *Ariel* are from the 1965 Faber publication. Page numbers for the poems as they appear in the 1966 Harper and Row edition are in parentheses. (The poems 'Lesbos', 'Mary's Song', and 'The Swarm', which appear in the Harper and Row edition, were not included in the Faber and Faber edition.)

---

[2] The Turret Press published this script in full (edition of 180 copies) with an introduction by Mr. Cleverdon. A short extract has been published in *Transatlantic Review*, no. 31 (Winter, 1968–69), 51–52.

The Play will be published eventually along with *Uncollected Poems* by Faber and Faber Ltd., and Harper & Row, Inc.

A

'Aerialist', *Cambridge Review*, vol. 90, no. 2187 (February 7, 1969), 245.

'Aftermath', *Arts in Society* (Fall, 1959), 66.
The Colossus, 29 (31).

'All the Dead Dears', *The Grecourt Review*, vol. 1, no. 1 (November, 1957), 36–37.
The Colossus, 27–28 (29–30).

'Amnesiac', *The New Yorker*, vol. 39, no. 24 (August 3, 1963), 29.

'Among the Narcissi', *The New Yorker*, vol. 39, no. 24 (August 3, 1963), 29.

'An Appearance', *Uncollected Poems; The Times Literary Supplement*, no. 3334 (January 20, 1966), 42.

'Apotheosis', *The Lyric* (Winter, 1956), 10.

'The Applicant', *London Magazine*, vol. 2, no. 10 (January, 1963), 15–16.
Ariel, 14–15 (4–5).

'Ariel', *The Review*, no. 9 (October, 1963), 12.
Ariel, 36–37 (26–27).

'The Arrival of the Bee Box', *Atlantic*, no. 211 (April, 1963), 70–71.
Ariel, 63–64 (59–60).
The New Poetry, ed. A. Alvarez, Penguin Books, Cox & Wyman, London, 1962, rev. ed., 1966, 67–68.

B

'Balloons', *Ariel*, 80–81 (79–80).

'The Beast', *The Colossus*, 83–84.

'The Beekeeper's Daughter', *The Kenyon Review*, vol. 22, no. 4 (Fall, 1960), 596.
The Colossus. 75 (73–74).

'The Bee Meeting', *London Magazine*, vol. 3, no. 1 (April, 1963), 24–25.
Ariel, 60–62 (56–58).
Tri-Quarterly, no. 7 (Fall, 1966), 29–31.

'The Beggars', *Chelsea*, no. 7 (May, 1960), 70–71.
Critical Quarterly, no. 2 (Summer, 1960), 156.

'Berck-Plage', *London Magazine*, no. 3 (June, 1963), 26–31.
Ariel, 30–35 (20–25).
'A Birthday Present', *Ariel*, 48–50 (42–44).
'Blackberrying', *The New Yorker*, vol. 38 (September 15, 1962), 48.
Uncollected Poems.
'Black Rook in Rainy Weather', *Granta*, vol. 61, no. 1173 (May 18, 1957), 9.
The Colossus, 42–43.
London Magazine, vol. 5, no. 6 (June, 1958), 46–48.
New Poets of England and America: Second Selection, D. Hall and R. Pack, eds., World, New York, 1962, 330–31.
'Blue Moles', *Critical Quarterly*, no. 2 (Summer, 1960), 156–57.
The Colossus, 49–50 (49–50).
New Poets . . ., 332–33.
'Brasilia', *The Review*, no. 9 (October, 1963), 4, 19.
'The Bull of Bendylaw', *Horn Book*, no. 35 (April, 1959), 148.
The Colossus, 27–28 (26).
'The Burnt-out Spa', *The Colossus*, 76–77 (77–78).

C

'Candles', *The Listener*, vol. 64, no. 1651 (November 17, 1960), 877.
Uncollected Poems.
'Child', *The New Statesman*, vol. 65, no. 1677 (May 3, 1963), 683.
'Childless Woman', *Encounter*, vol. 21, no. 4 (October, 1963), 50.
The New Poetry, p. 71.
'Circus in Three Rings', *Atlantic*, vol. 196, no. 2 (August, 1955), 68.
'The Colossus', *The Kenyon Review*, vol. 22, no. 4 (Fall, 1960), 595.
The Colossus, 20–21 (20–21).
Encounter, vol. 18, no. 4 (April, 1962), 56.
New Poets . . ., 328–29.
Tri-Quarterly, no. 7 (Fall, 1966), 14–15.
'The Companionable Ills', *The Spectator*, no. 6814 (January 30, 1959), 163.
The Colossus, 63₁ (65).

'Contusion', *The Observer*, no. 8955 (February 17, 1963), 23.
  Ariel, 84 (83).
'The Couriers', *London Magazine*, vol. 3, no. 1 (April, 1963), 30–31.
  Ariel, 12 (2).
'Crossing the Water', *The Observer*, no. 7271 (September 23, 1962), 25.
  Uncollected Poems.
'Cut', *London Magazine*, vol. 3, no. 1 (April, 1963), 28–29.
  Ariel, 23–24 (13–14).
  Tri-Quarterly, no. 7 (Fall, 1966), 28–29.

D

'Daddy', *Encounter*, no. 4 (October, 1963), 52.
  The Review, no. 9 (October, 1963), 4.
  Critical Quarterly Supplement No. 5, 1964, 2–4.
  Ariel, 54–56 (49–51).
  Time, vol. 87, no. 23 (June 10, 1966), 118.
  Tri-Quarterly, no. 7 (Fall, 1966), 32–34.
  The New Poetry, 64–66.
'Dark House', *The Colossus*, 81–82.
'The Death of Mythmaking', *Poetry*, vol. 94, no. 6 (September, 1959), 370.
  Tri-Quarterly, no. 7 (Fall, 1966), 11.
'Death & Co.', *Encounter*, vol. 21, no. 4 (October, 1963), 45.
  Ariel, 38–39 (28–29).
  Tri-Quarterly, no. 7 (Fall, 1966), 31–32.
'The Departure of the Ghost', *The Sewanee Review*, vol. 62, no. 3 (Summer, 1959), 446–47.
  (Cf. 'The Ghost's Leavetaking').
'Departure', *The Nation*, vol. 188 (March 7, 1959), 212.
  The Colossus, 18–19 (19).
'The Disquieting Muses', *London Magazine*, vol. 6, no. 3 (March, 1959), 35–36.
  The Colossus, 58–60 (58–60).
'Doomsday', *Harper's*, vol. 208, no. 1247 (May, 1954), 29.
'Dream with Clamdiggers', *Poetry*, vol. 89, no. 4 (January, 1957), 232–33.
  Granta, vol. 61, no. 1171 (March 9, 1957), 5.

'Eavesdropper', *Poetry*, vol. 102, no. 5 (August, 1963), 96–98.

'Edge', *The Observer*, no. 8955 (February 17, 1963), 23.
Ariel, 85 (84).

'Electra on the Azalea Path', *The Hudson Review*, vol. 13, no.3 (Fall, 1960), 414–15.

'Ella Mason and Her Eleven Cats', *Poetry*, vol. 90, no. 4 (July, 1957), 233–34.

'Elm', *Ariel*, 25–26 (15–16).
(Cf. 'The Elm Speaks'.)

'The Elm Speaks', *The New Yorker*, vol. 39, no. 24 (August 3, 1963), 28.

'Epitaph for Fire and Flower', *Poetry*, vol. 89, no. 4 (January, 1957), 236–37.

'To Eva Descending the Stair', *Harper's*, vol. 209, no. 1252 (September, 1954), 63.

'Event', *The Observer*, no. 8946 (December 16, 1962), 21.

'The Eye-mote', *Chelsea*, no. 7 (May, 1960), 70–71.
The Colossus, 12–13 (14–15).

'Face Lift', *Poetry*, vol. 99, no. 6 (March, 1962).

'Faun', *The Colossus*, 17 (18).
(Cf. ' Metamorphosis'.)

'The Fearful', *The Observer*, no. 8955 (February 17, 1963), 23.

'Fever 103°', *Poetry*, vol. 102, no. 5 (August, 1965), 292–94.
The Review, no. 9 (October, 1965), 10.
Ariel, 58–59 (53–55).
Tri-Quarterly, no. 7 (Fall, 1966), 26–27.

'Finisterre', *Uncollected Poems*.

'Flute Notes from a Reedy Pond', *The Texas Quarterly*, vol. 3, no. 4 (Winter, 1960).
The Colossus, 80–81 (84–85).

'Frog Autumn', *The Nation*, vol. 188 (January 24, 1959), 74.
The Colossus, 68 (70).

'Full Fathom Five', *Audience*, vol. 6, no. 2 (Spring, 1559), 33–36.
  The Colossus, 46–48 (46–47).

G

'Getting There', *Encounter*, vol. 21, no. 4 (October, 1963), 47–48.
  Ariel, 43–44 (36–38).

'The Ghost's Leavetaking', *The Colossus*, 42–43 (39–40).
  New Poets . . ., 333–34.

'Go Get the Goodly Squab', *Harper's*, vol 209, no. 1254 (November, 1954), 47.

'The Goring', *Arts in Society* (Fall, 1959), 66.

'Gulliver', *Ariel*, 42 (34).

H

'Half Moon', *Uncollected Poems*. (An unfinished poem in facsimile manuscript.)

'The Hanging Man', *Ariel*, 70 (69).

'Hardcastle Crags', *The Golden Year: The Poetry Society of America Anthology 1910–1960*, Fine Editions Press, 1960.
  The Colossus, 14–16 (16–17).
  (Cf. 'Night Walk'.)

'Heavy Women', *Poetry*, vol. 99, no. 6 (March, 1962), 346–51.

'The Hermit at Outermost House', *Audience*, vol. 6, no. 2 (Spring, 1959), 33–36.
  The Times Literary Supplement, vol. 23, no. 29 (November 6, 1959).
  The Colossus, 56–57 (57).

I

'I am Vertical', *Critical Quarterly*, no. 3 (Summer, 1961), 140–41.
  Uncollected Poems.

'I Want, I Want', *The Partisan Review*, vol. 24, no. 4 (Fall, 1959), 558.
  The Colossus, 39 (36).

'In Midas' Country', *London Magazine*, vol. 6, no. 10 (October, 1959), 11.

'In Plaster', *London Magazine*, vol. 1, no. 11 (February, 1962), 15–16.
   Critical Quarterly Supplement No. 5 (1964), 2–4.
   Tri-Quarterly, no. 7 (Fall, 1966), 16–18.
'Insomniac', *Cheltenham Festival Programme*, 1961. (Winner of Guinness Poetry Award at the Festival.)
   Uncollected Poems.

J

'The Jailor', *Encounter*, vol. 21, no. 4 (October, 1963), 51.

K

'Kindness', *The Observer*, no. 8955 (February 17, 1963), 23.
   Ariel, 83 (82).

L

'Lady Lazarus', *Encounter*, vol. 21, no. 4 (October, 1963), 49.
   The Review, no. 9 (October, 1963), 7.
   Ariel, 16–17 (6–9).
   Tri-Quarterly, no. 7 (Fall, 1966), 35–37.
   The New Poetry, 61–64.
'Lament', *New Orleans Poetry Journal*, vol. 1, no. 4 (October, 1955), 19.
'Leaving Early', *London Magazine*, vol. 1, no. 5 (August, 1961), 9–10.
   Harper's, vol. 225, no. 1351 (December, 1962), 82.
'Lesbos', *The Review*, no. 9 (October, 1963), 4–19.
   Ariel, 30–32 (30–32).
   Tri-Quarterly, no. 7 (Fall, 1966), 18–20.
'A Lesson in Vengeance', *Poetry*, vol. 94, no. 6 (September, 1959), 371.
'Letter in November', *London Magazine*, vol. 3, no. 1 (April, 1963), 29–30.
   Ariel, 51–52 (46–47).
'A Life', *The Listener*, vol. 65, no. 1675 (May 4, 1961), 776.
   Uncollected Poems.
'Little Fugue', *Encounter*, no. 21 (October, 1963), 50.
   Ariel, 71–72 (70–71).

'Lorelei', *London Magazine*, vol. 6, no. 3 (March, 1959), 34–35.
  Audience, vol. 6, no 2 (Spring, 1959), 33–36.
  The Colossus, 22–23 (22–23).
'Love Letter', *Poetry*, vol. 99, no. 6 (March, 1962).

M

'Mad Girl's Love Song', *Mademoiselle*, vol. 37, no. 10 (August, 1953), 358.
  Granta, vol. 61, no. 1173 (May 4, 1957), 19.
'Maenad', *The Colossus*, 82–83.
'Magi', *The New Statesman*, vol. 61, no. 1568 (March 31, 1961), 514.
'Main Street at Midnight', *The Spectator*, no. 6816 (February 13, 1959), 227.
'Man in Black', *The New Yorker*, vol. 36, no. 8 (April 9, 1960), 40.
  The Colossus, 52–53 (54).
'The Manor Garden', *Critical Quarterly*, no. 2 (Summer, 1960), 155.
  Atlantic, vol. 206, no. 3 (September, 1960), 52.
  The Colossus, 3–4 (9).
'Maudlin', *The Colossus*, 48.
'Mary's Song', *London Magazine*, vol. 3, no. 1 (April, 1963), 31.
  Ariel 45 (45).
  The New Poetry, 72.
'Medallion', *Critical Quarterly Supplement*, 1960, 20.
  The Colossus, 61–62 (61–62).
'Medusa', *Ariel*, 45–46 (39–40).
'Metamorphosis', *Poetry*, vol. 89, no. 4 (January, 1957), 234.
'Metaphors for a Pregnant Woman', *The Partisan Review*, vol. 24, no. 4 (Summer, 1960), 435.
  The Colossus ('Metaphors'), 41.
'Mirror', *The New Yorker*, vol. 39, no. 24 (August 3, 1963), 29.
'Mojave Desert', *The Observer*, no. 8891 (November 19, 1961), 28.
  (Cf. 'Sleep in the Mojave Desert'.)

'The Moon and the Yew Tree', *The New Yorker*, vol. 39, no. 24 (August 3, 1963), 29.
  Ariel, 47 (51).
  New Poems, ed. Lawrence Durrell, Harcourt, Brace & World, New York, 1963, 93.
  The New Poetry, pp. 66–67.
'Moonrise', *The Hudson Review*, vol. 13, no. 3 (Fall, 1960), 416.
  Colosuss, 66 (64).
'Morning Song', *Ariel*, 11, (1).
'The Munich Mannequins', *Ariel*, 74–75 (73–74).
'Mushrooms', *Harper's*, vol. 221, no. 1322 (July, 1960), 25.
  The Colossus, 37–38 (34–35).
  New Poets . . ., 331–32.
  Tri-Quarterly, no. 7 (Fall, 1966), 15.
'Mussel Hunter at Rock Harbor', *The New Yorker*, vol. 34, no. 25 (August 9, 1958), 22.
  The Colossus, 69–72 (71–74).
'Mystic', *The New Yorker*, vol. 34, no. 24 (August 3, 1963), 28–29.
'Natural History', *Cambridge Review*, vol. 90, no. 2187 (February 7, 1969), 244–45.

N

'The Net Menders', *The New Yorker*, vol. 36, no. 27 (August 20, 1960), 36.
'Nick and the Candlestick', *The Review*, no. 9 (October, 1963), 4–19.
  Ariel, 40–41 (33–34).
  Tri-Quarterly, no. 7 (Fall, 1966), 22–23.
'The Night Dances', *Ariel*, 27–28 (17–18).
'Night Shift', *The Colossus*, 7–8 (11).
'Night Walk', *The New Yorker*, vol. 34, no. 34 (October 11, 1958), 40.
'November Graveyard', *Mademoiselle*, vol. 62, no. 1 (November, 1965), 34

O

'On Deck', *The New Yorker*, vol. 37, no. 23 (July 22, 1961), 32.
'On The Decline of Oracles', *Poetry*, vol. 94, no. 6 (September, 1959), 368.

'On the Difficulty of Conjuring up a Dryad', *Poetry*, vol. 90, no. 4 (July, 1957), 235–36.

'On the Plethora of Dryads', *The New Mexico Quarterly*, vol. 27 (Autumn, 1957), 211–12.

'The Other', *Encounter*, vol. 21, no. 4 (October, 1963), 47.

'Ouija', *The Hudson Review*, vol. 13, no. 3 (Fall, 1960), 413.
  The Colossus, 52–53.

P

'Paralytic', *Ariel*, 78–79 (77–78).

'Parliament Hill Fields', *London Magazine*, vol 1, no. 5 (August, 1961), 7–8.
  Critical Quarterly Supplement No. 3, 10.
  Uncollected Poems.

'Poem for a Birthday', *The Colossus*
  Contains: 'Who', 80–81; 'Dark House', 81–82; 'Maenad', 82–83; 'The Beast', 83–84; 'Flute Notes from a Reedy Pond', 84–85; 'Witch Burning', 85–86; and 'The Stones', 86–88.

'Point Shirley', *The Sewanee Review*, vol. 62, no. 3 (Summer, 1959), 447–48.
  The Colossus, 24–26 (24–25).

'Poppies in July', *Ariel*, 82 (81).

'Poppies in October', *The Review*, no. 9 (October, 1963), 4–19.
  The Observer (October 6, 1963), 24.
  Ariel, 29 (19).

'Private Ground', *Critical Quarterly*, no. 3 (Summer, 1961), 140–41.
  Harper's, vol. 225, no. 1347 (August, 1962), 55.
  Uncollected Poems.

'Purdah', *Poetry*, vol. 102, no. 5 (August, 1963), 294–96.

'Pursuit', *Atlantic*, vol. 199, no. 1 (January, 1957), 65.

R

'Recantation', *Accent*, no. 17 (Autumn, 1957), 247.

'Resolve', *Granta*, vol. 61, no. 1171 (March 9, 1957), 5.

'The Rival', *The Observer*, no. 8847 (January 21, 1962), 31.
  Ariel, 53 (48).

'Sculptor', *Arts in Society*, (Fall, 1959), 67.
  The Grecourt Review, vol. 2, no. 4 (May, 1959), 282.
  The Colossus, 78–79 (79).
  Tri-Quarterly, no. 7 (Fall, 1966), 16.

'Second Winter', *The Lyric* (Winter, 1956), 11.
  The Ladies' Home Journal, no. 75 (December, 1958), 143.

'Sheep in Fog', *Ariel*, 13 (3).

'Sleep in the Mojave Desert', *Harper's*, vol. 224, no. 1341 (February, 1962), 36.

'The Sleepers'.

'Small Hours', *London Magazine*, vol. 1, no. 5 (August, 1961), 7.
  Critical Quarterly Supplement No. 5 (1964), 2–4.

'Snakecharmer', *London Magazine*, vol. 6, no. 3 (March, 1959), 33–34.
  The Colossus, 54–55 (55–56).
  New Poets . . ., 329–30.

'The Snowmen on the Moor', *Poetry*, vol. 90, no. 4 (July, 1957), 229–31.

'Soliloquy of the Solipsist', *Granta*, vol. 61, no. 1172 (May 4, 1957), 19.

'Sow', *Poetry*, vol. 90, no. 4 (July, 1957), 231–233.
  The Colossus, 9–11 (12–13).
  Tri-Quarterly, no. 7 (Fall, 1966), 11–13.

'Spinster', *London Magazine*, vol. 5, no. 6 (June, 1958), 46–47.
  The Colossus, 66–67 (68–69).

'Stars over the Dordogne', *Poetry*, vol. 99, no. 6 (March, 1962), 346–51.

'Stings', *London Magazine*, vol. 3, no. 1 (April, 1963), 26–27.
  Ariel, 65–67 (61–63).
  Tri-Quarterly, no. 7 (Fall, 1966), 24–25.

'The Stones', *The Colossus*, 82–84 (86–88).

'Stopped Dead', *London Magazine*, vol. 2, no. 10 (January, 1963), 14–15.

'Street Song', *Cambridge Review*, vol. 90, no. 2187 (February 7, 1969), 244.

'Strumpet Song', *Poetry*, vol. 89, no. 4 (January, 1957), 231–7.
The Colossus 35–36 (33).

'Suicide Off Egg Rock', *The Hudson Review*, vol. 13, no. 3 (Fall, 1960), 415.
The Colossus 51 (51).

'The Surgeon at 2 a.m.', *The Listener*, vol. 68, no. 1747 (September 20, 1962), 428.

'The Swarm', *Encounter*, vol. 21, no. 4 (October, 1963), 45–46.
Ariel (64–66).
The New Poetry, 69–71.

T

'Temper of Time', *The Nation*, vol. 181 (August 6, 1957), 119.

'Thalidomide', *Encounter*, vol. 21, no. 4 (October, 1963), 51.

'The Thin People', *London Magazine*, vol 6, no. 10 (October, 1959), 12–13.
The Colossus, 32–34 (30–32).

'Tinker Jack and the Tidy Wives', *Accent*, no. 17 (Autumn, 1957), 247–48.

'Times are Tidy', *Mademoiselle*, vol. 48, no. 3 (January, 1959), 34.
The Colossus, 75 (76).

'Totem', *Ariel*, 76–77 (75–78).

'Tulips', *The New Yorker*, vol. 38, no. 7 (April 7, 1962), 40.
Ariel, 20–22 (10–12).
New Poems, 94–95.

'Two Campers in Cloud Country', *The New Yorker*, vol. 39, no. 24 (August 3, 1963), 28.

'Two Lovers and a Beachcomber by the Real Sea', *Mademoiselle*, vol. 41, no. 10 (August, 1955), 52.
Granta, vol. 61, no. 1171 (March 9, 1957), 5.

'Two Sisters of Persephone', *Poetry*, vol. 89, no. 4 (January, 1957), 235–36.
The Colossus, 63–64.

'Two Views of a Cadaver Room', *The Times Literary Supplement*,
   no. 3010 (November 6, 1959), 29.
   The Nation, no. 190 (January 30, 1960), 107.
   The Colossus, 5–6 (10).
   The Golden Year.

W

'Watercolor of Grantchester Meadows', *The New Yorker*, vol. 36,
   no. 15 (May 28, 1960), 30.
   The Colossus, 40–41 (37–38).
   Tri-Quarterly, no. 7 (Fall, 1966), 13–14.

'Whitsun', *London Magazine*, vol 1, no. 5 (August, 1961), 9.

'Widow', *Poetry*, vol. 99, no. 6 (March, 1962), 346–51.

'Wintering', *Atlantic*, no. 211 (April, 1963), 70–71.
   Ariel, 68–69 (67–68).

'A Winter Ship', *Atlantic*, vol. 206, no. 1 (July, 1960), 70–71.
   Encounter, vol. 16, no. 2 (February, 1961), 23.
   The Colossus, 44–45 (44–45).

'Winter Trees', *The Observer*, no. 9950 (January 13, 1963), 22.

'A Winter's Tale', *The New Yorker*, vol. 35, no. 43 (December 12,
   1959), 116.

'Witch Burning', *The Texas Quarterly*, vol. 4, no. 3 (Autumn,
   1961), 84.
   The Colossus, 85–86.
   Tri-Quarterly, no. 7 (Fall, 1966), 38.

'Words', *Ariel*, 86 (85).
   Tri-Quarterly, no. 7 (Fall, 1966), 38.

'Words for a Nursery', *Atlantic*, vol. 208, no. 2 (August, 1961), 66.
   Tri-Quarterly, no. 7 (Fall, 1966), 21–22.

'Wreath for a Bridal', *Poetry*, vol. 89, no. 4 (January, 1957). 231.

'Wuthering Heights', *The New Statesman*, vol. 63, no. 1618
   (March 16, 1962), 390.
   Uncollected Poems.

Y

'Years', *London Magazine*, vol. 3, no. 1 (April, 1963), 32.
   Ariel, 73 (72).
'You're', *Harper's*, vol. 222, no. 1333 (June, 1961), 40.
   London Magazine, vol. 1, no. 5 (August, 1961), 6.
   Ariel, 57 (52).

Z

'Zoo Keeper's Wife', *London Magazine*, vol. 1, no. 5 (August, 1961), 5–6.

Forthcoming work and translations
The Bell Jar is published in Italy in the translation of Daria Menicanti by Arnoldo Monadore under the title *La Campana di Vetro*. The book includes the following poems: 'Gulliver', 'Letter in November', 'The Rival', 'The Laughing Man', 'Kindness' and 'Edge'. An edition of *Ariel* with *face en face* translation is planned for 1969.

Suhrkamp Verlag published *The Bell Jar* as Volume 208 of their series, 'Bibliothek Suhrkamp' under the title *Die Glasglocke* in the translation of Christian Grote. They also plan an edition of *Ariel* in the translation of Erich Fried.

'Elm', 'Tulips', and 'The Colossus' have been published in the Swedish magazine, *Rondo* (No. 3, 1962) in the translation of Siv Arb. Mrs. Arb is also at work on other poems, and her translations in *Rondo* arc accompanied by her own critical commentary.

The following poems were published in *La Nouvelle Revue Française* (No. 178, 1967), in the translation of Annette Lavers: 'Thalidomide', 'Childless Woman', 'Hanging Man', 'Kindness', 'Fever 103°', 'Poppies in October', 'Ariel', and 'Cut'.

American and English readers can look forward to an addition comprised of the radio play *Three Women* together with un-collected poetry and a small number of unpublished poems. A complete collected works is also planned.

'Surely the great use of poetry is its pleasure—not its influence as religious or political propaganda. Certain poems and lines of poetry seem as solid and miraculous to me as church altars or the coronation of queens must seem to people who revere quite different images. I am not worried that poems reach relatively few people. As it is, they go surprisingly far—among strangers, around the world, even. Farther than the words of a classroom teacher or the prescriptions of a doctor; if they are very lucky, farther than a lifetime.'

from 'Context'